THE THREE MUSCLETEERS

TO GREG.

WISHING YOU

HEALTH AND

HAPPINESS!

Ed Connors

SAN JOSE, CA

6 OCTOBER 2022

The Three Muscleteers

Ed Connors
Foreword by John Cena

Creators Publishing
Hermosa Beach, CA

THE THREE MUSCLETEERS

Cover art by Kenneth Bess (www.behance.net/kennethbess)

CREATORS PUBLISHING
737 3rd St
Hermosa Beach, CA 90254
310-337-7003

Library of Congress Control Number: 2022936318
ISBN (print): 978-1-949673-72-2
ISBN (ebook): 978-1-949673-73-9

First Edition
Printed in the United States of America
1 3 5 7 9 10 8 6 4 2

CONTENTS

To Winnie

With gratitude to the following for their help and support these past nine years:
Joan & Steve Cartwright, Roy Clauss, Connie Connors, Irv Gelb, Lisa & Ryan Haik, Judy & Tom Jackovics, Jordan Katz, Natascha & Mario Klintworth, Dr. John Livesay, Andrew Olson, Howard Mandelbaum, Cathy & Richard Pedersen, Joel Potter, Daniel Puder, Thresa & Keith Richardson, Leslie & Jack Wadsworth, Kurt Weber, Betty Weider, and Paul Ziert

I would also like to thank the people at Creators: Rick Newcombe, Alessandra Caruso, and Alexandra Nagy

"Every man's heart one day beats its final beat. His lungs breathe their final breath. And if what that man did in his life makes the blood pulse through the body of others and makes them bleed deeper and something larger than life, then his essence, his spirit, will be immortalized by the storytellers, by the loyalty, by the memory of those who honor him and make the running the man did live forever."

— The Ultimate Warrior

FOREWORD

I first met Ed Connors in the spring of 1999. While other college seniors spent their spring breaks in Cancun or Daytona Beach, I ventured to Venice, California, where I interviewed for an internship and visited the Mecca of bodybuilding, Gold's Gym.

One afternoon, as I finished up a training session and made my way across the parking lot, a man, yelling in my direction, came running out of the gym. As someone who grew up with four brothers, I knew what this meant: parking lot brawl. I turned around, ready for a fight, and came face to face with Ed Connors. It turned out he did want a fight — but not in the traditional sense. He challenged me to fight against the path of normalcy — the easy road; he challenged me to be a dreamer.

He encouraged me to move to California as soon as I graduated, and I countered with, "It's not that easy." These words were of course just a safety net I had cast to protect myself from the possibility of failure. Despite my excuses, Ed always offered a solution, and by the end of the conversation, I was left defenseless, standing in the Gold's parking lot, with a stranger handing me a "Gold's Ticket."

Although Ed offered encouragement, he made ZERO promises, guaranteed nothing, and stressed that any path I chose to pursue would be extremely difficult. But Ed saw potential in me and encouraged me not to waste it. Three months later, I arrived in Venice. Before I left, my father told me I wouldn't last two weeks, convinced that I would be taken advantage of. I later learned that he had made a similar trip early in his life that had a less-than-successful outcome. He was merely trying to protect his son from the world.

Ed, however, saw things differently; he had such passion for those who loved the iron game. He could speak in a language that made sense to me, but from a perspective that felt like it was elevated forty thousand feet, and I immediately became a sponge in his presence. He offered me a chance to train at Gold's Gym, and I bet on myself. I would not let him down. I vowed to stay around for more than two weeks.

During that time, Ed always challenged me but never spoke

down to me, or even bothered me for that matter. I enjoyed spending time with him and enjoyed how he would simply observe and comment on what he saw. This allowed me to absorb his wisdom and deduct my own takeaways. Even when I had some attempts with bodybuilding that were unsuccessful, Ed never abandoned me. He understood that the bodybuilding stage was not the only platform for turning one's passion for fitness into a livelihood.

Ed believed in me but certainly never sheltered or coddled me. For my first few months in Venice, Ed offered me a place to stay but explained that this lifeline was only temporary. When he sold his house, for the few weeks that followed, my home was a 1991 Lincoln. After that, I moved into a garage three blocks from Gold's. Still, Ed always inquired as to what I was doing and why, not just training-wise but in terms of my life as well.

I'm not sure if he knew it, but he was a driving force behind the molding of my values: Treat people well. Don't be a fuck up. Believe in yourself. Dream big. Not only did Ed encourage this behavior, but he walked the walk, and in doing so, made others believe in it as well. He was amazingly supportive of me taking a chance at professional wrestling (and one of the very few who was, I might add).

Ed is and always has been honest, yet not condescending, curious, but without judgment, and inspiring without any other motive than to see people become their best selves. I love him, and I'm thankful the universe put him in my path exactly when it did, because if there were no Ed Connors, there would be no John Cena. And for that, I am truly grateful.

PART I

THE BEGINNING OF THE FITNESS INDUSTRY

Gold's Gym Santa Monica, 1979

INTRODUCTION

I was one merit badge short of becoming an Eagle Scout. It was, however, the hardest one to get — at least for me. It was for personal fitness.

I was a fat teenager struggling with my weight. The last requirement called for me to perform different strokes in the water. This being Nebraska in the late 1950s in the early spring, the only indoor pool my Catholic scout troop could find was at the Jewish Community Center in downtown Omaha.

I had dyed my hair green for St. Patrick's Day, and now it had all came off in the pool. What was I thinking? I had just jumped in the water and turned it green! It wasn't exactly Moses turning the Nile red. It was not appreciated, and I was asked to leave.

Almost exactly forty years later, I'm on the fifty-ninth floor of the then Sears Tower in Chicago, selling a gym chain I started to franchise in 1980 to a private equity group out of Boca Raton, Florida, for $44 million.

Maybe it was all right that I didn't get that final merit badge for fitness. But I get ahead of myself.

Once, in what seems another life, I was one of the three owners of what became the largest gym chain in the world for twenty-five years. I was born before the end of World War II and grew up in the innocence and optimism of the '50s, when anything seemed possible. In the '60s, I was part of the free-speech movement at the University of California, Berkeley, before being sent to fight in Vietnam, where I served my country for twenty-one months. I worked as an architect at the end of the International Movement, in time to see the beginning of postmodernism and eventually contextual architecture. I was involved in the design of a dozen major buildings, including three high-rises in New York City and Los Angeles.

But many would argue that the biggest thing I was a part of was not the war in Southeast Asia that redefined America or the design of a high-rise but my part in building Gold's Gym into the largest international gym chain and the movement that made fitness terms part of everyday conversation.

I was part of taking weight training from something only a tiny group of male athletes engaged in — because everyone knew it made participants musclebound and slow — to something legitimate. Every athlete in every sport on the planet now pursues it, and every physician is expected to discuss it with their patients.

I knew Bruce Jenner, the 1976 Olympic decathlon champion, when he was on Wheaties boxes. I knew him because Bruce, like so many celebrities and professional athletes, wanted to be a member of my gym — and so did people like Sylvester Stallone, Dennis Hopper, Jodie Foster, Ed O'Neill, Jean-Claude Van Damme, John Cusack, Jimmy Caan, Keanu Reeves, Ray Liotta, Tony Danza, Magic Johnson, Lyle Alzado, Peter Dinklage — and the list goes on.

Even as I gathered my family for reunions at our annual Gold's Gym conventions with over fourteen hundred in attendance, they wondered aloud if I would ever get a real job.

My name is Ed Connors, and I was that self-conscious, chubby kid. This is the story of how my two partners and I went on to change not just our lives but indeed the lives of hundreds, probably hundreds of thousands, and possibly millions of people.

I was there at the start of the health and fitness craze in America when the fitness industry was in its infancy. I was there at the beginning of women's liberation and started women's bodybuilding with the first contest in 1979. I helped men's bodybuilding take off and change the American culture regarding fitness and working out. I was able to shape the face of bodybuilding by picking and encouraging its winners for twenty-five years, such as Mr. Olympia Jay Cutler and Ms. Olympia Cory Everson, along with celebrities in the wrestling and entertainment worlds such as The Ultimate Warrior, John Cena, and Joe Millionaire.

I was able to sell the gym chain in 1999 during the dot-com era, even though a gym was the ultimate low-tech business. When I exited in 2004, Gold's Gym was the largest gym chain in the world in forty-six states and twenty-six countries. Its seven hundred and four locations had over three million members and gross revenue exceeding a billion dollars a year.

We all begin with a mind and body to live a hundred different lives, but in the end, we live only one. This was my life.

For purposes of this book, it begins in 1979, the year my two partners and I bought a single Gold's Gym in Santa Monica, California.

THE WORLD IN 1979

The Soviet Union was the largest country in the world. China was the most populous. Both seemed like immovable monoliths of communist ideology. The Shah was ruling Iran. It would be ten more years before the Berlin Wall would fall and the Soviet Union would be broken up into a dozen different countries. China had become a capitalist nation on the verge of overtaking the US as the world's largest economy. And by the end of 1979, the Shah would be overthrown, and Iran would be a theocracy, with jihad being the new normal.

In 1979, the American economy was reeling from record inflation, exceeding one percent a month. The prime rate, which banks charge its most creditworthy customers, peaked at twenty-one and a half percent that year. People were in long lines at gas stations because of a gasoline shortage. To put those data points in perspective, inflation was two percent in 2020. The Federal Reserve Bank had set its interest rate at zero percent, mortgage rates were under three percent, and the US was the world's largest oil producer.

The change in the fitness industry, as it was to be called later on, may not be as crucial as the global shifts in power or the US economy, but it has been just as dramatic in many ways. If you were to pick up a phone book in 1979 and look at the yellow pages (the business listings), you wouldn't find a "Fitness Centers" category like you would today, assuming you could even find a phone book. Instead, you would have had to look under "Gymnasiums" or "Health Clubs."

At one end of the spectrum were the hardcore gymnasiums, or "gyms," such as Champion Charlie's Muscle Palace in my hometown of Omaha. At the other end were fancy spa chains such as President & First Lady Health Clubs or Jack LaLanne's European Health Spa. These health clubs were in big cities. If you lived in the suburbs or the country, your only hope might be a friend who had some equipment in the garage or basement, most of it homemade. The spas had fancy, chrome-plated equipment, such as machines with wood rollers that tried to beat off the fat. Compared to home gyms, they were almost a joke.

It was a big deal for men and women to work out in mixed settings, like at the YMCA, which had separate facilities for men and women. Or if they did allow men and women to train together, it was at most one day a week — usually Saturday. Men could use the facilities on Monday, Wednesday, and Friday. Women could come on Tuesday and Thursday. The facility was closed on Sunday.

ARNOLD SCHWARZENEGGER & GOLD'S GYM

Compared to the big-box gyms such as LA Fitness, 24 Hour Fitness, or even a lot of Gold's Gym locations today, Gold's Gym was small when it opened in 1965 in Venice, California. It was one of only four "gyms" serving Los Angeles's seven million people. It was like a garage gym, but it filled an entire house of forty-two hundred square feet, so it was ten times the size of a typical twenty by twenty-foot two-car garage space — huge for its time.

While it was filled with the standard free weights, it also had much impressive equipment, the likes of which no one had ever seen. It was all custom-made by George Pipasik and Joe Gold, who helped supervise its design and construction. Most pieces were constructed of solid steel stock, and all of it was black. It fit the names of hardcore gyms back then: The Body Factory, Ironworks, Steel Temple, Iron Religion, Iron Den, The Foundry Gym.

Nowadays, there are likely to be a half dozen choices for some kind of workout within the space of a mile in urban America. But in 1968, Arnold Schwarzenegger had to travel from Graz, Austria's second-largest city, to Venice to get a workout at "the Mecca."

In 1977, Arnold and Gold's Gym were immortalized in the movie *Pumping Iron*. It became a cult classic and cemented Gold's Gym's place in history. The movie was a star vehicle for Arnold, leading to his roles in *Conan the Barbarian* in 1982 and *The Terminator* in 1984. *Terminator 2: Judgment Day*, the first sequel, was the highest-grossing movie of 1991 and won four of its six Oscar nominations.

Perhaps you could say Gold's Gym grew up and matured alongside Arnold. It got civilized, especially when he became California's governor in 2003 in one of only two US gubernatorial recall elections ever to be successful. When Gold's Gym celebrated its fiftieth anniversary in 2015, Arnold was inducted into the Gold's Gym Hall of Fame.

Even today, Gold's Gym is still in its Venice location only

because Arnold has kept Google at bay, preventing it from making its building part of its Venice campus.

It wasn't even that there weren't that many workout facilities back in the '50s, '60s, and '70s, or that they were small. It was an entirely different mindset toward lifting: It might make you musclebound; it might even make you gay.

Even Arnold's father had worried about that when he saw his son putting pictures of scantily clad men on the walls of his bedroom. Ironically, it was a Joe Weider magazine where Arnold first saw those photos of bodybuilders at age fifteen, which became his blueprint for getting to America.

The three most popular sports — football, basketball, and baseball — never used weights. The coaches and trainers were against it. They said it slowed you down. It was no good. Doctors were against weightlifting because they said it was terrible for your heart. It gave you high blood pressure. Perhaps those were the same doctors who were featured in Lucky Strike cigarette ads, the ones who said, "9 out of 10 doctors who smoke, smoke Lucky Strikes." Everybody was wrong.

Fitness was even more radical for the women. The dominant scientific theory said that if a woman exercises too rigorously, her uterus will stop functioning. Or if she even touches a weight, she will get muscles and look like a man. It was a big deal for women to get together and sweat.

Health clubs charged differently back then as well. Most were expensive. Getting a membership was like buying a car. A prospective member was ushered into a room and, after an hour of browbeating, was pressured into purchasing a membership that could run as high as $3,000. So, for a family of four — with a slight discount, of course — it could run as high as $10,000. How long? Three years, five years, a lifetime. Who knew? It varied. No one asked how long the building lease was or whether the facility would still be there in a year. Many were not.

Banks wouldn't lend to gyms; they considered it a flaky business. Essentially, it was a cash business, after all. It was the ultimate scam: selling the same square foot over and over to different people, hoping they wouldn't all show up at the same time. No worries. They never did.

Franchise law prohibited Gold's Gym franchising from establishing membership pricing. But I started selling $19 per month memberships with my first gym. Of course, $19 is equivalent to $54 in today's dollars, but that was comparatively cheap and affordable in 1980. Remarkably, forty-two years later, there are Gold's Gyms, or former Gold's Gyms, still charging $19 a month. Rents certainly haven't stayed the same, nor has the cost of equipment. What has changed is the sheer number of people joining fitness centers to make this work. It is a testament to how many more Americans are working out and how much the culture has changed.

A chain such as Planet Fitness, which a former Gold's Gym franchisee started, is the penultimate high-volume, low-cost (HVLC) model today. One of every four Americans who work out is a member of Planet Fitness. Amazingly, they will pay at most $19 a month, exactly what I was charging forty-two years ago. Even McDonald's had to raise the price of its fifteen-cent hamburger to eighteen cents after twenty years.

Gold's Gym pioneered short-term memberships as well: a day, a week, a month, whatever the customer wanted. A short-term membership could be had for a reasonable price. There was no effort to lock someone into a long-term contract.

Gold's Gym franchisees helped enact laws in many states that would limit the ability of a health club to sell a contract over two years, or at most three. Gold's Gym turned conventional fitness industry wisdom on its head by combining low fees with high customer service standards to build Gold's Gym into the largest gym chain in the world.

SOUTHERN CALIFORNIA: LATE '70s, EARLY '80s

There are only three other areas in the world with a Mediterranean climate like Southern California's, and you probably would not want to live in two of them. With its mild, consistent weather, it became home not only to the entertainment and aeronautics and space industries but also the fitness industry. GIs going to and from the Pacific during World War II stopped in California. They found new lifestyles on the beaches of Los Angeles County. One of those beaches was the Santa Monica beach, with an area for weightlifting and gymnastics.

Los Angeles was the logical place in Southern California for it to develop and grow — and the timing was right. The stars were being aligned for Gold's Gym.

1975: The first issue of *Yoga Journal* was published. Richard Simmons was gyrating in his new exercise studio, "Simmons," in Beverly Hills, no doubt inspired by the aerobics show that Jack LaLanne and his wife, Elaine, put on TV.

1976: *Rocky,* starring Sylvester Stallone, was released, followed by *Rocky II* with a ripped Carl Weathers in 1979, and the first *Rambo* movie, *First Blood,* in 1982.

1977: Jim Fix's bestseller, *The Complete Book of Running,* was published, which started the jogging and marathon boom. The TV show *The Incredible Hulk,* starring Lou Ferrigno, debuted and went on for five years. The TV show *60 Minutes* covered the sold-out Mr. America contest Gold's Gym was putting on in Santa Monica, along with a parade viewed by a crowd second only to the Rose Parade that year.

1978: Warner Brothers released the big-budget superhero movie *Superman,* starring Christopher Reeve. The National Strength and Conditioning Association was founded in Lincoln, Nebraska, by former Mr. Nebraska Boyd Epley, the strength coach for the University of Nebraska football team. The American Machine and Foundry commissioned him to develop an entire line of strength-training equipment for college football. Blue Ribbon Sports changed its name to Nike. It went public two years later when it started manufacturing shoes in Taiwan.

1979: Chippendales, a new Hollywood nightclub, opened and began spawning imitators worldwide with hard-body performers. Gold's Gym even had its version of its hunk-of-the-month calendar for men and women as it pioneered women's bodybuilding. Arnold Schwarzenegger and Jim Lorimer launched the IFBB World Bodybuilding Championships (Mr. Universe) and Mr. Olympia and Mr. International contests in Columbus, Ohio. Jane Fonda opened The Workout in Beverly Hills. Two years later, in 1981, *Jane Fonda's Workout Book* was number one on the *New York Times* Bestseller List for a record twenty-four months. And in 1982, she began producing home workout videos, eventually selling seventeen million.

1980: Ted Turner launched CNN, and two years later added *Body by Jake,* with Jake Steinfeld.

1981: In November, *Time* magazine ran a cover that read, "The Fitness Craze: America Shapes Up." The front cover had photos of five people showing them working out. Having missed being involved with the *Star Wars* franchise, Mattel created *He-Man* and *She-Ra* in their "Masters of the Universe," complete with books, comics, TV shows, movies, and action figures.

1982: *Conan the Barbarian* was released.

1983: The June 9 cover of issue number 397 of *Rolling Stone* had a picture of a guy and gal working out, each holding a dumbbell with the headline "Mr. Goodbody: Health Clubs: The New Singles' Bars." Later on, the August issue number 402 had John Travolta on the cover flexing, wearing only briefs, with the headline "John Travolta, Sex, and the Single Star." Travolta appeared in the 1983 movie *Perfect,* grinding it out in his short shorts in an aerobics class.

The health craze was on at the same time as HIV/AIDS was raising its ugly head. Famous people wanted to associate themselves with fitness and health.

Then there was the debut of easy-to-use equipment like the StairMaster and activities like "spinning," both of which are still popular today. All this helped move fitness from a cult to an industry.

UNIVERSAL STUDIOS, SUPERHEROES, & PERSONAL TRAINING

In 1983, Universal Studios, located north of downtown Los Angeles in Universal City, was the biggest tourist attraction in LA County. The highlight of its amusement park was the scripted live-action shows featuring characters from current TV shows and movies. Gold's Gym often provided the larger-than-life cast members for these shows, many of whom had been houseguests of mine, such as Jack Wadsworth.

Jack was training at Gold's Gym after a long stint in Alaska. He had been there since 1973 and had come to LA this time after a big job in the oil fields in Prudhoe Bay, Alaska. I had initially met Jack in 1982 when he was competing at a contest we were putting on in Las Vegas.

I knew Universal Studios was looking for someone to play Conan, and like so many people I've met over the years, I encouraged him to go for it. Jack made a fateful call to Tony Christopher, the director, who learned that Jack could act and handle a sword at six feet, one inch and 250 pounds.

While playing Conan, he met his future wife, Leslie Faulkner, who was playing Red Sonja. The wedding on Conan's bejeweled and skull-laden set with some of the characters in full costume remains the most memorable wedding I have ever attended.

Later, Jack and Leslie toured the US playing He-Man and She-Ra for Mattel and MTM as part of the "Masters of the Universe Power Tour." The show played in twenty-six major US and Canadian cities, such as the Thomas Mack Center in Las Vegas and the Cow Palace in San Francisco. It sold out nineteen consecutive performances at Radio City Music Hall in New York City, a record that still stands today. It seems superheroes were big business.

When their lives calmed down, I became partners with them in what eventually grew into three Gold's Gym locations in the Seattle area. The leading club near downtown had the highest gross revenue per square foot of any Gold's Gym with which I was involved. This pattern of getting into the gym business with people who were passionate about fitness would be repeated many times, ultimately involving me in thirty-seven Gold's Gym locations in seven states: California, Texas, Washington, Oregon, Oklahoma, Michigan, and my home state of Nebraska.

Jake Steinfeld, another Gold's Gym member in both Venice and Reseda, California, was playing The Hulk at Universal Studios in the reenactment of that TV series. Movie stars would come over from the studio adjacent to the park and ask Jake how to develop their bodies. It was the beginning of celebrity trainers.

George Lucas would have Jake picked up at his home in the Valley in LA, chauffeured to LAX, flown to San Francisco, and then driven to Lucas Ranch in Marin to train Harrison Ford for his first *Indiana Jones* movie. This routine would be enhanced when filming occurred in exotic locations such as the Caribbean, even outfitting a cargo plane with a gym to maintain Ford's exercise routine. Jake was only twenty-four years old when Ted Turner put him on his fledgling worldwide cable network, CNN, with his show *Body by Jake*. Personal training was born.

Like no other one before him, Jake created the field of personal training and was the first to make it an occupation. Some people say there is no money in bodybuilding, but there are hundreds of thousands of young men and women all over the world making a living today from their knowledge of fitness. "Personal training" is currently listed as the fastest-growing occupation in America. Health and fitness will be even more important after the pandemic as it becomes known that the out-of-shape people were the ones most likely to die from COVID.

These personal trainers would eventually embrace the world of diet and nutrition. The Pritikin diet and scores of others like it started in LA. It's a rare trend in beauty and fitness that hasn't begun in Southern California. And those that didn't blew up there before moving into the mainstream.

The image of the LA body has been reshaped since the days when Muscle Beach was really for serious weightlifters and not just for tourists and ex-cons; and Gold's Gym was a small storefront on

Ocean Avenue in Venice; and before Joe Weider built a fitness empire. But it all started there; it had to start somewhere.

JOE GOLD OPENS GOLD'S GYM: 1965

If you were to look up the word "curmudgeon" in the dictionary, a photo of Joe Gold would suffice as a description. Like everyone in the gym business, Joe was ridiculously passionate in the beginning about what he did to a point where the average person would find him eccentric.

Joe was born in East LA, the son of a junk dealer. In junior high school, he led a group of friends in creating the Dugout Athletic Club, a "workout gym" in an auto repair shop. In his teens, he discovered Santa Monica's Muscle Beach, where stunt performers, acrobats, and bodybuilders gathered.

Joe Gold opened his first commercial gym "Ajax" in New Orleans, where he had spent time as a member of the merchant marines. Gold served in both World War II and the Korean War, where he sustained a back injury in a torpedo attack, something that would haunt him the rest of his life.

Joe returned to LA in 1954 to pursue bodybuilding, even becoming part of the famous Mae West nightclub act, which employed an eight-man chorus line of musclemen. He tried to work a deal with the Muscle Beach Weightlifting Club to open an enclosed gym after the city of Santa Monica shut down the outdoor area on the beach because of an alleged rape incident. When the club hesitated, he went it alone, opening up his gym in a private residence in 1965. He lived in the house adjacent to it and even had an enclosed passageway from his home into the gym.

He naturally called it "Gold's Gym." Bodybuilding had its church now, and it was located at 1006 Pacific Avenue in Venice. It became the "holy of hollies," a sanctuary for like-minded people. It became the Mecca.

After five years, Joe sold his gym and the buildings to Bud Danitz and Dave Saxe for $50,000 and returned to the sea. When Joe returned in 1976, he wanted to have a gym again, but having sold the rights to his name, he had to come up with a new one. He called it "World Gym."

Ric Drasin, who died in 2020 and had designed the original Gold's Gym logo with the bald weightlifter and bent barbell in 1973, came up with a new logo that replaced the man with a gorilla and used the same block lettering. It was so similar that people would often get the gyms confused, calling it "World's Gym."

In 1976, Joe opened his first World Gym on Main Street in Santa Monica, a few blocks south of where Gold's Gym was located at the time. He moved it back to Venice in 1987 and then finally to Marina del Rey.

Joe treated his gym like a private club and was not that concerned about membership numbers or revenue. He could do this because his operation was subsidized by his gym franchising revenue, which he copied after the model Gold's Gym had created.

Attorney Mike Uretz headed World Gym franchising. He would closely mirror what Gold's Gym did but never reach its numbers.

Undoubtedly, Mike's unwillingness to fly hurt their growth. His most extensive trip of the year was to travel by train from LA to Columbus, Ohio, for the annual World Gym convention, which was held in conjunction with the Arnold Classic. It was usually held too early in the year — before the midwest spring had a chance to bloom.

Many of our franchisees told me that the deciding factor in becoming a Gold's Gym rather than a World Gym was that our conventions were in Las Vegas and not Columbus. I often attended the Arnold Classic in March and experienced white-outs — blizzards unlike anything I knew growing up in Omaha.

After Joe Gold died in 2004 at age eighty-two, Mike Uretz sold its franchise operation two years later to Planet Fitness, which cherry-picked its better operators and then sold off the rest. World Gym closed its LA location on June 12, 2007.

KEN SPRAGUE: 1972-1979

Dave Saxe sold his share to partner Bud Danitz, who then sold the business — and the buildings — in 1972 to Ken Sprague, a twenty-six-year-old Mr. America finalist and porn star who worked under the stage name "Dakota" for COLT Studios.

Operating out of a motion-picture soundstage in Hollywood, Sprague had no problem letting director George Butler and author Charles Gaines use the gym to film their movie, *Pumping Iron.* Fortune smiled again as that is something Joe Gold would almost certainly never have allowed. The book *Pumping Iron,* which was on *The New York Times* Best Seller list in 1974, made bodybuilding chic.

Gaines and Butler, who died in 2021, spent six weeks filming in Gold's Gym Venice as Arnold, Franco Columbo, and Lou Ferrigno trained for the Mr. Olympia title held that year in South Africa.

Arnold would win his sixth Mr. Olympia title, and that movie would be the start of an incredible film career, peaking in the '90s when, at $25 million a movie, he was the highest-paid actor in Hollywood.

Perhaps because of the success and notoriety of *Pumping Iron,* Sprague saw the gym in a different light and moved it to a more prominent and more commercial location with parking three miles north to the Santa Monica business district. The storefront location at 1452 Second Street measured fifty by ninety feet, so at forty-five hundred square feet, it was slightly larger than the Venice location and similar in many ways, with two large windows flanking an entrance on the street.

It was one block away from what would become the world-famous Santa Monica Promenade. But back then, you could throw a bowling ball down the Third Street shopping mall and not hit anyone because it was so dead. (Ironically, you could do the same thing now, during the pandemic.) The gym's neighbor was the Pussycat Theater on Second Street, and a near-empty parking garage was across the street.

This was the era before cardio, so there wasn't even one bike in the gym. Members would use the elevators in the six-story parking structure rather than the stairs. Every ounce of energy was being saved for the gym.

The untimely death of Ken's wife, Maryon, made Ken decide to sell the business in February 1979. It ultimately ended up in the hands of an unlikely threesome: an architect and two competitive bodybuilders.

As Arnold would say about the architect, he had gone from "building buildings to building bodies." I'm that architect. My two partners and I would franchise Gold's Gym, and during our twenty-five years as caretakers of the brand, we would grow it to become the largest gym chain in the world.

That seemed a natural outcome, as my partner, Pete Grymkowski, became Mr. World. As he traveled the world, he realized that not everyone could visit Mecca. It only made sense for the Mecca to come to the people through a license or franchise of Gold's Gym.

PETE GRYMKOWSKI, ED CONNORS, & TIM KIMBER: 1979-1999

It was a fortuitous beginning. Had I been killed while serving in the Army in Vietnam, it likely would be a different world. Or had Pete Grymkowski not taken me up on my offer to come to California. Or had Pete not offered me the chance to buy in — or sold to someone else — things might have been different.

And then there was Tim Kimber, Pete's old training partner from Rochester, New York. Had he not been there to run things with me after I left being an architect full time, things might have been different. Tim's role was essential in making our threesome work.

The role of fate in my life — or anyone's, really — is something I often think about. It seems that life is fifty percent fate. The other half is what you do with what fate — some would call it luck — has dealt you.

After being discharged from the Army in 1971, I went to work for Kevin Roche John Dinkeloo & Associates, a prestigious East Coast architecture firm. I thought I would be working there for the rest of my life, but the architecture profession is fickle and vulnerable to recessions. I was laid off in the recession of 1975, the first of six I have lived through to date.

At one point, my quest for a job took me to Orlando, Florida, for an interview with Disney to work on the new EPCOT addition to its theme park. However, the humidity reminded me so much of Vietnam that I swore that I wouldn't take the job no matter what they offered me. But while I was in Orlando, I visited a friend I knew from New Haven who was working out at a small, local gym called Orange Avenue Gym.

That's where I met Pete Grymkowski, the biggest bodybuilder and best-built human being I had ever seen. The bodybuilding world was fresh in my mind because I had come from "the Mecca," where I had interviewed with an architecture firm for a job in LA.

I told Pete he would be the biggest guy at Gold's Gym, at least based on what I had seen the day I visited, and that he should move there to compete in Joe Weider's upcoming Mr. World contest. Pete said he would love to but that there was no way he could manage the move. He was going through a divorce, had very little money, and didn't even own a vehicle. I told Pete that I would get him out there. It wasn't long after that when I sent Pete a $186 one-way plane ticket that would change both our lives and the lives of many others.

Pete stayed with me initially in a cheap apartment in the Marina del Rey section of LA, adjacent to Venice. Back then, the Marina area had a bad reputation because of all the partying, mainly due to the pilots and flight attendants living there. It was minutes away from LAX, the primary airport serving LA. Pete would be my first "houseguest." Hundreds would follow.

Both Pete and I buckled down to work. Pete won his height class in Weider's contest and went on to win the Mr. World. He next started his own protein powder supplement line, something very novel at the time. He even had his own T-shirts with the motto "Think Big," along with bodybuilding courses.

I was busy, too — first as senior designer of the Neiman Marcus flagship store in Beverly Hills, which was the project that had initially brought me to LA. Several other significant structures would follow, almost all of them in Southern California.

Pete moved out on his own, like all of my houseguests would eventually do, but we kept in touch. After a long day at the office, I might have gone to Gold's Gym in Santa Monica to say hello to Pete, a night owl who often trained for hours in the evening. Then one day in February 1979, Pete called to see if I was interested in buying Gold's Gym with him. I assumed there were many other investors. There weren't. But I could remember walking into Gold's Gym for the first time and thinking how neat it would be to own it. Four years later, I did.

My religion was Catholic, but I had grown up with the power of positive thinking watching TV programs like Robert Schuller's *Hour of Power*, which was based on a philosophy similar to that showcased in Norman Vincent Peale's popular book *The Power of Positive Thinking*, which also had made a big impression on me.

I had never forgotten the very unpleasant experience of joining the Jack LaLanne European Health Spa when I was at the University of California, Berkeley. That facility was the successor to the first health club LaLanne opened in Oakland in 1936.

I was overweight and worried about being "cannon fodder," knowing I would be drafted for the war in Vietnam the moment I graduated. I can still remember having to go into a small office while the salesman sold me an expensive membership. In a classic move at the time, the senior manager, who was watching on a hidden camera, even called in on the telephone landline to privately tell his employee what he was doing wrong and to hurry up and close the deal. Somewhere in the back of my mind, I had made the mental note that if I ever could change that, I would — and I did.

I have been impulsive my entire life. Even though there was very little information about the business, I didn't hesitate when Pete called me about the sale. I told Pete I was interested. I had recently started my own architecture practice with a friend from back east who had also been laid off. Having a business and knowing what it was like to have to make payroll, I thought I knew enough: It's one thing to pay (or not pay) yourself, but quite another thing to have to pay an employee.

I had $15,000 saved to buy a new BMW. That money resulted from an investment in Twentieth Century Fox stock after seeing the first *Star Wars* movie in May 1977. I was a science fiction fan and felt that movie would change everything, like Stanley Kubrick's *2001: A Space Odyssey* had done a decade earlier in 1968. The stock split three times.

So, with Pete and another investor, Denny Doyle, I purchased Gold's Gym for $100,000 and the assumption of some liabilities the business had, mainly for unfilled equipment orders. When Ken Sprague learned I was an architect, I was given the additional task of converting the former Gold's Gym in Venice into a legal residence; he had been living in it. It was no easy feat, given the lack of windows in the former gym. (Hint: I used many skylights.)

Regarding the $100,000 purchase price, $50,000 was cash from the three of us, and the remainder was a loan to the business from Bank of America that I had secured and guaranteed. Given the reputation gyms had, it was not an easy loan to procure because gyms "came and went" in the banker's terms. Ironically, three of the franchises with Gold's Gym that I would later be involved with were in former Bank of America locations, ones that had come and gone but had pledged to support the community when they first opened. When I remodeled the spaces for gym use, I made sure to leave at least one former drive-in teller window in place as a memorial.

The initial business was off to a rocky start. It wasn't long before Tim Kimber replaced Denny Doyle. The percentage of ownership changed so that Pete would become the majority shareholder, while my and Tim's shares made up the remaining minority interest. Tim had been Pete's training partner in Rochester, and their chemistry was strong. Tim's relationship with me was also excellent.

Fate had landed us in the right place at the right time. But now it was time to do something with our good fortune.

I wasn't ready to leave working as an architect just yet, and Tim, with his people skills, was the perfect gym manager. So, we became "PET" in the office memorandums: Pete, Ed, and Tim.

Like so many new businesses, we lost money the first year: $15,000 on revenue of a quarter million dollars. The company couldn't afford to pay Pete or me, but there was enough to pay Tim a manager's salary, so it worked. I had my salary as an architect, and Pete had his income from seminars and selling his products. Tim's wife, Barb, and his mother-in-law also worked for the company filling the mail orders for clothing, doing excellent work for minimum pay — but everyone made enough to live. LA, especially for a big city in America, was very affordable then. Barb stopped handling mail orders and clothing in 1983 after their second child arrived.

It would be six years — 1985 — before I would feel comfortable leaving work as a full-time architect and devoting all my energy to Gold's Gym and my franchises. It was during this time, however, that I had quite a personal journey leading two, sometimes three lives as I worked for several different LA architecture firms besides being an independent consultant, all the while being one of the three owners of Gold's Gym and opening up some of my own Gold's Gym franchises.

There was even a two-week period where two different architecture firms employed me at the same time. I had given one a two-week notice, but the new firm wanted me to start immediately.

Given that they were each located in one of the two Yamasaki-designed twin towers in Century City (the same architect for the original World Trade Center in New York City), I was able to pull this off. I would tell the receptionist at one firm that I was going out for a meeting and then head to the elevator, go down to the main level, and cross the plaza to the other set of elevators to take me up to my other employer, who was located in the opposite tower. I'm sure I gave each of them a whole forty-hour week for those two weeks.

As my dad, a surgeon and emergency room doctor when he first started out practicing medicine, would say to me when I was young, "Forty hours a week is just getting started!"

JOE WEIDER

It was 1979 when I met Joe Weider. Weider magazines were an essential source of revenue for us and Pete, as well. Having won the Mr. World title, Pete offered protein powder and his bodybuilding courses for sale in the magazine. The small ads in the back of Weider magazines for Gold's Gym apparel were responsible for half our revenue in 1979. Six items were featured, including Gold's Gym tank tops and T-shirts for $8 each, plus $1 for shipping and handling. Our cost on each of those items was $2.50.

When those ads were mysteriously pulled, Pete went to the Weider offices to see Joe. I had two theories: First, the Weider people saw them as unnecessary competition. Second, Arnold, through Weider, wanted to pressure us to end the lawsuit Sprague had initiated against him after Arnold said on a nightly talk show that World Gym was a "penthouse" compared to Gold's Gym, which he called an "outhouse."

Whatever the reason, Pete's meeting didn't go well. I thought cooler heads might prevail, so I called Joe. When I introduced myself, and Joe found out I was an architect, he asked if I could see him at his home in the Hancock Park area of LA, which happened to be very close to the office of the architecture firm where I was working. He was having problems with some remodeling at his home and wanted my help. It was a quid pro quo: If I could help him with his remodeling plans, then Gold's Gym, and Pete, would get their ad space back. Thus began a relationship that went beyond his construction projects and lasted thirty-four years, until Joe died in 2013.

There was a priceless synergy between Weider and Gold's Gym. On June 22, 1979, we filed an Order of Dismissal for Joe Gold's Gym, Inc., vs. Arnold Schwarzenegger, et al. Case No. C 234 425, the lawsuit inherited from Sprague. It wasn't Pete's, Tim's, or my style anyway. We wanted to work with everyone.

Psalm 23 was on one side of the memorial card at Joe Weider's funeral service. The other side listed the dates of his birth and death: November 29, 1920, and March 23, 2013. My father had been born a year earlier, something I thought about often as Joe was already fifty-eight years old when I met him.

With his distinctive way of speaking — a kind of Canadian twang — he was a larger-than-life personality. People described his voice as a cross between a Hollywood gangster and a stand-up comedian. I thought of W.C. Fields, who I adored in his films with Mae West.

But Joe was serious, always serious about his business. He was such a workaholic that his wife, Betty, gave him a vanity license plate that read "TODO BOY" because every time she wanted to do something, Joe would respond by saying he "had too much to do." This was the license plate on Joe's Lincoln Town Car, the same vehicle Pete had taken a tire iron to after his argument with Joe regarding his ads and those for Gold's Gym.

Building Weider Enterprises was an all-consuming passion for Joe. It was not a career; it was his life. I hoped that I could be as passionate about what I was doing when I would be his age. Joe had grown up poor in the Jewish section of Montreal, where his father was a pants presser. He left school to work — and work out — as he, like Joe Gold, was bullied as a kid.

Weider was an avid reader of *Strength & Health,* the principal American fitness magazine Bob Hoffman published out of York, Pennsylvania. Around 1940, Weider decided to publish his own twelve-page newsletter, *Your Physique,* which had a subscription price of seventy-five cents a year. Not long after that, Weider was competing with Hoffman for control of the Iron Game.

After initially moving from Montreal to New Jersey with his magazine, now called *Muscle Builder & Power,* to further his publishing business in the US, Weider left for sunny Southern California in 1968 to better highlight the lifestyle his magazine promoted.

There was a natural synergy between his magazines and Gold's Gym Venice. He needed beautiful people, and Gold's Gym had them. Gold's Gym had already acquired an almost mystical reputation because it was so profoundly part of the bodybuilding culture.

Weider would bring people to Gold's Gym for Joe Gold to meet and help. One of those people was Arnold Schwarzenegger.

Joe was passionate about bodybuilding. He also had an eye for talent. He had seen Arnold compete in Europe and brought him to

America when Arnold was just twenty-one, becoming a father figure and mentor. No one would ever be on more covers of Weider's magazines than Arnold. And no issues sold better than those with Arnold on the cover. Joe would often show me the figures each month from newsstand sales to prove it.

My fondest memories of Joe were of him at work on his covers, either in the studio of the photographer taking the photos – usually an all-day affair at the studios of Bob Gardner, Harry Langdon, Ken Marcus, or Rick Zimmerman – or at his desk, selecting the final one to use for the magazine. He had an incredible eye for what looked right and would sell.

But Weider Enterprises was in danger of going broke in 1979 and even flirted with bankruptcy a few times. Until the 1980s, Weider was primarily a publishing company, and the magazines and the various products it advertised were under attack. The magazines were used as advertising to such an extent for Weider's various ventures that the postal service mandated that the percentage of ads would have to be decreased or it would be classified as an advertising piece and have to pay higher postal rates.

Then there were problems with the Food and Drug Administration, and Weider's claims for its supplement products. And the Federal Trade Commission found some of the Weider strength equipment claims were unsubstantiated and ordered the company to refund customers. The "Muscle Aids," like the "5-minute body shaper," was called worthless. So, in 1979, Ben Weider, Joe's brother who was based in Montreal, recommended that Allan Dalfen, who was fourteen years younger than Joe, come in as a consultant. After two weeks, Allan became president of Weider Enterprises.

Dalfen organized the company into four divisions: nutrient supplements, health foods, sporting goods, and magazines. Allan said, "I don't know a thing about bodybuilding, but I know everything about making money." Joe's mantra was, "Never trust anyone." Pete, Tim, and I didn't operate that way. But given what I saw at the Weider offices, I could see why Joe might say that.

Dalfen would later go to prison for embezzling money from the local synagogue. But Allan had the organizational skills. And Joe had the passion – and the ego. *The New York Times* reported, "His ego is Herculean. A single recent issue of *Muscle & Fitness* magazine contains at least 80 photos or likenesses of Weider and more than 110 mentions of Weider's name."

By the end of the '80s, Weider was marketing his home gym equipment in six thousand retail outlets and his nutritional products in twelve thousand stores in the US. Joe had come a long way from being a mail-order entrepreneur. The company was perfectly positioned to benefit from the exercise explosion, which it helped create. Weider had worldwide revenue of $350 million and four thousand employees by the end of the decade. *Muscle & Fitness* magazine had a circulation of 627,000 and, along with *Shape,* was in the top ten magazines in circulation in the US. *LA Business* magazine reported sales of all of Weider's magazines at the end of the '80s at $1.7 million.

Partly because of its enormous marketing power stemming from ad space at cost in all Weider publications, Weider Nutrition products started to take off in the mid and late '80s. There was lots of room for products and self-promotion, with a typical *Flex* at 150-plus pages and *Muscle & Fitness* running 250-plus, of which forty were devoted to company ads.

In 1994, Weider sold its sports equipment branch for $240 million. The publishing empire, which wouldn't be worth anything today, was sold for $350 million.

To its credit, Weider Nutrition also decided to establish itself as a producer and manufacturer to ensure the product quality of its supplements, even building a plant in Salt Lake City. Then it started buying up established companies in the supplement industry. By the end of the '90s, Weider was selling his supplements in at least sixty countries and grossing hundreds of millions of dollars for Weider's LA-based Total Fitness Company.

Schiff Nutrition, the successor company of which the Weider family owned seventy percent, was sold in 2012 to pharmaceutical giant Bayer for $1.2 billion. The interest of Big Pharma in the supplement industry continues to grow.

Joe Weider and the Weider publications were an integral part of the growth of Gold's Gym, along with bodybuilding and fitness in America and the rest of the world. If one were to stand in the lobby of Gold's Gym and ask the incoming, or potential, member why they were there, some might say, "Arnold," or, "the Hulk," "Lou Ferrigno," or perhaps, "The Ultimate Warrior." But the most frequent answer would be someone on the cover or in the pages of a Weider magazine.

When Weider Fitness Gyms, the Weider organization's attempt at gym franchising, failed, Gold's Gym became Weider's go-to gym. Gold's Gym was helped with that, even giving Chris Lund, Joe's favorite photographer, a studio and darkroom in the building in Venice. Those were the days before digital photography – and social media. We were probably one of the few gyms with a photography studio and most likely the only one with a darkroom.

All of the fitness magazines, not just Weider's, were the social media of the day. It was estimated that at its peak, a monthly issue of *Muscle & Fitness* was viewed by seven million people. Fitness fanatics read them over and over, like the Bible, in hopes of picking up the latest tips on how to get bigger and more muscular.

Jim Amentler, Alex Ardenti, Per Bernal, Ralph DeHaan, Bill Dobbins, Bill Comstock, Jerry Fredrick, Wayne Gallasch, Irv Gelb, Chuck Krall, Paula Crane, Jason Matthis, Steve Neece, Mitsuru Okabe, David Paul, Robert Reiff, Bill Reynolds, and Artie Zeller were some of the great photographers who shot at Gold's Gym. Each photographer had their style, so it was easy not to have favorites.

As the Catholic churches I attended preached, "All are welcome." John Balik and Mike Neveaux were given free rein for *Ironman* magazine. The same was true for Bob Kennedy with *MuscleMag,* and Steve Blechman with *Muscular Development.* Because these magazines had very few staff photographers and didn't pay for their people to travel to the various bodybuilding and fitness events, they waited for the talent to come to Gold's Gym Venice. Pete, Tim, and I were happy to help with that.

One of the first telephone calls I received after the sale of Gold's Gym International in 2004 was from one of those photographers. TRT Holdings, Inc., the new owner based in Dallas, wanted him to pay $350 to shoot in the gym. The new owners simply didn't get it.

GOLD'S GYM IN SANTA MONICA: 1977-1981

The storefront business at 1452 Second Street in Santa Monica was a couple of hundred square feet bigger than the original location in Venice. Like the Venice location, it had a couple of large windows facing the sidewalk where passersby could look in. There was a city parking structure across the street, so there was plenty of parking, at least for the time being, unlike the former Venice location.

I was working as a consultant on a parking structure down the street for the new Santa Monica mall that Frank Gehry was designing and realized that the halcyon days of empty streets and parking garages might be coming to an end.

Frank Gehry was relatively unknown but would become a "starchitect" — star architect — and one of the many celebrity members of Gold's Gym Venice. Ironically, the mall, which was at the southern terminus of the Santa Monica Promenade, became so successful that it was later demolished, enlarged, and opened to the sky to suit the latest mall design fashion. Even the six-story parking structure across from the gym was demolished and rebuilt to hold more vehicles.

Our landlord on Second Street was actor Robert Blake. He and his attorney were not the easiest people to deal with. They wanted to triple our rent. Perhaps it was because Blake was a loyal member of Vince Gironda's gym, the major gym in the Valley in Studio City, that he was being so difficult. Or maybe it was because his career had taken a hiatus. As a kid, I had enjoyed his starring role as a child actor in MGM's *Our Gang* (*Little Rascals*) film series, but his TV show *Beretta* had ended in 1978.

Whatever it was, between that and the parking, it seemed time to find another location. Twenty years later, Blake would be tried and acquitted for the 2001 murder of his second wife but be found liable in a civil court for her wrongful death. Terrible landlord, indeed.

GOLD'S GYM RETURNS TO VENICE: 1981

Again, my work as an architect played a huge role in the growth of Gold's Gym — along with Lady Luck.

I was working for the Office of Charles Eames in their design studio at 901 Abbot Kinney, located at the intersection of Brooks and Abbot Kinney Streets in Venice. Charles had recently died, and his wife, Ray, wanted help finishing some of their projects that involved more architectural design and not the furniture, exhibit, graphic design, or films for which that collaboration is so justifiably famous.

While working at the Eames Office, I noticed a warehouse a couple of blocks down the street at 358 Hampton Drive with an empty bay, fifty-three feet by 145 feet and nine inches, that had never been rented and had been vacant for several years. It looked perfect for the gym, with ceilings reaching twenty-five feet, and at 9,977 square feet with the mezzanine, it would be twice the size of the Santa Monica location.

The modern gym was being born. It would also mean bringing Gold's Gym back to its roots in Venice. It was only a couple of blocks from the original Gold's Gym and less than a mile from Muscle Beach.

Pete, Tim, and I didn't see the Muscle Beach weight pit as competition. After Universal Studios, Venice Beach was the second biggest tourist attraction in LA County. It was all part of the draw. The magic of Gold's Gym was that it was a block from the ocean. Bill Pearl's gym was in Pasadena — hot in the summer. Vince's Gym in Studio City was even hotter. Gold's Gym Venice didn't need air conditioning. Indeed, none of my three homes in Venice had air conditioning. And the heater or gas fireplace rarely had to be turned on.

Venice was created in 1905 by a developer looking for, to use a wrestling term, a "gimmick." Like its namesake in Italy, Venice came complete with waterways, bridged canals, and a turn-around for gondolas, along with a large amusement park on the beach. But by

1981, when Gold's Gym moved back to Venice to what would be its third and current location, it was not so charming.

Main Street, which had been a waterway, was now fronting on a seven-and-a-half-acre tract owned by the Southern California Gas Company, part of which was being used as a refinery. Later, when the site was being excavated for a three-hundred-fifty-car underground garage, it was discovered that the land had been badly contaminated. When Larry Field purchased the acreage for $3 per square foot in 1977, he constructed a production facility for Nabisco for their Rose Milk brand hand cream and lotion. After that came a manufacturing facility for Tristan Electronics on Main Street and Sunset Avenue. Then came the four-bay warehouse that Gold's Gym would occupy at Hampton Drive and Sunset Boulevard, one block east of Main.

Larry Field was the son of penniless immigrants when they arrived in New York City from Hungary. After moving to LA from the Bronx, Larry became an American success story, even having fun naming his real estate company NSB, which stood for "Not So Bad."

Perhaps because of his history, he was ready to take a chance on Gold's Gym, but I still had to personally guarantee the original lease and all the extensions that followed. We signed a twenty-year lease with three five-year options, which carried the space until 2016. I have learned that those twenty-year leases can go quicker than you might think.

Arnold took office space in one of the Gas Company's buildings. The Rose Cafe would ultimately take over the last remaining former Gas Company structure, where it still operates today.

Architect Frank Gehry eventually converted the Nabisco space into offices for the Chiat/Day ad agency, which gained worldwide fame with its "1984" ad for Apple, which was shown during the Super Bowl that year. They were a great neighbor and became Gold's Gym's ad agency for a while, producing groundbreaking material for us, ranging from TV commercials to the brochures for the tourist racks placed at hotels around the city.

Jay Chiat, one of the founders on Chiat/Day, next hired Frank to design its new headquarters across the street, including having Claes Oldenburg, the Swedish American sculptor, create a set of giant binoculars for the entrance to the underground garage that had been constructed on the ground contaminated by the Gas Company refinery. Digital Domain, a production company founded by James Cameron, the genius behind such movies as *The Terminator, Titanic,* and *Avatar,* eventually took over the old Chiat/Day offices. The neighborhood would evolve, but all this took time.

After being in the building for ten years, we would try to buy it every year, but Larry would inevitably respond, "I like to buy. I don't like to sell." I did manage to negotiate a deal to buy the four lots behind the gym from our neighbors for parking, and he became our 50/50 partner in those. I felt that would help strengthen our position with him because the buildings are all worthless without parking.

Also, I didn't fully trust Larry at this point. I had been disappointed when the former Chiat/Day warehouse space was leased to Digital Domain. We had been in serious negotiations for that site. I even had studies done regarding the feasibility of building a parking structure — my specialty — on that large site, one that would allow us to finally create a health food restaurant on the roof, the one we had dreamed of doing since the beginning. It would even have a view of the ocean.

Larry Field died in 2020 at eighty-nine, and now Google owns everything. Larry gave a lot to various charities during his lifetime. I can't help but wonder if some of that charity might have been extended to his tenants, perhaps allowing them to purchase the real estate they had occupied all those years — at a fair price, of course. They were the ones who helped make his fortune by faithfully paying the rent month after month, year after year. And, after all, Gold's Gym had changed the neighborhood.

When we moved back in 1981, Venice was dangerous. TV had made the Beverly Hills zip code, 90210, famous. The Venice zip code, 90291, sounded similar, maybe even glamorous, but it had the highest murder rate of any zip code in the United States. It was "Gangland," and it wasn't some section of Disneyland. Several gangs, like the Crips and the Bloods, were fighting each other for territory. You could pick up a hooker a block from the gym on Main Street. It wasn't safe.

In 1982, I purchased half of an unfinished duplex on a charming Venice walk street at 28 Paloma Avenue, two blocks from the gym. And I finally got that BMW I had saved for back in 1979 but had instead used the money to buy Gold's Gym. Those BMWs came with a standard Blaupunkt radio, which was a favorite target of car thieves at the time; one of those could yield $100 to buy drugs.

After AAA canceled my insurance when the radio was stolen — and the windows were smashed — for the sixth time, I turned my leased vehicle into the dealer. I said, "Now I know what BMW stands for: 'Break My Window.'"

I replaced that vehicle with a Ford Thunderbird, which I later sold to the wrestlers Sting and The Ultimate Warrior, who were then wrestling as the Freedom Fighters tag team.

Perhaps because I'm an architect, physical destruction bothers me more than most people. Vietnam was also fresh in my mind. While the loss of life was horrific, there was also the unexpected cost and waste of war. Walking around the gym parking lot and neighboring streets every day and seeing the piles of tempered glass on the ground from the previous night's break-ins was disheartening. It made me sick and angry. When some of the gym members caught a couple of gang members breaking into a gym member's car one night, I called the police. The person on the other end of the line said, "Can't you handle it? Aren't you Gold's Gym?"

One of the myths about bodybuilders is that they aren't as strong as they look. How many times had I heard that? True, they aren't Superman, but all you would have to do is watch some of them play with the 150-pound dumbbells — or 180s or 200s — in the gym to realize they're a lot stronger than the average person. And while not all bodybuilders are "fighters," their size and strength can make a difference regardless of how they feel about fighting.

I asked my manager to have the guys take care of them, perhaps teach them a lesson, and that the police had essentially given us carte blanche to do whatever needed to be done. After that, we never had a problem with the gangs. Even during the 1992 Rodney King riots, when supposedly a wave of rioters was heading toward the beach, destroying and looting everything in their path, we were left untouched.

Gold's Gym and its members transformed Venice, although it took time. It wasn't until 1985 — four years later — that The Firehouse Restaurant was brave enough to open. It's still there today with the same owner, Leiko Hamada. But now, thirty-seven years later, she had experienced break-ins from the homeless in the area during the pandemic even though they had been closed down for a while.

Sadly, it seems Venice has come full circle with the homeless as far as crime is concerned. But then, Gold's Gym was closed and not operating during the shutdown as well.

If one overlooked the gangs, which were more inland in the Oakwood area toward Lincoln Boulevard, Venice was what people liked to call "Bohemian." It seemed like a nice blend of San Francisco and Los Angeles: artistic and humanistic. This was the neighborhood during bodybuilding's golden age. It was composed of Jews, Latin immigrants, African Americans, writers, and artists. Anglos made up about sixty-four percent of the population, according to the 1980 census. A one-bedroom apartment costed $175 a month. Twenty years later, in 1999, that same apartment would rent for $475. Today, that rent would average $2,225 a month. Actor Dennis Hopper lived a few blocks from the gym and was a member, along with many others from Hollywood who lived along the Venice canals. Those canal houses went for $45,000 in 1979, $350,000 in 1999, and are selling for millions today.

The Gingerbread Court, a charming brick structure surrounding a courtyard just off the Venice boardwalk, two blocks west of today's Gold's Gym and near the duplex I purchased and remodeled for my residence, is a good example of the changes the neighborhood would experience. During the silent film era, it was the office of Charlie Chaplin's production company. Then it became a collection of shops and eateries during bodybuilding's golden age. More recently, it was the cafeteria for the employees of SNAP, one of the many high-tech companies that would move into — some say invade — Venice.

SNAP has since departed for Santa Monica, but at its peak, it took up 305,000 square feet of office space in Venice with forty-one different addresses. Google is there now with its seven thousand employees, one more reason why property values in Venice have risen eighty percent in the past fifteen years. Muscle Beach has become Silicon Beach.

The gym business comprises three elements: management,

capital, and location. You can theoretically change staff and add capital, but you can't do much about the location. However, the phrase "location, location, location" is much overused in the real estate world, at least as far as gyms go. It's hardly an impulse buy — not like fast food. McDonald's has determined that their average customer decides within twelve seconds whether to purchase a meal while driving by its golden arches.

With gyms, it's more a matter of convenience; it just helps to be close to where someone lives or works. Nowadays, internet-based programs will outline a twenty-minute drive time around a point on a map, along with incredibly detailed demographic information. Back then, information wasn't easy to come by. Gold's Gym Franchising, Inc. preferred that the market, defined then as a five-mile radius around the facility, have at least one hundred thousand people within that circle. (McDonald's started with fifty thousand.) That was close to Venice's market area, although half that area was in the Pacific Ocean. Venice is densely populated.

Supposedly, six to twelve percent of Americans worked out regularly in the '80s. That percentage varied depending on where someone lived, California being one of the higher-gym-use states. So, theoretically, there were twelve thousand potential members within that radius. If there were other choices for working out, say, two different facilities, you could then divide that twelve thousand by three and get four thousand members as an average number per club. The key, of course, was not to see that number divided equally three ways.

Gold's Gym Venice had twelve thousand members when it was sold along with Gold's Gym International in 2004. Joe Gold, who died that same year, had seven hundred members at his World Gym facility located about a mile away from Gold's Gym on Washington Boulevard in Marina del Rey.

One of the biggest myths or misconceptions concerning the gym business is that owners sell a membership hoping that the person never uses the facility. Nothing could be further from the truth, at least for the gyms I was involved in. You would think that with twelve thousand members there might be an overcrowding issue, but in my twenty-five years with the Venice gym, I received only one complaint regarding the gym being too crowded. And that came from Peter Paul, one of the Barbarian brothers, who wasn't even paying for a membership and could easily have come any time he wanted to avoid the crowds. Perhaps, like so many who fed off the energy of others, Peter and his brother, David, chose to go at 5 p.m. — prime time — to see and be seen. They were worth the price of admission, although Tim and I often had to reprimand them and threaten suspension for spitting on the floor.

The move back to Venice to that "expandable" warehouse space would be one of the most fortuitous moves imaginable. The gym would be able to expand into the entire four-bay warehouse over the next nine years. This was critically important as the fitness industry evolved during this period. While I designed the "new" Venice gym — the reincarnation of Gold's Gym in Venice and its third location — it was Tim Kimber who engineered the move in a brilliant negotiation with a TV production company.

Earlier, Tim had been cast in the movie *The Hustler of Muscle Beach* and had some familiarity with the entertainment industry. While occasionally starstruck, he was a tough negotiator. He made a deal with the producers of the TV show *Hart to Hart* to use the new gym space for filming before we moved from Santa Monica. Since the action was pending and announced to members, Tim put language in the contract that penalized the company for every day that delayed finishing shooting. Tim initially negotiated $5,000 a day for three days to film in the new location. But then Robert Wagner, the lead actor, strained his back, so shooting was delayed.

When the production company came back to seek more time, Tim asked for $12,500 a day for two more days. But then they needed a third day, so that was $25,000. In total, they spent $65,000 to film there — more money than the gym grossed in three months. The production company essentially paid for the move. The TV people even moved the gym equipment for free from Santa Monica to the new location three miles away. The gym also received a collection of "fake" weight plates from the production company. They were made out of balsa wood that carefully replicated the look of real metal plates. They would come in handy for the many photographers shooting in Gold's Gym; there was nothing "quick" about how most of them worked.

No doubt, those fake weights saved many athletes from significant injuries. We were glad to have them.

THE DESIGN OF THE NEW GYM

In those days before computer-aided drafting (CAD), the working drawings I drew for the new location took all of three two-by-three-foot sheets of paper. It was that simple: There would be a gym workout floor on the ground floor, with separate toilets for men and women. Additional toilets and sinks were on the mezzanine level, along with the men's and women's locker rooms and showers. With the extra square footage, the women would have an actual locker room, which they hadn't had in Santa Monica.

I can't imagine this design working for any other location in the US. It was that basic — crude, really. It would also be impossible today given the requirements in the Americans with Disabilities Act, which was enacted in 1990. We would have had to put in an elevator, which would have cost as much as the entire build-out. I have since argued for other gym projects that the money for an elevator would be better spent buying vans for the handicapped so they would be more mobile, but I have lost those appeals several times.

Imagine walking into a hearing room where five of the six people on the committee reviewing your project are in wheelchairs. Even so, I think Gold's Gym Venice had more members in wheelchairs than any other gym I've visited. I even sponsored Ludovic Marchand and Victor Konovalov, two of our handicapped members, in the first bodybuilding contest for athletes in wheelchairs. Both had lost their legs in motorcycle accidents. They went on to win several victories on the stage and in life. If seeing one of them on stage doesn't motivate someone to train, I don't know what does.

Gold's Gym Venice was like the stereotypical Chinese restaurant where the interior is ugly but the food is incredible. The simplicity of the design was so novel that it was later published in the March-April 1983 edition of the Italian magazine *Il Bagno*. It is every architect's dream to be published — and in an Italian design magazine, no less. I was flattered but surprised. It was the absence of any architectural style that became a style itself. And the layout has lasted forty years — with a few remodels in between.

I did experiment with the lighting, which is something that has changed the most over the past forty years. I used high-pressure sodium uplights rather than the strips of fluorescent lights I had seen in so many facilities and hated. The gym was big for the time as it was almost entirely filled with equipment, something I had to prove to the building department. This was 1981, and there was no classification in the zoning laws or building codes for "fitness centers." The only category that seemed to come close was "gymnasium," which the plan checkers assumed meant something like a large basketball court with bleachers filled with spectators, like something that might be found at a high school or college. I had to show them that this space could not be used as an "assembly area" with all the equipment in place.

Since it was a sports facility, green AstroTurf seemed appropriate for Gold's Gym Venice. It's hard to imagine now, but back then, there were many fitness facilities with shag carpeting, which seemed wrong, even gross, especially to Europeans. Later on, when the partners at Brockway Moran wanted to know why the early license agreements were only five years in length (while franchising stalwarts like McDonald's had twenty-year contracts), I got a laugh when I answered that was the likely life of the carpet in the gym. Gold's Gym Franchising Inc. wanted to have leverage over the owner to get a new agreement — and put down new carpeting or some other new flooring at the same time.

That new flooring became rubber flooring. In a matter of months, the AstroTurf was showing the cuts where weights had been dropped. The rubber flooring industry was in its infancy, so I used conveyor belt material glued to the building's concrete slab. It had a strong odor at first but did the job.

BIKES IN THE GYM

Cardio equipment was one of those "new" equipment requirements for a gym. When it all started in 1985, "bikes in the gym" might as well have been "snakes in the gym" because it was so foreign. But biking was common in the neighborhood and on the beach. The bike path edging the sand and fronting the Pacific Ocean was an integral part of the scene.

After I left my full-time job as an architect, I would often leave the gym office around lunchtime and go for an hourlong ride to clear my head and get some exercise. I had been a big fan of bicycles from an early age, after winning a fancy English racing bike in a coloring contest in Omaha. On the weekends, if I kept to the ten-miles-per-hour speed limit for bikes, I could cover forty miles in four hours, which would get me down to the beginning of Rancho Palos Verdes and back. Following the routine I had grown up with, I never wore a helmet or specialty gear.

Mike Mentzer, a Mr. America and Mr. Olympia competitor, and his brother, Ray, were two of the more prominent bodybuilders training at the gym in the mid-'80s. They, too, liked to cycle along the beach. They were big proponents of cardio.

Though it rarely rained, the thought occurred to Pete, Tim, and me that this activity ought to be brought inside for the days when it did.

I had already purchased some Schwinn squirrel-cage bikes at $350 each for my gym in San Francisco. It rained there, and the city was hilly, so it made sense. I had seen white bikes in my dad's medical office, and those are what I got.

Initially, the bikes were placed above the restrooms in the first room. They were accessible via the stairs that led to the mezzanine with the locker rooms. When that area became too crowded, bikes were added to the site on top of the gym's maintenance room at the back of the gym.

It was a boring activity, but someone on a bike could be entertained by looking down at the gym floor below from those vantage points. It was a great way to get an education as far as the use of the equipment was concerned. It was like watching an exercise video — except you could get caught staring.

Nine years later, when the gym expanded into the last of the four bays, a large area was dedicated solely for cardio. It was composed of stepped platforms constructed out of wood to accommodate the electrical wiring. One couldn't easily see into the gym and be entertained by the view, so the biggest TVs available were placed in front of the bikes. This arrangement would eventually be trademarked as "cardio theater," but back then, it was simply "bikes in front of TVs." Funny how Peloton insists it is a tech company, billing itself as "the largest interactive fitness platform in the world," but it still just looks like a bike with a TV on it to me. It seems like it's no longer good enough for companies to simply be what they are.

Nowadays, it's normal for a well-equipped gym to have more than a hundred pieces of cardio, many with TVs on them: bikes, recumbent bikes, steppers, treadmills, and more elaborate machines like ellipticals. But back in the beginning, that wasn't the case. The $100,000 it cost to equip the first Gold's Gym franchise in San Francisco would barely cover the cost of twenty treadmills.

AEROBICS: GROUP X

After cardio with the bikes, aerobics — group exercise — was the next significant activity to be added to Gold's Gym Venice when the gym expanded into the second bay in 1985, an area previously used for our apparel division. Aerobic studios had started to close because of higher rents and limited class schedules. Jane Fonda had wisely decided to concentrate on workout videos and not franchise her workout studios. It made sense to add that activity to the gym, especially if it brought in more women. The gyms could add it as an additional amenity as part of the regular membership price. Some of them, however, initially charged separately, even requiring members to have a paper ticket to enter a class.

Once again, my background as an architect played a role. Even though it was expensive, I went to the Vidal Sassoon hair salon on Rodeo Drive in Beverly Hills to get my hair cut and styled. I started going there because the salon had been designed by a famous East Coast architect who used the same materials I was given for the Neiman Marcus store I was designing in Beverly Hills: travertine, stainless steel, and bronze. I wanted to see how they had been used. My stylist was deaf and so was aided by an assistant, Maureen Meadows. When he died of AIDS — like so many people I knew in the '80s — Maureen became my stylist and so learned more about me, the "architect-gym owner."

When I mentioned that Gold's Gym was considering an aerobics program, she told me about her friend, Kathy Stevens, who was perfect for it. Kathy had been one of the first aerobic fitness program directors in Southern California and had developed programs for several other clubs. Kathy wisely realized that it had to be a different aerobics program to start with at Gold's Gym Venice. For this, she enlisted the help of some well-known personal trainers, such as John Richling and Francois Petit.

John was a competitive bodybuilder who I had encouraged to move to LA from Omaha and who was my trainer. He ended up teaching a class on posture and breathing. Francois was a martial artist and led the self-defense classes. Having celebrity members like Carl Weathers or Fred Dryer dropping in on the classes helped make them acceptable and cool, and the program took off. The aerobics room, like the gym, had the potential to be more like a social club where the workout is part of the experience but not the primary part of it. People today will want community like that more than ever after the pandemic.

Many gyms followed Gold's Gym's lead in adding group exercise. In the ten years following our introduction of aerobics, there was a forty-five percent decrease in the number of participants using independent aerobics studios in the US.

The business model was changing. Now it was time for fitness centers to add it to their facilities — if they had the room. Fate had given us the room, and we filled it. I can remember getting death threats when the announcement was made that we were adding aerobics to the Mecca. But aerobics is now "Group X."

People are afraid of change, but change is the constant. "If you're not growing, you're dying!"

ONE GYM FITS ALL

It is hard to imagine a time when it was essentially "one gym fits all." But when Gold's Gym Venice added the third bay of the four-bay warehouse to the gym in 1989, it set a standard for gyms, lasting nearly two decades, from 1990 to 2010. *The Santa Monica Evening Outlook* newspaper declared on August 4, 1989, that, "At 20,750 square feet of workout space, it is one of the largest gyms in the world." Today the health club industry is quite different and incredibly fractured.

Currently, there are at least five categories of gyms in America: high-end, luxury clubs like Equinox and Life Time Fitness, easily thirty-five thousand square feet and one hundred thousand square feet, respectively; big-box gyms like Gold's Gym, LA Fitness, and 24 Hour Fitness, in the twenty-five to thirty-five thousand square feet range; budget gyms, like Planet Fitness and Anytime Fitness, eighteen thousand and eight thousand square feet, respectively; boutique clubs, like SoulCycle, Orange Theory, and SNAP; and small, local hardcore gyms similar to the first Gold's Gym or ones utilizing CrossFit. It's quite possible a new category of fitness facility will be needed after the pandemic.

In 1990, on its twenty-fifth anniversary, Gold's Gym Venice entered the fourth and last bay. Nine years after the initial move back to Venice, Gold's Gym would occupy every square foot of the building, consisting of thirty-two thousand square feet, with the gym occupying 24,648 square feet of space. The wall between the first two rooms and the second set of two bays was an eight-inch-thick shear wall for seismic reinforcement for earthquakes, so only a small opening could be cut into it. But the barrier between the third and fourth rooms was a sheetrock-covered demising wall that could be removed so that the gym became three "rooms" in most people's eyes. Ironically, because of this, I think the gym area seemed larger than it was.

The gym offices were in the remaining space. The other businesses in the four-bay warehouse building hadn't thought Gold's Gym would last, but they were wrong. Gold's Gym had outlasted them all and had completely changed the neighborhood.

Pete, Tim, and I were not afraid to try new things. Tom Wilson, the gym manager, and Rich Minzer, Paul Grymkowski's assistant, cajoled the various equipment companies into letting Gold's Gym Venice become a testing ground and showroom for their equipment. At first, I don't think the manufacturers realized how invaluable the coverage they would get in the magazines along with Gold's Gym and its athletes would be.

I think this kind of exposure made companies like Hammer Strength almost an overnight success. The manufacturers told us that they could see wear and tear on their machines in a matter of months that would take years to show up elsewhere, so it indeed became a working laboratory. But it all came with the caveat that if it wasn't liked, it would be removed. Most of the equipment lines stayed, and as resistance machines evolved, they required more and more space. In the end, we had almost two million dollars' worth of "free" equipment.

BRANDING

In addition to architecture, graphic design was one of my passions. I first developed logo sheets for our licensees to clean up and standardize the Gold's Gym brand. The round logo — inspired by a weight plate — came a little later. Eventually, the bald man lifting the barbell, who we referred to as "Mickey," was replaced by "Oscar" to give the brand a more modern look, but both were in continuous use.

I had Barbara Stauffacher Solomon as a graphic design instructor at UC Berkeley. She had come from a Swiss-trained background, undoubtedly influenced by some of the same architects and designers employed by the Third Reich, who used powerful combinations of red, yellow, white, and black. I used them all. They worked for McDonald's. They would work for Gold's Gym. Above the mirrors in the gym, there was a continuous painted stripe consisting of red, black, yellow, and white in various formats, which read "GOLD'S GYM VENICE," along with the phrases "The Mecca of Bodybuilding" and "Serious Fitness for Every Body." It would be nearly impossible for anyone to take a photo or video in the gym without the Gold's Gym name and branding in view. This is true even today with social media photos. But back then, it was all about magazines.

Those bodybuilding and fitness magazines went all over the world. As a result, the Gold's Gym name went with them. The Weider magazines had the broadest reach. They were printed in thirty-seven languages — three alone in India, which now has over a hundred Gold's Gyms. A one-time, full-color ad in one of those magazines could cost as much as $35,000. But you could often pick up a copy of a bodybuilding or fitness magazine and see more than a dozen pages of full-page color photos showing beautiful, fit people working out, with the Gold's Gym name somewhere in the image. The individuals might even be wearing Gold's Gym clothing. There was so much of Gold's Gym in Weider's magazines that many people thought he owned it. These pictures became invaluable later on when Gold's Gym Enterprises needed proof of use of its brand to protect its trademarks both in the US and in foreign countries where it wanted to franchise or sell merchandise.

Gold's Gym Enterprises spent very little on advertising or marketing — less than $500,000 a year at its peak. Of course, the franchises made millions of impressions with their individual advertising budgets, but nothing quite compares to the free publicity Gold's Gym Venice achieved in the media. It was the ultimate grassroots marketing. It built the brand.

GIVE TO GET

Gold's Gym's marketing plan might as well be called "Give to Get." Pete, Tim, and I gave away a lot of discounted or free memberships and products. There were special arrangements for the police, fire rescue personnel, and sports and entertainment celebrities. I offered members of the clergy I met a complimentary membership; most accepted. As St. Francis had cautioned his fellow brothers: If the body is the temple of God, then it's best to take care of it. Catholic priests told me they heard confessions in the gym, and when a member was in the hospital or died, they practiced the corporal works of mercy by visiting them or helping grieving family members.

At one point, Joel Morse, our outside CPA for the critical last ten years of the business, asked us to keep track of the value of anything we gave away so he could quantify it for accounting purposes. This "goodwill" averaged $60,000 a month, even hitting as high as $80,000. "Standards & Practices," as the networks termed it, were more relaxed back in the '80s. If you were to give Eddie Murphy a Gold's Gym leather jacket, which he would end up wearing for the three hours he hosted the annual MTV Video Music Awards show, what would that be worth?

Famous people wanted to associate themselves with health and fitness. As long as Weider hired a stylist, makeup artist, and world-class photographer to shoot the celebrity for the cover of one of his magazines, no money changed hands. The same was true for Gold's Gym Venice. No star was ever paid to endorse the gym.

Tim said what was different about Gold's Gym Venice was that we were "family." For that reason, we were open on Christmas — maybe the first gym ever to do that. We knew that for some of our members, we were the only family they had. Our holiday hours were reduced to allow our staff to be with their families in the late afternoon, but that schedule worked for everyone.

My father was an emergency room surgeon, and the holidays were a hectic time of the year, when dysfunctional families got together and ended up hurting one another and sending family members to the hospital. I like to think that being open on Thanksgiving, Christmas, and New Year's allowed some of the members of those households an alternative to get out of the house for a while and relieve stress. Maybe lives were saved. And for our Jewish members, we gave them a place to go on Christmas besides a Chinese restaurant.

McDonald's didn't invent the hamburger; it just took it seriously. Pete Grymkowski, Tim Kimber, and I didn't create the gym business; we just took it seriously.

The driving concept of Gold's Gym was that there was no stereotypical bodybuilder or "muscleman," that everyone had muscle. The Gold's Gym franchises provided clean, well-equipped facilities with friendly staff, a novel concept at a time when "serious" or "hardcore" usually meant "dirty" and "unwelcoming."

Like McDonald's, Gold's Gym would be a good value for the money. When we sold to Brockway Moran & Partners in 1999, the Millennium Edition of the *Guinness World Records 2000* recognized Gold's Gym as the largest gym chain in the world, with 534 locations in forty-six states and twenty-four countries.

Gold's Gym succeeded on a grand scale because it had the wisdom and the courage to rely on hundreds of other entrepreneurs, including its employees, who were given tremendous freedom. Being the first, we were not bound by tradition. Joe Weider and his media empire changed the culture regarding physical fitness. Gold's Gym, along with Arnold, helped with that change.

PART II

THE GOLDEN AGE OF BODYBUILDING

Gold's Gym billboard in New Jersey

MEETING ARNOLD FOR THE FIRST TIME

I was thirty years old when I met Arnold Schwarzenegger in 1975. He wasn't yet in that elite group of people known by one name. In fact, his name was considered such a liability to future success in the entertainment industry that he was billed as Arnold Strong in his first movie, *Hercules in New York*. He was twenty-eight when I ran into him outside the original Gold's Gym in Venice. I had seen photos of him in Weider's magazines, so I knew who he was.

I asked him what he wanted to do, what his dream was. Arnold said three things: "I want to be rich; I want to marry well; and I want to be famous." I didn't doubt him for a second. If Arnold had told me he wanted to be governor of California or president of the United States, I would have thought, sure, he could be. That's the kind of charisma Arnold had. If Senator Ted Kennedy had lived a few more years, he might have gotten legislation passed that would have allowed Arnold to run for president, allowing a foreign-born resident to run for office if they lived in the US for at least thirty-five years. When Ted Kennedy died in 2009, Arnold had lived in the US for a total of forty-one years, more than half his life.

When Arnold won the Mr. Olympia title for the sixth time in 1975 — the subject of Charles Gaines and George Butler's book *Pumping Iron,* and George's movie of the same name — it marked the start of competitive bodybuilding on a grand scale in America. The book sold over six million copies. The movie was seen in almost every major American city when it opened in May 1977. It was followed by the National Physique Committee breakup from the Amateur Athletic Union. My partner, Pete Grymkowski, helped engineer that.

The AAU, which owned the Mr. America title, was guided by Bob Hoffman of York Barbell in York, Pennsylvania, a competitor of Weider's with weightlifting equipment and a magazine, *Strength & Health*. Besides the AAU, there was Dan Lurie's World Bodybuilding Guild and his magazine, and the National Amateur British Bodybuilding Association. But they were no match for the

International Federation of BodyBuilders, which Ben and Joe Weider used to support their international businesses.

At a meeting in Santa Monica, Ben Weider promised that if the NPC worked with the IFBB, the IFBB would not create its own amateur organization in the US, and the Weider magazines would publicize the NPC's events. Ben had done something similar in 1971 when he barred competitors from competing in both the NABBA Universe and the IFBB Olympia. They had to choose one.

Hoffman was more interested in competitive weightlifting than bodybuilding. His contests would go on for hours with weightlifting only to see the bodybuilding portion begin at the end of a long afternoon and evening, often starting after midnight. So, the split meant a new beginning for men's bodybuilding because now it would be on its own and have its own contests with no weightlifting. It was a messy beginning as each side fought for dominance: Ben and Joe Weider vs. Bob Hoffman; the IFBB/NPC vs. the AAU.

The emergence of competitive bodybuilding would be the spark to ignite a veritable explosion in health and fitness. It was bodybuilding's big bang moment, given the explosion of bodybuilding contests across the US. The start of Gold's Gym's expansion into licensing its brand for gyms in 1980 coincided with the rise and expansion of men's bodybuilding in America — and then Gold's Gym introduced women's bodybuilding — and gyms for both men and women.

THE BEGINNING OF THE GOLDEN AGE

Pete, Tim, and I did not start out to create the first gym franchise of its kind. But once we started, it was our goal that during the twenty-five years my partners and I were owners of Gold's Gym, it would be the largest gym chain in the world.

We were aided in this effort by the visitors to my homes, who helped make Gold's Gym Venice the Mecca and the most famous gym in the world. Some of these early visitors were great athletes who got caught in that transition between the AAU and NPC and never had the careers they deserved, people like NABBA Mr. Universe winners Jeff King and Matt DuFresne, Victor Terra, Jerry Scalesse, Bob Gosch, Mike Jaudes, Rich Roy, Frankie Vassil, and Mr. America Joe DeAngelis.

I brought them to my first home in Venice, where they stayed while getting photographed at the Mecca by magazines other than Weider's, such as *Strength & Health, Muscle Up, Iron Man,* and *Muscle Digest*. They carried the results and images from competing bodybuilding federations, like the AAU and NABBA.

In conjunction with the Jr. Mr. America, Gold's Gym held the first Women's World Bodybuilding Championship on June 16, 1979, at the Trinity Auditorium, a spectacular old theater located at 842 South Grand Avenue in downtown LA, now derelict. It was won by Lisa Lyons, a gym member who became an early spokesperson for women's bodybuilding. A year later, we held the American Women's Bodybuilding Championships in the Santa Monica Auditorium, along with the Mr. America contest — the last AAU-NPC joint venture — which Gary Leonard won, another early houseguest of mine.

In 1981, Gold's Gym promoted the Mr. America contest along with the American Women's Bodybuilding Championships. We were able to get the event televised, thanks to the help of Nick Martino, one of my early business partners in the gyms. Nick wisely recommended we create a "mixed pairs" competition to get HBO interested in covering it. Nick was an associate producer of the famous TV game show *Hollywood Squares*. Tragically, he was one of the early victims of HIV/AIDS and died at a very young age.

The NPC ended up winning the battle with the AAU. The NPC organization has endured and indeed prospered. Like great architecture or great design, bodybuilding can be very subjective.

Maybe it was my architect's eye, but it's uncanny how I was able to pick at least one person awarded an NPC pro card every year between 1983 and 2004 except for a couple of years in between. Some years there were even two or three whom I helped in some way to turn pro. It seems especially remarkable now because the NPC was awarding only three pro cards a year for most of that time.

It began with Bob Paris at the Nationals (NAT) in 1983, followed by:

- Rich Gaspari (NAT '84)
- Dave Hawk at the USAs (USA) in '85
- Gary Strydom (NAT '86)
- Mike Quinn (USA '87) and Dave Dearth (NAT '87)
- John Defendis (USA '88)
- Troy Zuccolotto (NAT '89), Eddie Robinson (USA '89), and Franco Santoriello (NAT '89)
- Aaron Baker (USA '90), and Jim Quinn at the North Americans (NA) in '90
- Mike Matarazzo (USA '91)
- Flex Wheeler (USA '92) and Tom Varga (NAT '92)
- Mike Francois (NAT '93)
- Paul DeMayo (NAT '94), Dennis Newman (USA '94), and Jeff Poulin (NA '94)
- Phil Hernon (USA '95)
- Jay Cutler (NAT '96) and Craig Titus (USA '96)
- Tom Prince (NAT '97)
- Jason Arntz (NAT '98)
- Aaron Maddron (NAT '99) and Mike Morris (NA '99)
- Jeramy Freeman (NA '01),
- Matt DuVall (NAT '03)
- Chris Cook (NAT '04)

This was bodybuilding's golden age. Unlike today, there was incredible depth in these events, like the 1991 Nationals: Kevin

Levrone placed first; Flex Wheeler was second; and Paul DeMayo third. Ronnie Coleman, who came in fourth, would go on to win the Mr. Olympia title eight times.

Nowadays, there are more trophies than competitors in most local and regional contests and even national events. That way, everyone gets a trophy.

Like the men I served with in Vietnam, most were from small-town America and had not gone to college. It is a wonder they dared to dream, given where they came from. They were driven away from their hometowns by the larger culture. They were considered freaks. If they had anyone who cared, their parents didn't understand them either. A survey would reveal an inordinate number of broken homes. Their peers underestimated them or tried to limit them for one reason or another, usually because of jealousy. All the people on the list above were in their twenties or right around thirty, adolescence being one great fight. Many started in the teenage division, where as many as sixty competitors were often competing.

Thirty isn't old. For most, it's the start of a new life, as it was for me. But for a bodybuilding career, it could be too late. Gary Strydom was considered an old man when he won the Nationals at twenty-seven. Mike Francois was twenty-nine when he finally got his pro card on the third attempt. Craig Titus was thirty when he got his. Jim Quinn was thirty-one. And Matt Mendenhall was thirty-one when he quit after going for a pro card six times.

They all wanted to grow beyond their birth circumstances and poverty and be something great — like a superhero. Superheroes could do impossible things, like Elon Musk being compared to *Iron Man's* Tony Stark today. Unbelievable things, indeed.

It was a time when the media was critical. The bodybuilding and fitness magazines defined this cultural moment, and these people were the face of bodybuilding in the magazines. They were also the face of Gold's Gym. On the covers or inside the pages of the magazines, they became larger-than-life characters, like the ones they had idolized growing up.

With its endless selfies and podcasts, today's social media makes them all-too-human. Listening to bodybuilders talk for hours — often to one another — upends this fantasy and destroys the illusion.

Some had never really felt special until they saw themselves on the cover of a magazine. This was a time when *Muscle & Fitness* and *Shape* magazines were in the top ten magazines sold in America, and you could find them at most supermarket checkout counters. I would get a kick out of seeing a houseguest purchase a copy, hoping that the clerk would recognize them on the cover. It was an extraordinary moment.

Because of the magazines, photos, and stories, they also became known to the NPC judges, who would undoubtedly be more likely to look at them on stage if they recognized the person from the magazines. I call it "lazy judging," but it was the reality. Their publicity, in turn, became publicity for Gold's Gym.

With most of them, all that was needed was some help, a little bit of encouragement, to push them over the edge to turn pro. With Rich Gaspari, one of the first, all it took was a little advice and then a job working at one of my gyms.

I met Rich when he was competing in San Jose. This was before the super heavyweight category was created, so at over 198 pounds, he was in the heavyweight class but didn't do well because of his height. At five feet, eight inches, he was overshadowed by the taller guys. It didn't matter how good he was. I told him he should drop down a weight class and invited him to work and train in Southern California at my Gold's Gym in Reseda. He ended up winning the following year. It helped that he was at a gym where other great bodybuilders trained, people like Gary Strydom, Matt Mendenhall, and Lee Haney, who had just turned pro. Lee would win Mr. Olympia, and Strydom would head up Vince McMahon's World Bodybuilding Federation. Rich learned from them.

In a letter on October 26, 1989, Dave Dearth wrote:

"Dear Ed, In 1986 you picked me out from a group of excellent competitors. You stood by me through the years, giving me the confidence and motivation I needed. You have been an extraordinary friend, and I am indebted to you."

As with Rich, I invited Dave out to California to work in one of my gyms where he could be closer to all the action. In the world of bodybuilding, bigger has often meant better — or at least an easier road to a pro career. Dave was one of only three middleweight competitors I ever encouraged; I felt they could all grow into a fitness career. They all turned pro. I felt like the Wizard in *The Wizard of Oz* giving the Cowardly Lion a medal for courage. Most of these athletes lacked confidence or suffered from low self-esteem. They did not lack heart like the Tin Man or brains like the Scarecrow. It takes much heart to be a competitive bodybuilder, and brains to figure out the right combination of everything to win.

It also takes the right genetics. While genetics may only be five percent of the makeup of a champion, without it, success is unlikely. Somehow I was able to spot that as well, so at times, I felt not like the Wizard of Oz but more like Yoda telling someone to "use the force" that they had it in them. They needed to find it and pursue it. And if someone didn't have that, I was honest about it. I would never lie to someone and say they had a future in fitness if I didn't believe it myself.

Matt DuVall, one of the biggest bodybuilders at five feet, eleven inches and three-hundred-plus pounds, wrote to me about the upcoming USAs in Las Vegas in a letter from July 1, 1997:

"... I feel confident that you can help to guide me in the right direction. In the past, I was very 'stand-offish' to anyone lending support or direction — all this due to insecurities — now I have conquered those insecurities and see the benefits of experienced direction. Thank you not only for listening but for giving honest opinions."

I had taken Matt to the Jr. Nationals in Orlando the previous year to show him that he belonged in the pro ranks. I did something similar with Evan Centopani. People respected me for always giving an honest opinion and being willing to put my wallet where my mouth was, which helped them know that I believed what I said.

While some like Gaspari, Strydom, and Dearth worked in Gold's Gym locations with which I was involved, for most of them — like Mike Matarazzo, Paul DeMayo, Tom Prince, Jay Cutler, Chris Cook, Matt DuVall, and Aaron Madison — it was a trip to Venice to train and get the exposure that made the difference in their careers. Nowadays, with Facebook, Instagram, Twitter, and TikTok, a person can gain publicity from anywhere. But back then, Gold's Gym Venice was the center of the universe for the fitness media. They were able to be photographed to become known worldwide — and to themselves.

When Nick Trigili, who turned pro in 2014, was flying into LA from Las Vegas in 2012, he wondered how long he would be staying.

I texted this message to his phone: "We will drive (back) to Las Vegas probably Thursday unless you get discovered in Venice and can stay. :)"

He texted back: "Lolol."

I texted: "It has happened. After 28 years living in Venice, nothing would surprise me."

He replied: "Lol, really?"

When Nick walked into the gym at the height of six feet, one inch and 285 pounds, he got discovered. After two days in the Venice gym, he had an offer of a job, a car, and a place to stay.

When I took amateurs to meet Joe Weider in hopes of getting a contract and being sponsored, Joe would often ask me, "How do you know they're going to win?" To me, it was obvious, like how I knew when I brought Dennis Newman and Mike Francois to see Joe, one of them would win that year, and the one who didn't would most likely win the following year — which is precisely what happened.

I met Dennis when he was a teenager. He was a frequent visitor to Venice, as he lived in California. Mike had come in second place two years in a row. When I contacted him to ask what it would take for him to win, he said he needed to train twice a day and get a nap during the three months before his contest. Mike needed a sponsor. He lived in Columbus, Ohio, so I invited him to meet Joe. When Joe hesitated with him, I introduced Mike to Mike Zumpano, the owner of Champion Nutrition, a rival but much smaller supplement company. Zumpano hired him on the spot. When Francois won later that year and got his pro card, it eventually cost Joe twice as much to get him as a Weider athlete.

I invited Joe to visit Gold's Gym Venice more often to meet the guys himself. But it wasn't easy getting him to come to Venice from either his office in Woodland Hills in the Valley or his home in Hancock Park, an area west of downtown LA.

Venice is an acquired taste. You have to be a "Venetian" to live there — or apparently even to visit. During the nearly three decades I lived in Venice, I will admit that I never had one visitor to my various homes on Halloween. After buying treats to hand out the first couple of years, I gave up on having trick-or-treaters. Halloween was nothing special in Venice. As it turns out, it was amateur night.

Most of my visitors had been top athletes in high school sports like baseball, track, football, and wrestling, and very few went on to college. They were not your stereotypical ninety-eight-pound weaklings who joined a gym to put on muscle. Nor were they fat kids growing up, like me, who started working out to burn calories and lose weight. Physiques had come a long way from the days of Charles Atlas getting sand kicked in his face in the comic book ads or Steve Reeves in *Hercules* and the gladiator movies. This was a different breed, starting with Arnold. These bodybuilders became real-life superheroes to their fans. There was nothing small about them. This was the era of HUGE. They were larger than life.

Thanks to steroids, the evolution of GI Joe dolls from a fit soldier to a mountainous, V-shaped hulk was increasingly achievable. Ironically, steroid use among athletes was labeled "pandemic" back then. By the beginning of the '90s, it was estimated that 350,000 to a half-million high school students were using steroids.

Quite a few of these athletes attended the Gold's Gym conventions in Las Vegas and the amateur and pro bodybuilding contests held in that city, like the USAs and Mr. Olympia. I would make a point of taking them to see the copy of Michelangelo's *David* that was on display at Caesars Palace. I have seen the real *David* several times in Florence, where it is displayed in a rotunda similar to Caesars. Like Michelangelo's masterpiece, the reproduction is gigantic — seventeen feet tall, three times the size of an actual man, and weighing six tons. *David* was a giant marble god, except he was a man — a perfect man. It is probably the greatest piece of sculpture ever created, and Michelangelo, the greatest sculptor who ever lived; there is no one who compares to him.

These modern gods, these bodybuilders from the golden era, had the symmetry and proportions of a classic physique but had added incredible mass to their structure, something unimaginable before Arnold, let alone five hundred years ago, or two thousand years before that with the Greek and Roman sculpture that so inspired the Renaissance artists. When the movie *Pumping Iron* premiered in New York City, Charles Gaines and Richard Butler had Arnold and other bodybuilders from the movie pose at the Whitney Museum of Art. They were presented as living works of art, like *David*. The trick is to put on that size and retain the art and elegance of that statue.

Unfortunately, most pro bodybuilders onstage these days have left that aesthetic behind. With the hindsight of four decades, I can say that while there is now incredible size, there is little beauty.

"It's unacceptable the way bodybuilding is going. We don't want to see stomachs sticking out. We want to see the most beautiful man, the most aesthetic man," Arnold has said.

People call them "mass monsters." With the advent of classic bodybuilding, it may now be "back to the future" as that older look is revived. The same thing may happen to the gyms post-COVID.

As Chris Bell, a former front counter employee and, as it turns out, resident genius at Gold's Gym Venice documents in his groundbreaking documentary movie, *Bigger, Stronger, Faster,* these bodybuilders were like nothing that had come before them. And as it turns out, the physiques during this golden age have a look that may never be seen again.

But the world has changed for a lot of professional athletes. It had once been simply about getting in shape and learning to play with your teammates if it was a team sport. But now, it's assumed that that's a base from which you must go higher.

Pro bodybuilders, along with many other professional athletes these days, often have an entire team of advisors working with them called gurus. Genetics for bodybuilding is critical, and basic skills are taken for granted, but you are expected to take that to a whole other level. It has become something simple: Getting better at getting bigger.

This was bodybuilding's golden age, but I encouraged a few others after those two decades: Joel Thomas and Brad Rowe in 2007 at the Nationals, when the NPC was giving out two pro cards in each weight class. After that, there were a few others: Seth Feroce, Jeff Long, and Evan Centopani at the Nationals in 2009, Brian Yersky at the Nationals and Dallas McCarver at the North Americans in 2012, and Caleb Blanchard and Nick Trigili in 2014 at the USAs.

It is essential to put these pro cards in perspective by comparing them with today's competitive bodybuilding scene. When the NPC started, there was only a men's bodybuilding overall winner and a women's overall bodybuilding winner — two pro cards — and there were only three pro qualifiers a year. Compare that with the current state of affairs: The NPC gave out 614 pro cards in 2019 in the following categories:

- Masters Men's Bodybuilding (BB) 40+: two classes
- True Novice: one class
- Novice Men's BB: two classes
- Unlimited Men's BB: seven classes: bantamweight, lightweight, welterweight, middleweight, light heavyweight, super heavyweight
- Masters Figure 35+: one class
- Masters Figure 40+: one class
- Masters Figure 50+: one class
- Unlimited Figure: five classes
- Women's Physique: one class
- Master's Men Physique 45+: one class
- Master's Men Physique 35+: one class
- Teen Men's Physique: one class
- Novice Men's Physique: three classes
- Unlimited Men's Physique: seven classes
- Master's Bikini 35+: one class
- Masters Bikini 45+: one class
- Novice: six classes
- Unlimited Bikini: eight classes

There are weight or height classes within these various categories, so many subdivisions that there are usually more trophies than competitors. For example, men's physique initially had six height classes: A, B, C, D, E, and F, and then added a seventh, G. In short, everyone gets a trophy. Depending on how many categories they enter, some even get two or three trophies. A typical NPC promoter might have three hundred competitors but twice as many entry fees as competitors choose to enter more than one division: six hundred entries at $300 per entry fee is $180,000 in entry fees alone.

There's almost no incentive to sell tickets, which tend to be outrageously priced anyway. The cheapest ticket at the Olympia in 2019 was $150. The eight-thousand-seat arena at The Orleans Hotel was half-empty. Most of the people who had gone to Las Vegas for the Olympia weekend watched on their laptops in their hotel rooms.

There were no entry fees when Gold's Gym put on contests in the '80s. The competitors were the show. It seemed like double dipping to make them pay to compete. And the ticket prices were priced fair enough that the three-thousand-seat Santa Monica auditorium was sold out.

The NPC has recently added even more categories, such as "true novice," for competitors who have never competed before, a "heroes" category for former military, and a "wellness" class for women who feel somewhere between a bikini and physique competitor. At just one contest in 2021, the NPC could potentially give over two hundred pro cards, all of which come with an annual renewal fee of $250.

There are just too many trophies, too many medals, too many pro cards. It reminds me of when I walked into Joe Weider's headquarters in Woodland Hills for the first time. I was stunned by the number of bronze statues Joe had on the shelves in his office. These were figures, typically of men on horses, approximately two feet in height, created by the great American artist Frederic S. Remington at the end of the nineteenth century. His subject was the American Old West.

When Joe asked me what I think, I said, "You have so many that they look like kewpie dolls at the state fair!" (The Joslyn Art Museum in my hometown of Omaha had one Remington on display.)

But Joe had an eye for beauty — and value. After he died, his collection of Remington bronzes brought over $5 million at auction.

My encouraging bodybuilders wasn't limited to the United States. One of my favorite subjects in school was geography. My grandparents paid $1,100 for a six-week trip to Europe in 1962 with some of my high school classmates as a graduation present. At that time, only ten percent of Americans had ever been on a plane. I often thought about that gift and experience of travel and how it changed my life, especially when inviting someone to visit the Mecca.

I knew there was a whole world out there, no doubt with talent equal to or surpassing what was to be found in the US. I also knew that class differences are more entrenched in most European countries.

Birth is destiny. There are marked differences between the classes, and rarely do class lines get crossed, which seemed especially true in England. While today in America there is a growing economic disparity, it is still taken for granted that class lines are fluid, and a person can break out with their talents and have a different life if that is what they want. For most foreign bodybuilders, I knew the best chance they had to realize their dream was America. Arnold was the shining example.

Name the top German or Austrian bodybuilder and he would likely have been someone I invited to the US to train at Gold's Gym Venice. Being different was particularly frowned on in both countries, and they were considered even more a freak in their homeland than as a bodybuilder in the US. Some felt they belonged here and ended up staying.

German Frank Hildebrand, who won his pro card in 1989 at the world championships, wrote:

"Ed, thank you for everything. I could not have had a better time. When I get back, I'll realize how great everything was. You were right, I belong here, and I would have never known how far I could go without your help. You are a great friend, don't change, neither will I.

Love, Frank"

There were other Germans and Austrians like Frank, no doubt inspired by Arnold: Karin and Jurgen Huber, Achim Albrecht, Markus and Monika Becht, Lambert Bohm, Roland Cziurlok, Daniel Hill, David Hoffman, Heiko Kallbach, Dirk Karrengarn, Roland Kickinger, Mario Klintworth, Michael Kocikowski, Stephan and Regina Norte, Alfred Krautgartner, Ron Matz, Markus Mueller, Markus Ruhl, Carmen and Gunter Schlierkamp, Armin Scholz, Mike Sehr, Marco Wiebelt, Roger Walterscheid, and Katja and Dennis Wolf.

Eventually, Japan and India would have more Gold's Gym locations, but during that time, Germany had more Gold's Gym franchises than any other foreign country other than Canada.

Rainer Schaller, the founder of McFit Gym, said he was influenced by Gold's Gym Venice when he opened his first McFit facility in 1997 in Wurzburg, Germany, ironically the ancestral home of the German side of my family. He even created something similar to our Motion Picture & Entertainment Division, calling it the McFit

Talent Agency to help his gym members get recognized.

McFit is now the largest gym chain in Europe, and Rainer Schaller's RSG entity is the new owner of Gold's Gym International, which he purchased out of bankruptcy in 2020.

Unfortunately, there were a number of great bodybuilders from other European nations who didn't have the careers I think they should have had because of their inability to speak or learn English, such as Marko Savolainen from Finland. At twenty-three and five-eighths inches, Marko's biceps tied for the biggest I have ever taped — but they were the freakiest. I called them the "Alien biceps" because just when you thought you had seen his bicep peak, another portion popped out, like the Alien's teeth in the eponymous movie; just when you thought you had seen it all, another set of teeth appeared. Thanks to YouTube, these images can be easily accessed and are not lost — certainly one of the pluses of today's technology.

When Alicia Paz, our receptionist for many years, told me there was someone on the phone whom she was having a hard time understanding but whom she said was "hungry," I immediately figured out that one of my houseguests from Hungary was calling from my home phone. At least a half-dozen Hungarian bodybuilders I met over the years were world-class bodybuilders but were held back because they couldn't communicate, such as Peter Molnar, Jeno Kiss, Elek Joba, Istvan Horvath, and Krisztian Bereczki.

I felt like a proud father when I saw the poster for the 2014 Arnold Classic in Columbus, Ohio. It prominently displayed images of the two main competitors: Flex Lewis from Wales and Dennis Wolf from Germany. I brought both to America in 2004.

Flex was my last houseguest in Venice when I moved permanently to the desert area east of LA. Dennis and his wife, Katja, were my first guests in my new home in Rancho Mirage. Now they were competing on the same stage in different categories ten years later. I got much gratification standing in the back of the auditorium behind sixteen hundred screaming fans and seeing them compete. Both won — Flex in the 212 weight category and Dennis in the open. It was one of those Wizard of Oz, man-behind-the-curtain moments.

Flex and Dennis settled in Las Vegas with their families, where Flex opened Dragon's Lair Gym. They were different culturally from most of my other foreign guests in that they dared to live the American dream and make the big permanent move to America, the country Germans in their travel posters advertise as "Amerika: das Land der unbegrenzten Moglichkeiten" — "America, the land of infinite possibilities."

When I asked Dennis why he chose to become an American citizen, he said, "How can you not love a country where you can get a driver's license for $35 after a short test?!" It could often take a year and $1,000 worth of driving lessons in Germany.

The first two decades of the NPC were a simpler, more innocent time, with fewer than a half dozen pro cards given out in men's and women's bodybuilding during the year. You had to win your weight class at the Nationals, or the overall at the North Americans, the USAs, or the World Championships. The contests have since become money-making machines and a way to buy oneself a trophy, take a photo or two, and have something to post on social media.

But back then, before 2006 and the creation of the iPhone, those pro card winners were the stars and the faces of bodybuilding in the magazines, which was the only media of the day and the only way to learn. They helped immortalize Gold's Gym. Today they would be called "influencers," comparable to social media stars Sergi Constance and Calum Von Moger.

Sergi had eight thousand followers on Instagram when I brought him to the US to be photographed by famed photographer Ulrich Oehmen in Miami and try out for the WWE professional wrestling organization. He now has over five million followers.

Calum's numbers are similarly impressive; he has over three million followers on Instagram. He was also someone whom I sent to the WWE tryouts in Orlando. While both turned down offers to pursue professional wrestling from the WWE, they have done quite well as entrepreneurs.

MY HOUSEGUESTS

For my houseguests, my home was the haven where they could pursue their dreams in the hope of learning the magic by which their goals might be made real. In this era before the internet, they were in my home communicating with like-minded individuals — dreamers — perhaps for the first time in their lives.

Sitting around my kitchen table, which was five feet in diameter, is not the same as sharing an email or text. In the confines of my house, there was no ability to construct a carefully crafted version of themselves on Facebook, Instagram, Twitter, or TikTok. There were no personal communication devices to distract them. They were fully exposed. All it took was a look in my refrigerator to see what they were eating, what supplements they were taking. When they sat around in my home, they talked to one another, or they watched bodybuilding videos together — over and over, like some of my friends' children watching Disney's *Frozen* again and again.

There can be a wonderful vibe you get when you're in the presence of like-minded people, especially if they share the same craft. I enjoyed seeing two bodybuilders meeting for the first time and "downloading" information to each other on how they train. It was like what I imagined two computers might do to exchange intelligence.

They became the bodybuilding superheroes for generations of fans, the owners and managers of gyms, or the fitness trainers of the world. I helped twenty-one athletes get into professional wrestling, such as Daniel Puder, Chris Mordetzky ("The Masterpiece"), Rob Terry, Kurt Angle, Sting, The Ultimate Warrior, and John Cena.

And then there were the ones who made it on to television, such as Jessie Godderz in CBS's *Big Brother;* Jessie Pavelka in *DietTribe* on Lifetime TV, *Biggest Loser* on NBC, *Obese: A Year to Save My Life* on British network Sky1, and *Fat: The Fight of My Life* on Sky Living HD; and Evan Marriott in *Joe Millionaire*. Then there are the characters on *American Gladiator* and *Battle Dome*, such as Billy Smith, Mike O'Hearn, Steve Henneberry, Raye Hollitt, and Scott Milne.

Some of the above have amazing careers beyond their initial

athletic achievement. After rising to the top of as many as ten thousand other athletes seeking to compete, Daniel Puder won the WWE Tough Enough competition in Venice Beach after beating a couple hundred finalists. He went on to compete in MMA after a one-year stint in wrestling. He has created the Transformational Technologies Academy and opened a half dozen schools in Florida designed to support the needs of at-risk middle school and high school students, who make up about twenty-five percent of the students in America.

I opened up a string of gyms. Daniel opened up a string of schools. No one can tell how far he will get with this project, but his dedication and drive are simply amazing.

Perhaps because we failed to produce a successful line of supplement products during my twenty-five years with Gold's Gym, I am particularly impressed by the success of my houseguests who helped transform America's over-the-counter supplement industry: Rich Gaspari of Gaspari Nutrition, Gerard Dente with MuscleMeds/MHP, Chris Cook of Unique drinks, Jeramy Freeman of Freeman Formula, Rich Piana of 5% Nutrition, Dave Palumbo with Species, Sean Greene of Max Muscle, Jeff Long with Like A Pro Supplements, Neal Spruce with Apex and dotFIT, along with Jay Cutler, Ben Pakulski, Flex Lewis, Brad Baker, Dave Enders, and Dan Freeman. If you took the best year's sales for each company and added them up, you would have total revenue exceeding $1 billion.

During the past forty-five years, my houseguests numbered around 528. In learning about them, I also learned things about myself and the world of fitness. Very few people realized it at the time, but those houseguests were helping to make Gold's Gym Venice the Mecca, and Gold's Gym the largest gym chain in the world. I, in turn, hoped the visit would give them an opportunity they would otherwise not have had and change their lives for the better. For most, it did.

FLEX LEWIS FROM WALES

Flex Lewis said it best when he responded to my comment on an Instagram post in September 2018. I wrote:

"I didn't discover Flex Lewis; I just opened the door in 2004 when I met him online and invited him to America, the land of dreams and dreamers. So happy for his success!"

Flex responded:

"You have a massive part in my success; you say you didn't discover me? Well, we can exchange that word for opening my eyes to the world of endless potential, that if [you] put force, hard work, and relentless pursuit to goals and dreams, things can get achieved. So regardless, if it weren't for YOU, I wouldn't have seen what I had and be where I am going...@gymarchitect love you mate."

I had seen a photo of Flex on the cover of a British bodybuilding magazine in the Gold's Gym "library" and contacted Flex online. Despite all the technology and information available online — or maybe because of it — Flex was skeptical about the invitation to come to America to pursue his dreams. But I was persistent.

After three months of back-and-forth messaging, Flex agreed to come over. He returned to Great Britain briefly to get his pro card, and then on October 14, 2007, I received this email from Angela Lewis, his mother:

"Hi Ed, Just a short note to inform you that James (Flex) has just won the overall championship in the UKFBB Notts (Nottingham, England) tonight. He is now the newest IFBB Pro. We, as a family, would like to take this opportunity to thank you for all the support and faith you have shown James over the last few years. I hope that this evening has made you very proud. Looking forward to speaking to you sometime this week.
Steve and Angela Lewis, Flex, Craig, and Luke."

KLAUS RIIS FROM DENMARK

Klaus Riis, a young bodybuilder from Denmark, was easier to convince after reading one of his posts on social media that his dream was to come to America and be in a Weider magazine. I could make that happen. I thought Klaus had "that look." I invited him to visit. The result was an eight-page exercise spread in *Muscle & Fitness* that would jump-start his fitness career and change his life.

After Klaus returned to Europe, he wrote the following in a December 20, 2006, email:

"Hey Ed,

Thank you for everything.

The trip became more than what I had imagined. I have learned a lot, social and nutrition-wise, but I have also learned a lot about myself and my own body.

Maybe the most important thing I have learned is to enjoy life and enjoy what you are doing at any particular time – and to learn to sell me and be honest and confident while meeting and getting into contact with many new people.

The trip will forever be memorized, and once again, thanks for giving me a chance and a start in this big industry. It is up to me to follow that up and take those steps further to become prominent in this small world.

Keep in touch, Ed. 'I WILL BE BACK!' :)"

GRANT HENDERSON: MR. ZIMBABWE

There were others like Flex and Klaus whose lives were just as dramatically altered but who chose not to pursue a fitness career. Regardless, bodybuilding changed their life. I think it made it better, maybe even saved them.

One of those people was Grant Henderson, Mr. Zimbabwe, who I first saw in a foreign bodybuilding magazine when he was competing for the Mr. Universe title. Grant looked like a younger version of Steve Reeves, whose *Hercules* movies made a strong impression on me while growing up.

Before the internet, it wasn't easy to contact people, and phone calls were expensive. I was able to locate a number where I could send a fax to his gym, and so in 1993, I wrote to Grant:

"Bulawayo, Zimbabwe sounds to me like some sort of jungle paradise. You would seem to be leaving a lot. Venice, CA is not for everyone; but perhaps for you, it could be where you reach your full potential."

Grant made the move, ending up at my home with Paul DeMayo, who coincidentally had been one of his childhood heroes. While Grant did not have the career I had imagined, the trip to LA took him out of Zimbabwe, formerly Rhodesia, before its descent into madness with its president-for-life dictator Robert Mugabe. Zimbabwe went from being the breadbasket of Africa to being a basket case, with economic and social change so drastic that Grant's parents later sought refuge in South Africa. Grant's brother, Justin, followed him and became a successful trainer in LA, even making the *Playgirl* magazine cover, which certainly demonstrates the role genetics play.

Grant hoped to bring his parents to America as well. A life — an entire family's life — changed because of bodybuilding. Others like Justin followed their brothers to a new life in California. Berry DeMey's brother, Jorgen, is a successful trainer in LA and has authored several training books. Doug Dearth, brother of pro bodybuilder David Dearth, is another one who became a trainer to the stars while working in the entertainment industry.

Of course, I was always looking for the next Arnold, all the while knowing that there could never be another Arnold. After all, Arnold is a seven-time Mr. Olympia winner and a movie star. Maybe Flex Lewis, a six-time Mr. Olympia in the 212 class, is something to be proud of. Or perhaps John Cena has come closest in terms of celebrity status in the entertainment world; more movies starring him are yet to come. And Evan Marriott's last episode of pioneering reality TV show *Joe Millionaire* was seen by forty-three million viewers.

DAVE ENDERS

People would ask me how I could see in certain people what others couldn't seem to notice. I just knew. It could be almost comical at times, like the day when I happened to be visiting Dave Enders, a former houseguest, who was undergoing stem cell therapy in Santa Monica. After Dave was finished, we went next door to a hole-in-the-wall hamburger joint for a quick meal before Dave returned to Orange County and I to Venice. The place was empty except for Dave and me and a group of guys in the corner, one of whom was white; the others were Black. They were rather rowdy, making a lot of noise, so I found myself staring at the group, wondering what was going on.

Finally, I said to Dave, "That one white guy sure has a great look."

Dave, who is thirty years younger than me, said, "Ed, that's Justin Bieber!"

At that moment, a big, black SUV pulled up, and the group got in. Talent discovered!

I had one former houseguest, Christian Boeving, who had been a bodyguard and trainer for Bieber. Oh, the stories he had. I was proud of the fact that he had quit after refusing to break the law on Bieber's behalf by taking a monkey into a foreign country without first quarantining.

Dave Enders, originally Dave Skrbin, had his own incredible story. Like so many of my houseguests, his biological father was nowhere to be seen, one reason he left early for LA from Pittsburgh on basically a wing and a prayer — and some false promises. He was so disappointed in his father that he later had his name changed to his mother's maiden name as it was her parents, his grandparents, who played a significant role in his life.

I had overheard Dave use my name at the front desk to get a discounted membership, yet I had never met him, so I started asking questions. Dave was in a somewhat desperate situation, so I invited him to stay at my home while he got his life in order. At the time, two other people were staying with me: Sam Smith, a young bodybuilder from Canada, and Justin Lopez from New Jersey.

When listening to the dreams Justin and Dave had for their

lives in California, which weren't working out yet, I said, "If I looked like either of you, I would stand on a corner on Rodeo Drive in Beverly Hills in a tight-fitting shirt and wait to be discovered."

Taking it one step further, Dave and Justin did just that but went to a nightclub in Beverly Hills. The following day, when I saw Justin, I asked where Dave was. Justin replied, "Dave met someone."

Dave was gone for several days, and I was either too busy or was so confident that Dave could handle himself that I didn't worry. I was not like today's helicopter parents — nor were my parents. When I was outside my garage in the alley washing my car later in the week, Dave pulled up in a beautiful, deep blue Lamborghini with Sophia, an Asian American woman, in the passenger seat. Dave had found love. Sophia had found hers. Nearly twenty years later, they are still a team and have been involved in many successful businesses together. One of them was a supplement company, something I think Sophia would never have tackled without Dave's involvement.

Justin Lopez went a more circuitous route but lived part of his dream. His IMDB, internet movie database, shows he has appeared in twenty-two movies and TV shows during the past fifteen years.

GUESTS BEFORE AIRBNB

The number of houseguests I had didn't seem so strange at the time, but it now seems unusual, even remarkable in hindsight. It was kind of like hitchhiking, which I saw pretty often growing up — I even did it myself — but is not common now. Or maybe it's called Uber or Lyft now, and people pay money for a ride. Perhaps I was just ahead of Airbnb with a not-for-profit model. That realization came because I am, more recently, a guest in someone's home. I'm not surprised when it's apparent that I am my host's first guest outside of family.

The key to making a free-market economy function is the ability or willingness of people to move for work. I did that in 1975 when I got laid off, but not many are willing to go that route. Once we settle into adulthood, even small moves can seem inconceivable. Or it's impossible, as happened in the 2008 recession when people couldn't sell their homes to leave for opportunity elsewhere.

I learned a lot from several newspapers and magazines I read regularly. *The LA Times, The New York Times*, and *The Wall Street Journal* were invaluable, especially when it came time to sell the gym. *The New Yorker* and *The Economist* were two of my favorite magazines and are still in print.

One of my other favorites, *American Demographics,* which like so many is now gone, reported one statistic I would often share with my houseguests: Only one out of every ten Americans ever end up living permanently outside a hundred-mile radius of where they were born.

That statistic seemed hard to believe. But every time I went back to Omaha for my high school reunions, I was struck by how few of my classmates had ever moved out of the state. This is especially remarkable because I went to a Jesuit prep school, and most of my classmates went away to college. However, my latest high school newsletter for 2020 indicated that at least three of every ten alumni are now living out of state, so things are slowly changing.

My houseguests ran the whole gamut, although they all had a passion for fitness as a common denominator and the potential to realize something in that field as I saw it. And they tended to be big. My fellow architects thought all of my friends — the ones who visited the architect offices where I worked between 1975 and 1985 — were huge. I said it was all relative. To me, they were normal, and my architect associates were small.

My projects in the architecture office could be in various stages of development: schematic, preliminary design, design, working drawings, and construction. So, too, were my houseguests in different stages of development. Some were unsure of pursuing a fitness career; others were pre-contest or post-contest; but all were focused on fitness. Perhaps a big reason I didn't consider my gym friends freaks was that I was used to extremes not only in bodies but in buildings as well. The heads or founders of almost all the architecture firms I worked for would be considered "starchitects" today — freaks of architecture and design, really, like the people at the Eames Office. Once you've seen one of the many Eames chairs, it suddenly puts that entire category in perspective. How can you have an average if you don't have extremes?

If I had known what would transpire over the past forty-five years, I might have thought about keeping a diary or at least a visitor's log. But a journal writes in the moment, with no insight into the future. A record of houseguests, with photos, would have come in handy but now seems so calculated and formal, basically a sign-in sheet. What I did was more spontaneous, formed by how I was brought up.

I was raised by a mother who often said, "There but for the grace of God go you or me," when she saw someone less fortunate or who needed help. I grew up in a home where my mother would let anyone visiting know they were welcome and loved — and if they were hungry, she gave them something to eat. My mother's parents died when she was very young. She and her five siblings were raised by an unmarried aunt who worked as a librarian. Despite their limited means, my mother and her brothers and sisters had a tradition growing up of sharing, inviting anyone they wanted to their home for Sunday dinner.

Maybe because I was allowed to view so little TV growing up, the few shows I did watch made such an impression on me. Besides *The Loretta Young Show,* another series called *The Millionaire* was influential in my life. The premise dealt with what might happen to someone if they were anonymously given $1 million tax-free. How might it change their life?

I never gave anyone $1 million. Pete's one-way ticket was $186. But even getting on a plane could be life-changing. Despite how big most of the guys were, it was a white-knuckle ride for many, as it was their first time flying. But it taught them the value of traveling and exploring new worlds and new opportunities.

An important lesson I learned after selling out of Gold's Gym in 2004 was that too much help, primarily financial, could cripple someone. The net effect of giving someone a plane ticket or a temporary place to stay — room and board, help with food and supplements — could be just as life-changing and more beneficial.

MY FIRST HOUSEGUEST, PETE GRYMKOWSKI, & CORY & JEFF EVERSON

Pete Grymkowski was my first houseguest, but I quickly learned there were more people like Pete out there who wanted to make the journey but didn't have the means to do it.

One of the earliest houseguests after Pete was Cory Everson. Cory, an interior designer from Wisconsin, knew I was an architect and wondered if I could help her find a job in LA. I offered Cory and her husband, Jeff, a place to stay at my home while they looked for work and a place to live. They settled in the Valley after moving out.

Life in California seemed to ignite Cory's passion for fitness. She won Ms. Olympia six times from 1984 to 1989, an achievement that no one else has come close to matching.

After introducing Jeff to Joe Weider, Jeff became editor-in-chief of *Muscle & Fitness*, whose offices were in Woodland Hills.

Those were magical times, the beginning of bodybuilding's golden age.

Jeff's position at Weider's probably didn't hurt the chances that Cory — and Gold's Gym — would be omnipresent in the major Weider magazines. Cory had over five hundred magazine covers in those and other fitness magazines.

After Cory, all the Ms. Olympia winners seemed to pale by comparison. But I remember some extraordinary women after her, such as Diana Dennis and Debbie Kruck. Debbie stayed at my home several times with Lee Apperson, a champion bodybuilder and her boyfriend at the time.

As with the male bodybuilders, it's about more than lifting weights. Personality counts a lot. Cory, Dianna, and Debbie all had it. And now, forty-two years later, with the advantage of hindsight, women's competitive bodybuilding is almost dead.

THE GOLD'S GYM LIBRARY

Gold's Gym Venice received fitness magazines from all over the world. I don't ever remember subscribing or paying for any of them. Perhaps the publishers of these magazines felt the Mecca should have a copy of their publication.

I enjoyed reading anything. I grew up in a house with ten people living in it — five siblings, my parents, and my father's parents — and one bathroom. While waiting to use the bathroom, I sat on the stairs in the attic that led to my bedroom, which I shared with two brothers. On those steps were piles of magazines, all from my dad's medical office waiting room, most the result of numerous magazine subscription drives, which were popular at the time with Catholic schools and charities. Maybe because a librarian raised my mother, the Connors family was the last household in the neighborhood to have a television. Books and magazines were valued over TV; there were many, and they were diverse.

In what amounted to the Gold's Gym library, I was fascinated by the images of Gold's Gym that started showing up in the foreign publications. They, too, were many and diverse. Some were original stories, but most of the time, the images were stock photos purchased — or stolen — by the editors from American magazines like *Ironman,* or from photographers like Irv Gelb, most of whom shot exclusively at Gold's Gym Venice. That's where the action was, and the photographers were welcome. Ironically, all these images in these magazines became invaluable later on as Gold's Gym expanded throughout the world.

Because the Weider magazines were printed in thirty-seven languages, they were proof to any foreign trademark office that Gold's Gym was known from an early date in that country and was an American brand. It also helped that Gold's Gym Merchandising had shipped T-shirts and tank tops to most of these countries as well through its mail-order ads in those very same magazines.

GUNNAR ROSBO, MY FIRST FOREIGN HOUSEGUEST

I was intrigued seeing photos of foreign bodybuilders I had never heard of and, in all likelihood, were unknown in America. It only made sense that Europe, with a population greater than the US, would have its share of talent. That gave me the idea to invite some of this talent to the US. Not only would they get to experience the Mecca and return home with that memory but they would be a draw at the contests the gyms were promoting.

It was not uncommon in the '80s for gyms to put on bodybuilding contests to market for new members. This coincided with the rise of the NPC. Having a "guest poser" — much like a guest speaker in today's world — to boost attendance was the norm. At a local level, it still happens occasionally. It was a great way to get publicity without spending much money.

Competing gyms would put up the poster for the event with the guest poser on it and essentially advertise their competition. Dick Ferris, one of my partners in Gold's Gym San Francisco, and I spent much energy — and money — producing some beautiful posters. And so it was that in August 1982, I invited Gunnar Rosbo from Norway to guest pose at a contest the SF club was promoting: Mr. San Francisco, which was being held at the Palace of Fine Arts, an ersatz classical Greek structure in San Francisco's Marina District. Its eleven hundred seats would typically be sold out at our contests. Gunnar would be the first of dozens of foreign houseguests I would eventually invite, most of whom became very well-known.

Indeed, Gunnar's five weeks in California and his photoshoots with Weider on the beaches in LA would cement his place in bodybuilding history.

I had been warned that Gunnar had a problem with alcohol. But I couldn't imagine how someone could look like him and have a drinking problem. Gunnar was the closest thing to Arnold I had ever seen — and I was still looking for that next Arnold. Gunnar was about the same height and, at 285 pounds, might even have weighed more than Arnold did at his peak, when I saw him compete. I could never quite believe the numbers given for what Arnold supposedly weighed. I thought they were low.

When Gunnar would be on Venice Beach, a couple of houses away from my first home in Venice, people would shout, "Hey, Arnold!" Gunnar didn't like that. He was Gunnar, but the resemblance was striking.

A dozen years would pass before I had another houseguest with a similar look: Roland Kickinger, who, like Arnold, was also from Austria and had an identical accent. And another couple of dozen years would pass after that before I met the third Arnold look-alike: Calum Von Moger, from Australia. All fascinating yet different stories.

Roland came to see me when he first arrived in America. He wanted my advice regarding a bodybuilding career. At six feet, four inches, I thought he was too tall for competitive bodybuilding and suggested pro wrestling or acting instead. I had been around bodybuilding long enough by then to know that a pro bodybuilding career for anyone over six feet, two inches would be challenging and not something I could easily recommend.

Roland starred in *Son of the Beach* and numerous other TV shows and movies, even playing a young Arnold in one of the *Terminator* sequels. He now owns a string of supplement stores in California and Arizona, and is still making movies and even trying out stand-up comedy at one of the clubs in LA.

Calum nailed it playing a young Arnold in the biopic on Joe Weider, *BIGGER: The Joe Weider Story*.

I was still working as an architect when Gunnar stayed at my home on a Venice walk street. It wouldn't be until 1985 that I left that career. So, every morning before driving twelve miles into the mid-Wilshire, Miracle Mile district of LA to work, I would put some chicken breasts in a Crockpot along with a half-can of soup so Gunnar would have protein to eat during the day.

People at the gym told me that when Gunnar worked out, he smelled like a whiskey still. It wasn't until Gunnar left after six weeks in the US that I figured out why. While cleaning under my kitchen sink, I noticed that every bottle of alcohol stored there was depleted to within a quarter of an inch of the bottom of the bottle. Back then, a common practice was to give a dinner host a bottle of alcohol, most often a dessert liquor because wine wasn't that popular. I must have had thirty bottles in the cabinet. All were nearly empty. Mystery solved! That's where Gunnar was getting his fats and carbs!

While some of my other houseguests who helped out Gunnar have their own stories, I remember one time when Gunnar seemed to get out of control. I was at a Sunday brunch in Marina del Rey with several other people when Gunnar decided he wanted some coffee and couldn't wait. Before anyone knew what was happening, Gunnar went over to the waiter's station, picked up a forty-cup coffee urn, and carried it over to where he had been sitting. When the waitstaff ran over to stop him, I warned them that it would be best to leave him alone.

While cradling the enormous stainless steel cylinder in one arm, Gunnar used his free hand to turn the spigot to gently fill his coffee cup. The only houseguests I ever met with similar-sized forearms were Casey Viator and Frank McGrath, both with forearms eighteen and a half inches in circumference.

While I occasionally cooked for my houseguests — if a Crockpot counts as cooking — most of the time I lived in Venice, the more common practice was to take whoever was at my home to a restaurant once I got home after my twelve-hour days. I figured my time was worth hundreds of dollars an hour, and so between going to the grocery store, preparing and cooking dinner, and then cleaning up, it was a costly meal. By comparison, eating out on the Westside of LA was comparatively inexpensive. There were even a few restaurants, like Dinah's, that had all-you-can-eat nights where you could keep ordering endless amounts of fried chicken. They eventually had to post signs saying, "No Bodybuilders Allowed." But it was fun while it lasted.

When we went out to eat, I could spend quality time with my guests, discuss their day and life in general, and relax. One of the fun things we often did at a restaurant was to decide beforehand whose birthday it was going to be so I could tell the server ahead of time and we could then get a "free" dessert, as is the custom in most restaurants in the US. Other than cheesecake at The Cheesecake Factory, we rarely ordered dessert, so if one was shared for the table, it was OK, and no one had cheated on their diet. It made a nice finish to the evening.

In learning about your guests, it is amazing what you learn about yourself even regarding something as simple, or taken for granted, as eating out at a restaurant, or was often the case, "dinner and a movie." I learned that eating at a restaurant where you sat down and were served a meal was a new experience for many of my houseguests. It was the first time for many, like getting on a plane.

I quickly learned that my childhood was quite different from the one most of them had experienced. It wasn't just that I was white, male, and had grown up in America. I was blessed with parents who made a point of taking their six children to a restaurant when they were young to teach them basic table manners. We didn't go out often, but it was a big treat when we did. For that reason, I wasn't judgmental and I never criticized my guests, other than offering constructive criticism. I had to show quite a few basic table manners, especially those having lunch or dinner with Joe Weider. Certainly, one of the joys of having foreign houseguests was to show them some of the fantastic restaurant choices in LA, like Sunday brunch at a major hotel or prime rib at Lawry's in Beverly Hills, where a massive slab of beef is rolled out on a silver cart to be carved and served to the customer.

MEASUREMENTS & EVAN CENTOPANI

As bodybuilding started to take off, there was, and still is, much controversy regarding judging because it is so subjective. There was an early attempt to make it more objective by having "Ironman" contests where the competitors scored points by placing in various powerlifting events. Not a bad idea and something certainly worth exploring again.

Seeing someone like Jeff King come down the stairs of my first home in Venice with thighs bigger than his waist got me thinking about measurements. How is a prize-winning physique quantified? What made a champion? Perhaps because I was an architect, I focused on measurements and proportions, just as so many architects have since ancient times: the golden rectangle, entasis, etc.

This was an era where the guys still had tiny waists, and I remember Jeff's thighs taping around thirty-four inches, several inches more than his waist — something unheard of today. I can only think of a couple of guys — Rich Piana and Paulo Almeida — with thighs equaling Jeff's. However, their waists were much bigger.

Taping athletes is something I would continue to do for the next forty years. With so many guys claiming to have twenty-inch biceps, Rich would say my measurements were the only ones he trusted. I can assure you twenty-inch biceps are a high hurdle.

Like Gunnar Rosbo's forearms or Jeff King's thighs, I focused on measurements because it also made many of the bodybuilders I met feel that what they had previously perceived as unobtainable now seemed possible. Again, it was like I was the Wizard of Oz, giving them the courage or confidence to compete. They might even have been at that key mark already, like when I met Evan Centopani in Las Vegas and encouraged him to "go for it!" Like so many I had heard it from, Evan's first response to me was that he wasn't "big enough" to compete.

I taped Evan. Chest: fifty-four inches. Waist: thirty-six inches. Forearms: sixteen inches. Biceps: twenty-one inches. Thighs: twenty-seven and a half inches. Calves: nineteen inches.

This was off-season, long before Evan had even thought about competing. By comparison, Arnold's published measurements when he first competed in 1968 in Mr. Universe, supposedly weighing 235 pounds at the height of six feet, two inches, were: Chest: fifty-seven inches. Waist: thirty-four inches. Biceps: twenty-two inches. Thighs: twenty-eight and a half inches. Calves: twenty inches.

I told Evan that at five feet, eleven inches and 265 pounds, his measurements were already very close to a typical pro's onstage. I offered to fly him to Atlanta to see the NPC Nationals in 2005 to convince him that's where he belonged. Evan took me up on my offer. After viewing the competitors on stage, he agreed with my assessment and competed the next year, coming in second. The following year, 2007, he won and got his pro card.

I was always reluctant to encourage someone — like Evan, in this case — to change directions if that person seemed to be doing well enough with their current job. And Evan was unusual in that he had a college degree. This measurement centered around income. When I asked Evan about his work and how much he was making, he said he was employed by a residential title company and making around $60,000 a year. That was a good income and gave me pause. The next time I ran into Evan and asked him if he still had his day job, he told me he had been let go due to the 2008 housing crisis. That made me feel a lot better about the gamble he had taken. It isn't all about money, but money can buy some measure of freedom.

Universal Supplements has sponsored Evan since he got his pro card. It has allowed him to do many other things with his time besides training.

BERRY DE MEY, RON MATZ, JIM QUINN, & VINCE McMAHON

Berry De Mey from Holland and Ron Matz from Germany were my next foreign houseguests after Gunnar. Matt Mendenhall was at my home at that time with Berry. By this time, I had purchased the other half of the duplex I was in, and Ron was staying in that section with his girlfriend. Jim Quinn, a former Dallas Cowboys football player who had injured himself playing ball and now wanted a career in bodybuilding, or maybe wrestling, was also staying with me.

Pro wrestling was much on my mind those days. In 1985, Pete, Tim, and I had gone to Kansas City to meet with Hulk Hogan and Linda and Vince McMahon of the World Wrestling Federation to talk about them potentially buying Gold's Gym. Vince created the World Bodybuilding Federation instead and then the World Football League. Both only lasted a couple of years, and Vince ended up losing more money than what Pete, Tim, and I were asking for the business – probably more than twice as much, as he lost close to $100 million with the football league alone. It would probably have been a lousy marriage anyway, or at least not what Vince would've had in mind.

THE WORLD BODYBUILDING FEDERATION

Joe Weider said, "We've worked with bodybuilding since its infancy to create a respectable, dignified sport, a well-organized sport that we want to be part of the Olympics. But the WBF wants to turn it into a freak show!" (Joe and his brother, Ben, had been on an eternal quest to get bodybuilding into the Olympics.)

Vince McMahon had created larger-than-life characters and superheroes out of the bodybuilders he had hired for the WBF, like Aaron Baker as Batman or Dave Dearth as The Wild Child. Eight of Vince's thirteen paid athletes had been houseguests of mine:

- Gary Strydom, a South African immigrant who had worked with his wife, Alicia, in one of my gyms in El Paso, Texas.
- Berry De Mey, who I had brought to the US from Holland and who, unlike Gunnar Rosbo or Ron Matz, had stayed in America.
- Troy Zuccolotto, a former Mr. California from Orange County.
- Jim Quinn, a former pro football player from Long Island.
- Eddie Robinson, an Ohio bodybuilder who I had met when he was nineteen.
- Vince Comerford from Arizona.
- David Dearth, a former employee of mine in San Bernardino.
- Mike Quinn, who stayed at my first home along with Joe Meeko. Joe was a terrific bodybuilder from the AAU era who tragically died early from Lyme Disease.

Matt Mendenhall, another great who I also brought to California at that time, just missed out on that action. Joe Weider kept promising him riches from the free ads he was giving Matt in his magazines in exchange for appearances related to Weider products. Like the movie studios when they first began in LA after World War I, the magazines could create media stars. Matt, to this day, remains the greatest bodybuilder who never turned pro. He died in 2021 at age sixty-one, probably from an overdose of painkillers due to recent back surgery after a bad fall.

Even though it was short-lived, Vince McMahon's World Bodybuilding Federation injected some money and life into the competitive bodybuilding scene, which was significant. When it was all over, Weider ended up having to pay a total of $1.5 million a year to twenty-four bodybuilders to appear exclusively in his magazines.

JIM HELLWIG, THE ULTIMATE WARRIOR & STEVE BORDEN, STING

Jim Hellwig was one of those early houseguests in the mid-'80s whose dream was to be a professional bodybuilder. I saw photos of Jim after he won Mr. Georgia and invited him to Venice to train for his next contest, the 1983 Jr. USAs, a national-level show. But after coming in sixth place in that event, he got discouraged and went back to Atlanta to become a chiropractor. It was only later that I realized that at six feet, three inches, the road to a bodybuilding career was challenging. It is hard to pack on the size at that height to create the illusion onstage to win. Amazingly, at six feet, two inches, Arnold was at that magic cut-off point that made for a great bodybuilder. But the small screen adds the appearance of size, and so Jim and Arnold on TV or in the movies looked even bigger, maybe thirty pounds bigger.

Besides expressing interest in buying Gold's Gym, it was during this time that Vince McMahon was buying up minor, independent wrestling leagues and consolidating them under his WWF banner. When the World Wildlife Federation — the other WWF — objected to its name, he changed it to World Wrestling Entertainment, probably more appropriate anyway.

When Ted Turner got into the wrestling scene a little later with his organization, the WCW, he allegedly called Vince to let him know, to warn him, that he was getting into the wrestling business. Vince's response was said to have been, "Good. Because I'm in the entertainment business."

I have a similar reaction when people say they're in the gym business. I will tell them I'm in the people business. And then there's the classic retort when Ray Kroc would ask people what business they think he's in. They would say, "fast food, hamburgers." He would respond, "real estate." McDonald's is one of the largest real estate holders in the world.

Televised wrestling and the wrestlers were a big part of Gold's Gym's notoriety, so big that it was one of the primary reasons Vince and Linda McMahon and Hulk Hogan were interested in buying

Gold's Gym, even creating the World Bodybuilding Federation.

Hulk Hogan and many other wrestlers would often train in the Gold's Gyms popping up around the country and then go into the ring in the city they were visiting, rip off a Gold's Gym T-shirt, and throw it to the crowd. A ruined shirt, but much free publicity for Gold's Gym. There weren't strong "Standards and Practices" for television.

I thought having our own wrestling team would be even better, so a Gold's Gym team was formed. One of the four wrestlers was Steve Borden, my twenty-one-year-old manager at the Gold's Gym in Reseda. Steve and his tag team partner were the bigger of the four wrestlers, and that was key. When Steve's partner quit (who was the same height as Hellwig), I called up Jim to see if he was interested in professional wrestling. It would only pay $100 a night, but it would work compared with what Jim said he was earning in Atlanta. So Jim came to LA for wrestling school, teamed up with Steve, and then went on the road.

Success didn't happen overnight. It took almost two and a half years. I connected with them in some of the small towns in the South and Southwest they wrestled in and saw the early struggle and dedication myself. I remember being with Jim as he was getting ready to enter the arena. When the announcer asked Jim what weight he wanted to be announced at, Jim said, "285" and turned to me smiling and said, "If only it were that easy!" He had exaggerated his weight a little, but unlike most of the other wrestlers on the road, Jim and Steve did everything they could to maintain their physiques — their gimmicks — like getting in enough sleep, training, and eating the right meals.

There were some fun, crazy moments when I was with them on the road. I had a chance to witness firsthand the havoc that a couple of bodybuilders can wreak.

Scott and Ric Steiner, the Steiner brothers, were University of Michigan wrestlers who had qualified for the US Olympic wrestling team but never got a chance to compete because of the US withdrawal from the Olympics that year. Now they were on the road with Steve and Jim before they became Sting and The Ultimate Warrior — and before Scott Steiner would go it alone as Big Poppa Pump.

Ric and Scott were larger-than-life characters at five feet, ten inches and around 265 pounds each. Either one of them could have been a top competitive bodybuilder. They were big fans of Gold's Gym, and I had reciprocated by trying to help them with their gimmicks.

When Steve and Jim decided they were more tired than hungry, I went with Ric and Scott to a local bar to get some food and, of course, talk bodybuilding. All eyes were on them when we entered the local restaurant bar in a small town in Louisiana. I don't know that I heard anyone mumbling "steroids," but there was loud talk about "fake" wrestling. And, of course, there were a lot of "beer muscles" looking to show off. It wasn't long before the brothers found themselves in a fight with a couple of dozen patrons.

People ask me what I think of the superhero movies so popular nowadays. I say, "Not much." No CGI comes close to matching reality once you've seen a bar fight with the Steiner brothers.

Like so many bodybuilders I have known, Jim idolized superheroes, which was crucial to his success. Bodybuilding was his lifestyle. Jim took that lifestyle on the road with him when he wrestled. He got to the next town early enough to get his meals and training in while some of the other wrestlers might still be in bed, having stayed out late partying. Jim even took a blender on the road.

One of the most significant changes in the fitness world in the past forty-five years has been the quality of over-the-counter supplements. Back then, what was on the label wasn't necessarily what was in the container. The supplements, such as the protein powders, didn't mix well. And the final product didn't taste good either.

Today, you can make a protein drink in a shaker bottle that tastes great and is good for you — a complete meal replacement. But back then, Jim would empty a can of tuna fish in the blender, throw in some eggs, a couple of scoops of protein powder, and finally, some orange juice, then turn the blender on high and chug down the mixture.

He was hardcore, dedicated, on a mission.

Part of their eventual success was the face paint both of them adopted. It concealed their good looks. This is hard for people to remember as they did it as part of their gimmick when they were a tag team, but then they split up early and went their separate ways, even to separate wrestling organizations. But both kept the face paint.

Back when they started, the wrestling leagues were giving the "heels," the bad guys, the "push." The "babyfaces," the good guys, were thought to be secondary to the action. The babyfaces were typically the better-looking guys, both in face and physique.

I remember buying Steve and Jim their first makeup kits at a costume store on Pico Boulevard in LA, which still exists.

Before The Warrior died in 2014, I had a chance to talk to him about that gimmick. I heard for the first time The Warrior speak about the toll that makeup had taken on his face after all those applications.

An easier gimmick to maintain was The Warrior's bands on both arms, just above his biceps. Jim had been in enough bar fights to be self-conscious about the scars on his arms from broken beer bottles. Those straps of red fabric helped conceal that; later, he would get tattoos.

In the early days before the WWF, he was The Dingo Warrior, and the name was embroidered in yellow on the red fabric band. Later, Vince McMahon, a marketing genius, would change Dingo to Ultimate, and thus The Ultimate Warrior was born. The Warrior became a household name after beating Hulk Hogan in the 1990 WrestleMania VI, the highlight of his thirteen-year professional career.

In my opinion, wrestling fans weren't interested in seeing "ordinary," like someone they could see walking down the street. They wanted to see freaks. Jim became a superhero freak in real life, even legally changing his name to Warrior in 1993.

In a 2009 email, he wrote:

"It (my name) represented my feisty, determined, disciplined, hard-working and never-ever-quit philosophy of life."

The only question I typically asked when I first met someone like Jim was what motivated him to work out, what did he want to do or be. I didn't ask about their circumstances growing up unless they volunteered to share. It was only later that I learned Jim had grown up poor, basically in a trailer home, that his father had left him when he was nine years old.

Just as Arnold had told me about wanting financial success when I first met him, so, too, Jim was focused on money and rewarding himself with some nice things when he had the financial resources to do it. Like so many I knew, Jim's childhood poverty had robbed him of his self-esteem, and buying things was one way to "redeem" himself.

By 1986, Jim was making enough money to lease a 1985 Mercedes 380SL, the longest-running nameplate in Mercedes-Benz's production car history. (The initials stand for "Super Leicht," or "Super Light," a German superlative for sportiness.) But he had leased his dream car without ever trying it out. So, not too long after getting it, he called me up to ask if I would be interested in taking over the lease. At six feet, three inches and 275 pounds, Jim was just too tall and big to be comfortable in it. I had never owned an expensive car, so it would be a big step.

I was just leaving the architecture world to work full time at the gym office. I had sold my 1983 Ford Thunderbird to Jim and Steve when they went to wrestle and needed a more reliable vehicle for traveling on the road, but then bought another. At about the same time as Jim's request came, I overheard someone in the Gold's Gym Venice parking lot commenting about the cars Pete and Tim were driving and wondering where my car was.

Both Pete and Tim had their own parking spaces, filled with some nice cars over time. Pete had a custom Silver Shadow Rolls-Royce, a second Silver Shadow, and three specially built Porsches. Tim even had a Ferrari at one point. I didn't want my own space, as I typically walked to work. Pete lived in Victorville, and Tim lived in the Valley.

But that remark got me thinking. That was back in the day when what you drove in LA mattered. Now it's shifted from sports coupes (and every other luxury vehicle category) to SUVs. So, The Warrior's vehicle became my first "luxury car," and I would go on to have two more Mercedes convertibles after that, as I thought they were the most beautifully designed convertibles ever made — if you weren't over six feet tall.

Ironically, it was seeing me in The Warrior's Mercedes when I visited the gyms I was involved with in Santa Barbara that helped Sebastyn Jackovics, a freshman at University of California, Santa Barbara, decide he wanted to be like me and pursue the gym business. Sebastyn convinced his parents, Tom and Judy, to go all-in with Gold's Gym. The Jackovics family en masse eventually took over the territory I had in San Francisco and currently own and operate eight world-class fitness facilities in the Bay Area. And Sebastian's garage has quite a collection of cars much more exotic than my Mercedes. I guess what I drove was important.

The Warrior's relationship with Vince McMahon and the WWE had its ups and downs. But, fortunately, The Warrior was inducted into the WWE Hall of Fame in 2014, just twenty hours before he died at age fifty-six. While his lifestyle wasn't conducive to a long life, his father and grandfather died in their fifties, so there was undoubtedly genetics at work here.

In his Hall of Fame acceptance speech, he mentioned me and John Cena, who was in the front row. I had told The Warrior that he was the one who had inspired Cena when he was young, so in many ways, it felt like the torch had been passed.

Fifty-six is too young an age to die. But if The Warrior had never lived, there might never have been Cena to inspire more millions of fans.

In one of his last emails to me, The Warrior wrote: "There are some who die early but live to get the most out of their life, and then, there are those who get more time but never really live."

I felt that applied to many people I knew and rephrased it: "Many will die never really having lived."

Perhaps Mark Twain said it best: "The fear of death follows from the fear of life. A man who lives fully is prepared to die at any time."

Jim went beyond emulating the superheroes of the past. He created a new one.

LEAVING WORK AS AN ARCHITECT

During this 1979 to 1985 period, I lived three lives: one as an architect, another as a parking garage consultant, and a third as a gym owner. It was a lot of hundred-hour weeks, but I was having the time of my life. I tell people that I am likely to be the only architect/gym owner they will ever meet. Some of the architect employers never knew of my "other life" with the gyms. Others ended up finding out or were told by me at some point during my employment with them.

It was a very productive period, especially for a young architect. Most architects' careers mature very late in life. Fortunately, most architects also live long lives. Kevin Roche, my first employer out of the Army, died in 2019 at age ninety-six.

It was probably because I had worked on designing a Neiman Marcus store while at Roche Dinkeloo Architects that I was offered the job in LA to create the new Beverly Hills store. Fate. A store in Las Vegas would follow.

While neither was great architecture, they were good buildings. More significant was the headquarters for the Port of Los Angeles in San Pedro while with John Carl Warnecke and Associates, my work on California Plaza in downtown LA while with Arthur Erickson & Associates, and then my design role on Fox Plaza in Century City with William Pereira Associates, the latter two both thirty-four-story office buildings. Fox Plaza would be immortalized in the first *Die Hard* movie as "Nakatomi Plaza."

After Ronald Reagan left the presidency, he had offices on the top floor of Fox Plaza. When I met President Reagan's Secret Service team, who were training at the gym — for free, of course — and told them I had worked on the building, they asked if I wanted to meet President Reagan and see his offices. I said sure, even giving the former president a box of golf balls with "Gold's Gym" stenciled on them.

While working as a senior designer on Fox Plaza in 1985, I decided to quit working forty-plus hours a week for an architectural firm. It was no longer fun. Working as an architect has its rewards, but it can be tedious: five percent inspiration, ninety-five percent tedious work. I worked in that senior designer position for two years, and the design and working drawings were finished. I was proud of all the buildings I had worked on, but I could see my life would be more meaningful if I were full-time at Gold's Gym.

I compared watching the Fox Plaza under construction to a bodybuilder walking onstage and posing. It's no coincidence that so many high-rises look like a giant phallus. Most bodybuilders are probably less exhibitionistic. With them, it's more existential. They look in the mirror to find imperfections, not just to look at themselves.

STEROIDS, HGH, & PAIN KILLERS

Unfortunately, it is impossible to write about the history of this period in bodybuilding without talking about steroids. It is the elephant in the room, or maybe the big bodybuilder in the room, who everyone sees and assumes those muscles are from steroid use.

My introduction to steroids began in the late '70s, when Pete Grymkowski asked me to give him a shot for the first time. I told Pete that I was concerned I might be hurting him. Pete said to me, "There's only one thing you need to know: I would rather be dead than small."

And so it went. Up until the end of the '80s, steroids were legal, and there were doctors all over the country who specialized in sports medicine who prescribed them. In LA, Dr. Jekot, a pediatrician, was one I knew well. One side of his office was a waiting room for the mothers and their children, the other half for his bodybuilder patients. I am sure that there was some mixing of the two over the years, no doubt making for some troubled marriages. Dr. Jekot even made house calls to my home for emergency cases if someone was sick and needed immediate help. He was one of the good doctors. Even when it was legal, the doses were not as strong as they are now.

While steroids impacted activities as diverse as professional baseball and the Olympics with major scandals, they helped make it the golden age of men's bodybuilding. People would often whisper "steroids" when they saw me with one or more bodybuilders, usually at a restaurant or movie theater. Of course, those who said it usually did it loud enough that everyone could hear them. Indeed, if it were that simple — taking a pill or a shot — then we could all be superheroes. But they were quick to attribute all that hard-earned muscle to drugs.

Maybe it's because Jimmy Quinn had been a bouncer on Long Island that he always seemed to have the best retorts when he heard that word. I remember being with him in a theater lobby when a man's wife or girlfriend muttered "steroids" loud enough for everyone to hear. Jimmy went over to her — I think the guy she was with was beginning to wet his pants — and said very politely, "Thank you, I must be getting close," and smiled.

Another time, at a fast-food restaurant, probably a Carl's Jr.

with its charbroiled chicken sandwich, baked potato, and salad (something Gold's Gym got them to offer for a while in Southern California), an obese father told his very young son, who was infatuated with Jim's physique, that all that muscle eventually turns to fat. Jimmy — all 285 pounds of him — got up, went over to the table, and said, "Well then, you must have been Mr. Olympia since it looks like your chest is now around your waist. But since you're not Black, I don't think so." (This was during the era when Lee Haney was winning the Mr. O year after year — and indeed, his chest was his best body part.)

If the person were both obese and smoking, then they would get a double whammy from Jim when he would say, "You can't be both fat and smoke; so, since you can't drop fifty pounds that quick, then maybe you should put out that cigarette."

He's embarrassed now by those memories, but I loved it — and still do. Whenever I see a fat person smoking, I can't help but think of Jim. He was not afraid to tell it like it was — or still is. I grew up having never smoked. Architecture firms weren't hiring smokers because of the risk of burning a hole in the drawings.

Obesity is a serious issue that is often underestimated in the US. For example, our government failed to tell us that fat people were the ones dying most from COVID.

I was disappointed when I heard President George W. Bush label steroids as a serious issue in the US in his 2004 State of the Union address. What about smoking and alcoholism? Steroids certainly seem to be a victimless drug compared with the havoc wreaked on families by alcoholism. In 2012, when I asked pro bodybuilder Dallas McCarver, one of my last visitors, what motivated him to start lifting weights and get big, Dallas said it was to protect himself and his mother from his alcoholic father. After over forty years around bodybuilders, nothing had changed. That answer was all too common.

Steroids were first manufactured in the '30s to treat depression and chronically ill people whose catabolic or destructive metabolisms could not produce protein, causing them to lose weight. Medical researchers knew that the male hormone testosterone causes the retention of nitrogen, the source of amino acids and protein, which increases muscle mass. They thought synthetic versions of testosterone would reverse protein depletion in their catabolic patients.

My father, a surgeon, dealt with many burn patients and prescribed steroids as part of their recovery. They worked. But the medical community determined that the negatives outweighed the positives.

The American College of Sports Medicine, an organization for physicians and researchers, even declared that the drugs had not been shown to increase muscular strength. When you open a typical box containing a steroid for injection or for taking orally, the warning on the printed material inside usually says something like, "This does not increase or enhance athletic ability." If adding fifteen to thirty pounds of muscle in months doesn't increase strength, I don't know what does. How can you scare people with labels if they are filled with lies?

Indeed, after forty-five years, I am still amazed at how quickly a bodybuilder can change his physique. One benefit of time is being able to see the truth more clearly. It's strange how people would say steroids don't work back then, but nowadays, when anyone wants to emphasize the potency of something, they will say it was like it was "on steroids."

And then there's the even bigger lie that they may cause sterility or impotence. I don't know anyone for whom this is true. But enough steroid users believed that it was and so treated it as a male contraceptive. They were surprised later when they had been able to get someone pregnant.

I was with Mr. America Joe De Angelis at the Marina del Rey Hospital when he was having an abscess on his shoulder from a dirty needle checked out. As usual, the doctor gave him the customary lecture about using steroids, including not making babies.

Finally, Joe said to him, "Doc, you want to hurry it up. My wife is down the hall giving birth to my son." True story.

In 1987, a former British track star and thirty-three other people were named in a 110-count federal jury indictment as an alleged nationwide black market dealing in bodybuilding steroids that had been smuggled into the US from Tijuana. The charge was led by US Attorney Philip Halpern in San Diego, who made this his career. It named some members of Gold's Gym Venice, several of whom had been houseguests of mine. The indictment alleged a conspiracy to manufacture and distribute anabolic steroids to a market that grew when the FDA narrowed the list of approved steroids that may be sold legally.

It had many similarities to the attempted prohibition of alcohol, in my opinion. In 1990, Congress amended the Controlled Substances Act, making the possession or use of anabolic steroids a federal crime. Steroids are grouped with opium, morphine, and amphetamines as "Schedule III" substances under federal law.

In his book *Legal Muscle,* Rick Collins calls steroids the "orange in the apple crate." States have gotten into the steroid regulation act, with penalties that vary widely, not unlike the current marijuana use and possession laws.

The phone company GTE informed me on August 7, 1991, that my phone had been tapped from August 26, 1988, to December 26, 1989. Agents from the DEA interviewed me in the Gold's Gym Venice offices, wondering where my money came from. It was like the scene from the movie *The Ten Commandments* when Moses pulled back the curtain to reveal the obelisk going up in honor of the pharaoh. I pulled back the curtain in an upstairs office to reveal our clothing operation in the warehouse below. That's where the money came from. They left satisfied.

In my forty-five years around bodybuilding, I can honestly say I don't know anyone whose death was directly caused by steroids. I am not advocating their use. I am simply stating my experience, my history.

When Vince McMahon and the WWE were on trial in 1991, steroids were blamed for turning pseudo-athletes like Hulk Hogan into "freakishly muscular cartoon action figures." I was hoping that McMahon might initiate a massive clinical study regarding the use of the drugs, but nothing happened.

More bad press came the following year when Lyle Alzado died at age forty-two. Lyle was the closest thing Gold's Gym Venice had to a mascot. Steroids were blamed for his death, but more likely, they added ten years to Lyle's football career. They didn't kill him.

Later, in 1996, a study published in the *New England Journal of Medicine* showed few adverse effects in people taking controlled doses of steroids over ten weeks. I think there is a fascination in the bodybuilding world with steroids and deaths because people want to believe that what they did to become who they are also ended up killing them. As it turns out, there were many causes other than steroids.

I can't say the same thing about synthol, human growth hormone — GH, IGF-1 — or insulin. None of these were in use in the '80s, and GH, or HGH, didn't become widespread until the mid-'90s. As befits the media for the time, the new world of supplements was announced in the December 1993 issue of *Flex* magazine with a photo of Dorian Yates on the cover, and a headline announcing, "Dorian Yates 'SHOCKING PICTORIAL' 269 lbs. & BIGGER THAN EVER!" There were full-page photos inside showing the transformation he had made in one year. (Dorian is five feet, eleven inches.)

Regarding synthol, a doctor told me that you cannot inject impure fluids into your body and not expect trouble. It is a synthetic oil injected underneath the skin to mimic muscle; it is not restricted and easily purchased. It's derived from an Italian steroid called Esiclene, which acted primarily as an inflammatory muscle agent, giving the muscle a more prominent, fuller appearance.

I think synthol may be responsible for the death of at least nine former houseguests; Nasser El Sonbaty is perhaps the most well-known. Why they thought twenty-two-inch biceps weren't big enough and had to inject something in them to get to twenty-three inches is beyond my comprehension, especially when it's so obvious — and ugly. A lot of the guys suffer from "bigorexia." They look in a mirror and see a small guy, not what the public sees.

I do not believe in "roid rage" either. If a person is naturally aggressive, that aggression may be heightened, but it's not like a switch being turned on or off and someone going from Dr. Jekyll to Mr. Hyde. *A Body to Die For,* a 1994 movie starring Ben Affleck as a steroid-using high school football player gone berserk, is to steroids what the scare movie *Reefer Madness* was to marijuana during my era at UC Berkeley. It created a lot of harmful stereotypes and myths.

Many bodybuilding careers were ruined because of actions by law enforcement bordering on entrapment. Several were even killed due to their involvement in the drug trade, including Steve Krader and

German bodybuilder Markus Mueller.

The big problem with steroids is that no one has adequately addressed the post-cycle period, when many guys turn to recreational drugs or painkillers to counter the effects of being off everything. Benjamin Franklin's, "There are no gains without pains" seems to have morphed into, "No gain without Nubain" – or something more substantial, like fentanyl, which is eighty times stronger than morphine. The combination of painkillers, anti-depressants, and sleeping aids is what doctors call the "Trinity." Professional wrestlers simply call it the "Death Cocktail."

Over the past forty-five years, recreational drugs have only gotten more prevalent, potent, and dangerous as fentanyl is being laced into many of them. And as ever, the more people try anabolic steroids, the more the traffickers take over.

MIKE MATARAZZO: 1991

Mike walked into my office in February 1991. Tim and I shared the same space most of the time we worked together, but Tim would joke that you needed to have twenty-inch biceps to enter my half. If that were true, Mike would have gotten in easily.

Mike knocked on my door that day because his training partner back in Boston, Paul DeMayo, had told him that if he needed help while in LA, he should "go see Ed." Like a number of my houseguests, Mike had been encouraged by Lou Zwick, the producer of the TV show *MuscleMania*. But somewhere along the way, Lou had left Mike stranded — like so many — so Mike needed help.

This was around the same time several Santa Monica City College football players were coming to the gym. I thought Mike was one of them and still wearing his shoulder pads when he came into my office. I teased Mike and said, "You don't need to go into my office wearing your pads." When Mike said he wasn't, I said, "You're not leaving here until you turn pro."

To which Mike replied, "You better talk to my parents."

I flew back to Boston to meet Mike's mom and dad at an Italian feast in their home, maybe on Easter Sunday. What made the visit more special even after these years was that Mike had some of the most loving parents I have ever met. By the time I left California, forty years after buying Gold's Gym, I had had over five hundred houseguests, and yet out of that group, I had talked to fewer than a dozen parents, let alone shared a meal with them. Was that how many cared about what their child was doing out in LA?

But that day, Mike's parents, Mary and Big Mike, wanted to talk and learn what I had in mind for their son. I predicted that if they let Mike stay with me and train with my other houseguest at the time, Achim Albrecht from Germany, there was a good chance he would win the USAs in July and get a pro card.

What would that mean? I boldly forecast that Mike would earn $300,000-plus a year if that happened. Mike's dad said that seemed like a good gamble since Mike was unemployed and gave his blessing.

Mike, along with Achim, shared my half of the duplex — about sixteen hundred square feet — for the next five months. All

Mike did was eat, sleep, and train, but that's what it took to win — and he did. Mike's parents and his sister were there in Santa Monica when he won the USAs and got a pro card. I still remember Mike's dad grabbing me around the neck and giving me a big Italian hug in the auditorium after Mike's win. Mike, who tragically died too early in 2014, remembered it as the happiest day of his life.

Achim was the first of several dozen fitness competitors from Germany who I would eventually have as visitors to my home in California or Nevada. They were all very friendly and pleasant but at the same time very German. I remember the standard refrain from them: "I must eat, I must train, I must sleep!" But that's what Mike did. They were a perfect match at the time, despite an occasional miscommunication due to language.

After his pro career with Weider, Achim went on to a wrestling career as Brakus with the WWE and is now working as a personal trainer in San Francisco, where his clients include people like one of the founders of Airbnb.

CRAIG TITUS

During the '90s, photographers like Irv Gelb, who primarily submitted photos to *MuscleMag,* would introduce talent to Tim or me. Unlike Pete, we were in the office most of the time. We would likely give the person a complimentary membership and maybe some clothing for a photoshoot. I might even provide a place to stay.

Irv introduced me to Craig Titus in 1991 when he was in LA competing in the Ironman contest in Fontana, located just east of the city. Not everyone I met and encouraged who got a pro card had a successful bodybuilding career — or life. Craig was one of those people.

I initially told him he could stay at my place anytime he was in town to get photographed. During those visits to my home, Craig met people like Mike Matarazzo, Lee Priest, Matt DuVall, Tom Prince, and Mike Francois — a veritable who's who of bodybuilding who could help guide him on a successful career path.

Craig had that all-American look that I knew was marketable. In 1998, Craig even tied Mike O'Hearn's record for the largest number of magazine covers on the newsstand at one time: four. Mike was another bodybuilder I had encouraged to move to California after seeing him at a Gold's Gym in Seattle in which I was part owner.

Back in the day, when there were newsstands and fitness magazines, I could walk by the display of magazines and often see a half dozen former houseguests on the covers, sometimes even several who were still living at one of my homes. Being on three covers at one time was the "trifecta" of bodybuilding and could ensure a fitness career.

Craig had eighteen covers before he even turned pro. I know because I had them framed for him.

Like several former houseguests, Craig had been arrested for selling drugs. But in Craig's case, it wasn't steroids; it was ecstasy, or molly. He was arrested while he was living in Houston. I wasn't judgmental and was all for giving people a second chance, especially if they had paid their dues by serving time in jail. When Craig was arrested a second time in 1996, I even gave up three weekends to drive to Lompoc, California, where he was in federal prison, to see him.

Craig's last letter from Lompoc, dated February 16, 1999, was full of optimism and hope:

"Dear Ed,

Hey bud!! I can't even sleep because my mind is going a smile a minute. I'm ready to get MASSIVE!!

See you in a few days,

Craig."

Craig and I made plans to resurrect his career when he got out. Craig even asked me not to have any other houseguests while he was there so he could concentrate on a new start. But after leaving prison and returning to LA, I saw Craig for all of fifteen minutes before he left for Las Vegas.

Ten years later, in August 2009, I received this letter from Craig, who was now in jail in Nevada for murder:

"I'm hoping you'll forgive me for being such an awful friend over the years after being released from Lompoc. I've had the last four years of my life to truly reflect on my errors in life and the regrets I have to live with. I'm not sure why I didn't keep my family and friends close to me while I was rebuilding my life back in 1999 but it tears at the depths of my soul in the fact that I was a terribly selfish and self centered person. Ed, for that I am truly sorry. But I will tell you that I did not commit murder or kidnapping."

I believe Craig is innocent and is likely covering for his wife, Kelly Ryan, who was released from prison in 2017. He is not entirely innocent, as he participated in the botched attempt to cover up the murder, but I doubt very much that Craig killed Melissa James, his live-in assistant, by himself.

I had to suspend Craig's membership at Gold's Gym Venice three times — a record — for fighting in the gym. Despite their size, some bodybuilders are all talk and no action, but Craig was not like that. He certainly wouldn't have used a Taser and pushed Melissa down the stairs if he wanted to kill her. That wasn't Craig's style.

Craig had a problem with women, having at least more than one relationship simultaneously. In the beginning, Tim, Derek, and I would give the spouses of pro bodybuilders a complimentary membership, even extending it to their girlfriends. But after Craig seemed to have a "girlfriend of the week," and the number of complimentary memberships got out of hand, I had to tell Craig that he needed to be married to the person to receive that perk.

LEE PRIEST FROM AUSTRALIA: 1993, 1994

One of the joys of working in the offices next door to Gold's Gym Venice was the unpredictability of each day. Every morning, I would write down a "Top 10" list of things I hoped to work on that day. A lot of it was usually carried over from the previous day. Some days I would make it through all ten items, but other days I might not get past the first one on the list.

When I was working as an architect, I might have been juggling three balls at one time: one building might be in the concept phase, another in advanced design, and the third project under construction. But they were all known entities that I might have been involved with for several years. There were few surprises.

At Gold's Gym, I never knew who or what might walk through the door. Every day was different.

One of the biggest surprises during those twenty-five years was Lee Priest, all the way from Australia. Even coming from down under, he grew up wanting to look like a superhero — in his case, He-Man, whose real identity, as he will tell you, was Prince Adam of Eternia. Later on, he would gravitate toward Superman, including a Superman tattoo and an apartment filled with Superman memorabilia.

But the He-Man action figure had resonated with him as a kid. Weighing 215 pounds at five feet, three inches with twenty-one and a half-inch biceps and blond hair, he was the closest thing to a real-life action figure I had ever seen — and certainly one of the greatest bodybuilders of all time.

Lee had been encouraged by Lou Zwick to put a plane ticket on his uncle's credit card and fly to LA from Melbourne. He was told he would be reimbursed. At twenty years old, Lee was pretty gullible — but then, Lou did convince him with his *American Muscle* credentials.

Lou had tricked many into believing he wanted to help them, including Mike Matarazzo two years earlier. At one point, I had three "Lou Zwick refugees" staying at my home simultaneously. Paul

DeMayo and Mike Francois promised each other that they would each grab a leg and make a wish if they ever saw Lou again together in person. Francois even sued him over some prize money from a *MuscleMania* contest and won in court. Like all the others, Zwick had left Lee stranded in Venice.

Fortunately, Lee was seen in the gym by photographer Irv Gelb, who was always looking for new individuals to photograph. You might say he was my number one talent scout.

Some magazines paid separately for a cover photo or an article with pictures, so an independent contractor like Irv had to be creative and work hard. After hearing Lee's story, Irv brought him to the corporate offices to meet me.

With one look at Lee, I immediately took him down the hall from my office to the photo studio used by Chris Lund, one of Weider's main photographers. Chris would use it when visiting from England. I snapped some Polaroids of Lee to FedEx to Weider.

In a matter of days, Lee and I were having lunch with Joe in Woodland Hills, where the Weider offices were located. As fate would have it, Jim Manion, head of the NPC, was also in LA at that time. He contacted Paul Graham in Australia to ask Paul to grant Lee a pro card since Lee had won the Mr. Australia twice. That meant that Lee could compete in the upcoming pro contest in Niagara Falls.

I knew Joe was more likely to offer Lee sponsorship if he had pro status. When I took the Canadian bodybuilder Paul Dillett to meet Joe and get a contract, I later learned that the only reason Joe sponsored Paul was that he thought he was already a pro. How that mistake happened, I do not know, but I was happy for it. And indeed, Joe offered Lee a contract that would be enough to live on and start a life in the States.

But Joe had many people around him at the office who thought they needed to protect him from himself, so nothing was automatic — or quick. A contract and the release of money would take some time.

A dozen of my former houseguests have written books. Lee is one of them. Chapter seven of Lee's memoir begins with the heading "Edward Connors Saved My Arse." During this waiting period, which lasted almost five months, Lee was a guest at my home in Venice, which was right on the beach about two hundred yards south of

Muscle Beach and three-fourths of a mile from Gold's Gym Venice. There was no need for a car. Lee could settle in pretty quickly until the money started to flow.

The only major trip was to the grocery store. I knew to simply drop my foreign houseguests off and tell them I would be back in a couple of hours to pick them up. At first, they didn't understand, but it became clear once in an American supermarket. It might as well have been a trip to Disneyland for them. A visit to Costco was like dying and going to heaven. It was that entertaining. Whereas in their home country they might find a couple of choices for something like rice cakes, they would discover many feet of rice cakes on the shelves here in America. And then there was all the nutritional labeling — the calories and fat content — to make their lives that much easier. Everything was right there on the package.

Lee was one of the first visitors to my third and last home in Venice, where I lived for eleven years. When I was traveling and checking into a motel or hotel and had to give my address, I would say, "2311 Ocean Front Walk." Sometimes the front desk person might say, "That sounds wonderful." It was one of the few homes in Venice that fronted the boardwalk that didn't have commercial activity in front of it. There was the house, twenty feet of boardwalk, a bike path, and then sand. The Pacific Ocean was about one hundred yards away, usually crashing on an outcropping of rocks that was part of the Lifeguard-Maintenance building near my home.

The TV show *Baywatch* was filmed nearby. Some of my houseguests even made money from the show when they needed background people to create the Venice Beach scene, which everyone knew meant Muscle Beach — even if the houseguest was from the other coast or another country.

Some even complained to me — or at least expressed guilt — that they were posing as a California bodybuilder when this was their first time in the state. I told them, "This is Hollywood, the land of make-believe. Take it."

Indeed, my home, like the gym, had its own agent for rentals to production companies. At $3,000 a day, it made more some weeks than I did appearing in made-for-TV movies, where it might be the MTV house one week or the fugitive home of a Nazi the next.

This particular house of mine had four bedrooms and three and a half baths in about forty-seven hundred square feet. The bedrooms were all usually filled. I offered Lee the basement bedroom, which seemed to be everyone's favorite — ironic because it was one that I had added after I moved in. It was just off the six-car underground garage, which was a rarity for the beach given the difficulty of excavating sand. It did have some small windows that opened to allow the sound of the waves crashing on the beach at night to be heard, but there was no view. However, the room could be made dark during the day, unlike all the other bedrooms, which were flooded with natural light.

But Lee wanted to be upstairs, which meant he'd have one of the "Jack and Jill" bedrooms — ones with a shared bathroom — at the back of the house on the alley side. My bedroom was on the same floor but facing the beach at the other end of the house.

One of my other houseguests at that time was Scott Young, a teenager I had met at one of the gyms I was involved with in East LA. Scott's family couldn't afford college for him. But he was tall and big for a teenager, so I thought he might get a football scholarship if he put on some weight. I invited Scott to spend the summer training at Gold's Gym Venice. Indeed, he could learn a lot from Lee, who was only a couple of years older but one of the best bodybuilders ever.

It was only many years later that I learned that Scott was so intimidated by Lee that he never used the bathroom they had in common during the entire summer. Scott made do with the powder room downstairs next to the kitchen and showered at the gym. Lee kept the bathroom door locked from his side, so Scott had little choice and didn't object or say anything to me the entire time he was there. Scott eventually got that scholarship in law enforcement and became a policeman in Las Vegas, where I suspect he is no longer so shy — or intimidated.

Louis Coulombe, a French-Canadian bodybuilder who had come to LA seeking a new life and the American dream, was another houseguest during this time. Louis wasn't big but had a great look and a personality to match. As I would say, "It's not just lifting weights. It's the whole package."

I was looking out not just for the next pro bodybuilder or the next pro wrestler but the next star. I knew what Joe Weider had done for Arnold. I saw people like Kevin Sorbo struggling to make it and training in Venice and then becoming Hercules on TV. Jean-Claude Van Damme was another one who had lived in his van in the gym parking lot. There were enough people like them that I believed anything was possible.

When Lee's fiancee visited from Australia, Louis found her knocking on his door one night. Lee was training for the Ironman contest, and whether Lee wasn't interested in sex at the time or Louis was just too good-looking to resist is unknown.

Louis informed me about his surprise night-time visitor. When I told Lee what had happened, he was in denial. It wasn't until after his contest, when she took his prize money and split for Australia, that Lee figured out she wasn't suitable for him. She was one of a number of the girlfriends or wives of houseguests with whom I would talk to, usually in the kitchen, so often I called it my "kitchen talk." They would say things to me like, "I'd love him even if he didn't lift weights or look the way he does. I'd be happy if he just had a forty-hour week factory job." To which I would say, "BS!" I would tell them that you can't separate that much physicality from the person, that a lot of what they must have loved was the look and the passion to obtain it. These women simply didn't understand.

I would have let Lee stay longer, but the increasingly frequent trips to my home by Ms. Fitness America Laurie Donnelly had me worried. I had previously been sued by the parents of one of my houseguests' girlfriends, who alleged their daughter was raped and had gotten pregnant in my home. This resulted in a painful settlement, and I wasn't anxious to see that repeated.

When Lee opened up a letter from Australia and a baby picture fell out, my first thought was that I didn't want him making babies at my place. As it turns out, he had gotten someone pregnant before leaving Australia, and he was learning about its consequences that very day I saw him open the letter.

When director Joel Schumacher contacted Lee about playing Bane in his 1997 version of *Batman & Robin,* Lee had a chance at breaking into Hollywood. But because Bane's protagonist in the movie, Uma Thurman as Poison Ivy, was so tall, Schumacher chose Jeep Swenson instead.

Jeep had been a houseguest and wrestling candidate of mine.

He would have been my pick for the Gold's Gym team if he had stayed in California for two more weeks before returning to Texas ten years earlier. But with Jeep gone and impossible to reach, I called Jim Hellwig instead. Fate. Jim became The Ultimate Warrior.

Jeep died in 1997 at forty years old, the same year the Batman movie was released. When I asked the doctor at the UCLA Medical Center if there was some way to save him, like a heart transplant, he said that was impossible given the size of Jeep's heart, which was probably due to so much growth hormone. At six feet, four inches, Jeep was obsessed with size, going way over the four-hundred-pound mark. When I had my picture taken next to him, I told him I was happy to do it because he made me look small. Jeep said, "Don't say that." He joked with me and said he told people I weigh three hundred in the photo. Jeep had one of the biggest hearts — figuratively and literally — of any of the big guys at Gold's Gym Venice.

Jeep's enlarged heart issue reminded me of Lee's time at my home a few years earlier, when growth hormone had been a topic. The gossip mill pre-internet was alive with talk of this freak, this dwarf, training at Gold's Gym Venice, who most certainly must be taking massive amounts of growth hormone. Lee and I eventually figured out this talk, mainly from the East Coast, was about him. We both got a big laugh out of it because Lee wasn't using growth hormone. And indeed, I remember him telling me later that he spent $300 on his most recent cycle.

Genetics and what the person did growing up is a small but essential part of what makes a great bodybuilder. Lee finds the current state of bodybuilding to be sad. "Bigger is not always better," as he says in his book. And in my opinion, he rightfully accuses the judges of being the primary cause of this.

Lee eventually left Gold's Gym for World Gym when he and Flex Wheeler were at odds with each other, and it was difficult for him to train in the gym when Flex was there. As a result, Joe Gold became a surrogate father for Lee. I was happy with how all this turned out as I didn't have the time to mentor Lee. (Lee's father, like a surprising number of my houseguests, had come out as gay and, because of the sentiment at the time, was out of Lee's life early. I also had houseguests whose mothers were lesbian and were raised by lesbian couples, perhaps one reason they trained to be stronger to fight given the taunts from fellow classmates.)

Lee and Joe were so close that Joe left his two dogs to Lee when he died. During this period, I became co-owner with Flex Wheeler in a duplex, so perhaps Lee felt that he couldn't resolve the situation with Flex given my relationship with him.

I had seen Flex drive up to the gym one day in an expensive Mercedes. When I asked Flex if he even owned a house, Flex said no, that he didn't know how. I said I would show him. So we became partners in a duplex at Wavecrest and Ocean Avenues in Venice, just one house south of the original Gold's Gym. For many years, it was my "overflow house" when the three extra bedrooms on Ocean Front Walk weren't enough. People like Gunter Schlierkamp, Jack London, Mike Matarazzo, John Cena, Geir Paulsen from Norway, Roland Cziurlock from Germany, and Roland Kickinger from Austria stayed there various times.

Ken Fisher from Mississippi was another houseguest during this period. Between Lee's thick Australian accent and Ken's southern accent, there were a lot of memorable moments together ordering at restaurants. You could also add in Louis's French-Canadian accent.

Each time the waiter or waitress asked Lee to repeat his order, Lee would get more and more upset, finally saying, "Can't you understand me? I'm speaking English!"

Ken later invited Lee to Mississippi for his first guest posing in America, and so Lee got to experience the real South early on in his visit to the US.

Lee turned twenty-one at my home on July 7, 1993. I remember that birthday well as he wanted an ice cream cake. Lee had a sweet tooth, one of only three houseguests for whom I can remember having to worry about dental work. He would live in the US for the next decade before heading back to Australia.

GETTING TO PLAY "GOD"

"If you do good, people will accuse you of selfish, ulterior motives. Do good anyway."

"The good you do today will be forgotten tomorrow. Do good anyway."

— Kent M. Keith

Like Hollywood, with its actors and actresses seeking fame and fortune and going to LA to be discovered, Gold's Gym Venice became a magnet for anyone with a dream to make it big in bodybuilding.

Unfortunately, also because of Hollywood, people assumed I was gay and had a hidden agenda. No doubt, a number of the fitness people I tried to encourage to pursue a bodybuilding or eventually an acting career was discouraged because of the "casting couch" and having to sell themselves to succeed. I'm sure a number of the people I approached refused my "advances" because they assumed I wanted something more out of the relationship than simply helping them — or Gold's Gym. And, of course, what I was dealing with — bodybuilding, pro wrestling — was essentially a male-dominated world. It also didn't help that many of the people I approached came from broken homes where their fathers had abandoned them early. If you can't trust your dad to be there, who can you trust?

My therapist called it the "stray dog syndrome," but I would characterize it more like "playing god" — god with a small "g" — rather than trying to save a stray dog.

Pets had never been my thing. I didn't grow up with any. When people would ask why I would spend several thousand dollars trying to help someone, I would tell them that, according to the 2010 US census, the average American spends $16,000 on their dog during its lifetime. The people I've told this to would then usually tell me that number seems low. (It was previously listed at $12,000 in the 2000 census.) But for much less than that, I could potentially make one human being's life a little better. Sometimes it cost me nothing but my time.

My favorite movie is *Groundhog Day,* with Bill Murray. The premise of the film begs the question, what would you do if you lived the same day over and over until you got it right?

There's a beautiful scene where Murray says to co-star Andie MacDowell, "I'm a god. I'm not THE God, but I'm a god" because of what he knows.

Because of what I knew, I could change a life. I could play god.

There were times when I could play god, when it wasn't even necessary to bring a certain person to California. I could see something that no one else seemed to be able to see, like with Rob Terry, Flex Lewis's occasional training partner in Wales.

Rob was working as a bank guard in the Welsh city of Swansea. At six feet, five inches and nearly three hundred pounds, I considered that a waste of his talents and suggested he meet me in London. The WWE was staging a two-day event there, and I would be in the city to meet the new owner of Gold's Gym London. When I introduced Rob to Vince McMahon at the WWE event, he hired him on the spot, something he told me he had never done before.

Vince, who is my age, also told me that Rob didn't need to dress the way he did. But I like to tell the guys when they go to events, "You're not there to read poetry. People want to see muscle." So, I asked Rob to dress to impress. And he did — enough to impress Vince.

Talent and opportunity coincided — or collided — that day, and Rob realized his dream of going to America. Later, his girlfriend joined him, and she has had a successful career modeling in the States. They are now married with two children and live in Florida, like many Brits.

Maybe I was following Martin Luther King's interpretation of the Good Samaritan parable, which tells us when confronted with someone in need to ask not, "If I stop to help this man, what will happen to me?" but instead to ask, "If I don't stop to help this man, what will happen to him?" Maybe I was a good shepherd, a shepherd of talent.

At age seventy-six, you would think something would have happened, but I've been celibate most of my life. Sex isn't that important — at least for me. I never wanted a marriage to a woman any more than I wanted a relationship with a man.

To say, however, that I have never known what it is to live with someone or have children would be a mistake. I have had my houseguests. I don't like living alone, and my houseguests have filled that need and given me a relationship with the larger world.

The internet is the venue for mean-spirited thinking and talk now with all of its "haters." Mike Bergsma from Kent, Washington, is a tragic example of the consequences of this kind of hate.

I met Mike at a contest in 1985 and thought he had pro potential, so I invited him to LA to get some publicity. Shortly before he was to come down the second time for a Weider photoshoot, Mike and his father were killed in a gas explosion while working on a fence with propane torches.

After the funeral, I went over to the gym where Mike trained. I saw a crude drawing on the bulletin board in which someone had written "Mike" over a person kneeling, giving a person labeled "Joe Weider" a blow job. Even though it was the greater Seattle metro, this was the kind of small-town behavior I found repugnant and that altered people's lives — sometimes tragically. I castigated the gym owner for not taking it down.

Mike had delayed his trip because of that kind of vicious gossip and innuendo. The thought of Mike going to LA and potentially doing something different with his life was enough of a threat to someone in that gym that they felt that they had to do everything possible to sabotage his trip. They did. He delayed and died.

Something similar had happened with Paul DeMayo, one of the all-time greats in bodybuilding. I initially met Paul when he was only nineteen while visiting the Venice gym after winning a local Gold's Gym Classic contest in Boston. He was another Lou Zwick refugee. I encouraged him to come back out to LA and go for his pro card and get it before turning twenty-one. That would be an achievement only four of my houseguests had garnered: Rich Gaspari, Eddie Robinson, Lee Priest, and Dallas McCarver.

He went back to Boston but, like Mike Bergsma, received so many negative comments about going to LA that he didn't make a move. It was only after Mike Matarazzo, his occasional training partner at the local Gold's Gym in Malden, Massachusetts, came out to stay with me and got his pro card that he changed his mind. Then Paul had been goaded by his fellow gym members with taunts of, "Well, if you're so good, then why aren't *you* a pro like Mike?" I hired his girlfriend, Jill, to work in our accounting office, and Paul flourished in the Southern California environment.

A few of the guys — very few — could go months without training. Paul was not one of that group. Like most of the great bodybuilders, he was obsessed with exercise.

A typical ninety-minute leg day looked like this:

- Squats, five to seven sets of twelve reps
- Hack squats, three to five sets of eight to twelve reps
- Thigh extensions, three to five sets of ten to twelve reps
- Lying leg curl, three to five sets of eight to twelve reps
- Stiff leg deadlift, three to five sets of ten to twelve reps
- Standing calf raises, three to four sets of twelve to fifteen reps
- Seated calf raises, three to four sets of twelve to fifteen reps

With the moniker "Quadzilla" given to him by bodybuilder, writer, and fitness contest MC Lonnie Tepper because of his freakish legs, Paul was in demand for guest posing at competitions all over the US. He had nineteen engagements the first year he lived in Venice before getting his pro card three years after Matarazzo. When he stepped onstage at the Nationals in Orlando in 1994, he weighed 252 pounds at five feet, nine inches. There was nothing small about the guys from this era.

Paul died tragically at age thirty-seven in 2005 from a heroin overdose. I can't help but feel that if he had come out to California earlier — and stayed — his life would have ended differently.

When I flew back to Boston for the funeral, I was shocked to see the poor Boston neighborhood where the funeral was held, with street signs everywhere indicating it was a "No Oxy Zone," referring to Oxycontin. I learned at his funeral that Paul had switched from that drug to heroin because it was cheaper.

His training partner died one day after he did. They owed the dealer around $18,000, and he was making an example of them by giving them a lethal batch. I tried to get one of the Boston papers interested in the story since it was essentially murder but had no luck.

Because there were so many jealous haters out there, I avoided publicizing that I had houseguests and asked my guests not to mention me in interviews they gave publicly. They could thank me later if they wanted.

With shows like *American Idol* and *America's Got Talent,* it's easier now for people to understand another one of the reasons I avoided publicity: There were a lot of people out there who thought they had a future in fitness but had nothing I could honestly or legitimately endorse or encourage. I wasn't going to lie to them, nor did I want to be mean or cruel. Just as you might wonder what sound system the person on one of those TV shows was listening to that made them think they could sing, so, too, I wondered what kind of mirror people were looking into that made them believe they had potential in bodybuilding.

But then, I even had serious complaints about the mirrors at Gold's Gym Venice. People asked me if we had "trick mirrors" — mirrors that made them look smaller. Many would tell me they looked bigger back home. While the thickness of the glass can make a slight difference, I assured them that that was not enough to matter, and all our mirrors were a standard thickness.

I suspect they were no longer the biggest fish in the pond when working out in Venice, and they felt small. And indeed, this was a problem for a number of my houseguests. They enjoyed being the biggest guy in the club back in their hometown rather than one of many at Gold's Gym Venice. I knew they were not likely to stay.

There was another, darker reason I avoided publicity: My houseguests might be targeted by men and women who could harm them. Granted, given their size, it is hard to imagine that anyone could make them do something they didn't want to do.

There was a time when I shut down my Facebook account because several women were preying on the younger friends they saw on my page. I call one of them the "Black Widow" because she would mate with her prey and effectively kill them — either their careers or cause them to contemplate suicide. Fortunately, I believe none of them went that far, but a couple came close. She would fly the guys to San

Francisco, secretly videotape having sex with them, and then try to blackmail them.

As far as I know, she wasn't after money. She wanted to play with them, to ruin their lives. She destroyed a couple of budding careers. She even messed with Rich Piana when he was in his forties.

Somehow she had wormed herself into Rich's life enough to go with him to Germany to work his 5% Nutrition booth at FIBO, the biggest fitness trade show of its kind, held yearly in Cologne and attended by nearly 200,000 people. When I saw her there, I was shocked but didn't want to say or do anything. It was only after Rich told me he had tied her up in his hotel room and left her there while he returned to the States that I told him the history my houseguests had with her. With Rich, she had tried to steal a lot of money while working his booth, so it was primarily financial with him, although he was initially drawn to her romantically.

She died in a head-on car crash in 2021.

Another one of the female stalkers on Facebook would pretend to be with Gold's Gym corporate and contact the guys wanting to sponsor them, only to string them along so that in the end, they had wasted much time and come up with nothing.

There were male predators as well. One lived near Muscle Beach, a few hundred yards from my last home. He would recruit guys to do gay porn, most of it shot in the Valley area of LA, which is famous for that. Again, a lot of dashed dreams and altered careers.

Sometimes characterizing what my houseguests might expect staying in one of my homes was a lot less dramatic, even funny. When Dave Dearth, along with his brother, Doug, came out to stay with me before going to work at the Gold's Gym I owned in San Bernardino, and before he became a pro, we were having lunch at The Firehouse Restaurant, which was a block away from the gym and the most popular place to get a meal before or after a workout. The back portion of the restaurant has a patio with seating for twenty off of an indoor area with tables for about thirty.

Dave and I were sitting amid a packed house inside when he said to me, "So, what's it like to be a houseguest of Ed Connors?"

I told him he could ask either party to the right or left of our table — or half the people in the room. All had been houseguests of mine. Everyone got a big kick out of it when I asked the fellow "alumni" to welcome Dave into their group.

FIVE CATEGORIES OF HOUSEGUESTS

If one were to categorize the fitness-related careers of my 528 houseguests, it would break down like this: a hundred and two were pro bodybuilders, sixty-six became gym owners, twenty-two started nutritional supplement companies, and twenty-one went into professional wrestling.

In addition, a few became fitness models and actors, and many became personal trainers. Some of those bodybuilders who saw the potential of personal training early on in Venice took it back to where they had come from and became pioneers — or evangelists — of fitness, such as Mike Hubon in Perth, Australia, or Mike Jaudes with Fitness Edge Personal Training, which he started in St. Louis in 1984 — way ahead of its time.

Then there were those personal trainers who took it to another level, like Alfred Krautgartner, originally from Austria, who trained Tobey Maguire for *Spiderman,* and Brad Rowe, who got Mike Tyson back in shape to fight.

Fifty-six are deceased who I know about, mostly from solo traffic accidents, most likely falling asleep at the wheel while driving late at night. Up until the opioid crisis, traffic accidents were the most common cause of death of white males between ages twenty and thirty in America. More recently, many of my former houseguests have died from overdosing on pain killers like fentanyl. In 1999, just under seventeen thousand Americans died from drug overdoses. That number reached over ninety thousand in 2020.

Not all my former houseguests were saints. At least three have been involved in murders, and two were killed in what I believe were drug hits, one involving mistaken identity.

Each of these categories might be broken down into three more: those whose lives I believe were permanently changed because of me; those for whom meeting me had little or no effect; and those for whom I'm not sure, like Jay Cutler.

JAY CUTLER

Jay swears that he is where he is today in the bodybuilding world — at the pinnacle of success as Mr. Olympia — because of me and Joe Weider. In his book and videos, Jay says that when I met him at twenty, I told him he could be Mr. Olympia. I don't remember that moment, but the important thing is that Jay does.

Jay was another one of those people I "discovered" in the gym. But as with Christopher Columbus and America, he was already there.

Like Paul DeMayo, Jay was from Massachusetts and had won the local Gold's Gym Classic bodybuilding contest. He had come out to Venice because the local newspaper had misprinted an ad for air travel, and the airline chose to honor the low fare.

When I saw Jay in the gym, I went up to congratulate him and told him to let me know if he ever needed anything. I also asked where he was staying. When he gave me the motel name and location, I said he needed to move out right away because it was unsafe. I offered Jay and Kerry, his future wife, my home. It would be the first of several visits by Jay, some of them lasting for over a month.

In his podcast episodes, Jay credits the invitation to stay at my home the second time as a critical point in his bodybuilding career because that's when he decided to pursue bodybuilding and not law enforcement, which was another career path many of my visitors chose to follow. He says he learned a lot from the other guests during those visits, mainly about food, supplements, and training. In hindsight, he wishes he had explored more of LA than just my home, the beach, and the gym, but he was young and on a mission.

Jay was flexible, open to new ideas, and willing to learn, unlike some guests. He would come down the stairs at my three-story home on Venice Beach from his upstairs bedroom and shout, "Who wants to go train?"

At least that's what a bodybuilder from the East Coast might say. One from the Midwest would probably say, "Who wants to go lift?" to which cynics, of course, would ask, "Lift what?" And the West Coast guys would say, "Who wants to go workout?" That was probably a hangover from Jane Fonda's days, making the term "working out" famous from her videos. Many were getting a training partner for the first time in their life, something they couldn't find at home and that could be critical for success. The language in each case was a little different, but the results were the same. And off they would go to the gym, which was less than a mile away.

Those were the days before the internet — or the fitness gurus. It wasn't easy to get information or start a conversation. Even running into someone in the gym was usually unproductive. People don't want to be bothered while they are working out. It's rude. But while living under the same roof for a while, it was easy. It was hard to hide what you were doing as far as eating and supplements are concerned.

It's funny to think of it that way, but in today's world of gurus or trainers, my home was a "guru house," a fraternity of like-minded people. Unfortunately, the internet hasn't been the help I thought it would be. It is filled with misinformation, negativity, and hate.

Jay is one of the greats from the golden age who has made the leap from the covers of bodybuilding magazines to social media with 3.8 million followers on Instagram. He has become an influencer while also promoting his supplement line.

GUNTER & CARMEN SCHLIERKAMP

I initially met Gunter in Germany at a fitness event. I knew Weider would like Gunter's look, so I invited him and his girlfriend at the time to come to America to further his career. Gunter didn't speak a lot of English, so his girlfriend did all the talking, basically saying, "We do not need to go there."

Later on, with now-wife Carmen, Gunter finally made it to the US — not to California but to New Jersey. It wasn't working out for them. When I ran into Gunter at a bodybuilding contest in San Jose, he was ready to quit and go back to Germany. I was sitting next to him in front of the auditorium. There were ten finalists on stage; Gunter wasn't one of them. I asked Gunter how many Caucasians he saw onstage. Gunter said three: Lee Priest, Eddie Robinson, and Troy Zuccolotto, all of whom had been houseguests of mine. Then I asked Gunter how many were taller than him. Gunter said, "None."

I said, "See? There's a market for you!"

But Gunter and Carmen were stuck on the East Coast with a rather unscrupulous supplement company owner who was their host. Because of Gunter's lack of English, I tried to make his situation as graphic as possible. I drew a classic bullseye pattern with concentric rings and explained to Gunter that they lived in one of the outer rings, away from the center of the bullseye: Venice.

Like so many I've met, Gunter said there was no way he could make a move. It would be too costly. Staying in a motel room along with eating out while looking for an apartment could take several weeks and drain all the savings most had, savings that would have to be used for the deposit and first month's rent. And, of course, Gunter had no job. So I offered Gunter and Carmen a place in my home on Venice Beach and told him I would introduce him to Joe Weider to get a contract. The only bedroom other than mine with a TV was the basement bedroom, and so they stayed there, perfect for Gunter as he could then watch movies and learn English.

During this time, I introduced him to Joe Weider, as I had done with many people. Joe initially offered Gunter $30,000 a year. I told Gunter to hold out for more money and that he was welcome to stay as long as was needed. Gunter eventually got more than twice that amount, but it took five months. In the meantime, however, Gunter's English got much better.

One of the lines I used to get Gunter to LA was to tell him that he looked like a movie star. Ironically, once he was in LA, people did come up to him wondering if he was a movie star. No doubt part of that was due to his size at six feet, two inches and 275 pounds — but he also had a great face. This discovery led Gunter to seek an agent.

All three of the houses I owned in Venice were within walking distance to the gym, and the closest grocery store was only seven blocks away. Gunter and Carmen got around on their bikes. When those were stolen, they took the bus.

Gunter and Carmen took the bus to a talent agent I recommended Gunter see, which involved transfers and took hours, this being LA in the '90s. After the interview, when the Hollywood agent asked Gunter for his parking ticket to validate it, Gunter told him they had taken the bus. The agent was so impressed with their determination that he said then and there that he would take him on as a client.

Indeed, Gunter did get some parts in commercials and movies, such as *Beerfest*. It was income that was hard to depend on but wonderful when it did happen.

When agencies would cast their net looking for tall bodybuilders, Gunter and Rich Piana were often the only ones who showed up. Gunter said for every ten of those casting calls — "cattle calls" — he would land one. I told him that's about the same ratio as when I went after architectural commissions.

The point is that if you want to get a job, it's best to go for as many attempts as possible. Again, it was luck combined with persistence. The harder you work, the luckier you get.

At six feet, one and a half inches, Gunter would be the tallest pro bodybuilder on stage most of the time, like Arnold — that near-perfect height. Though Gunter never won the Olympia, he placed high and had a long, nine-year career. He was also one of the few pros to get a standing ovation at the Olympia when he retired.

Gunter may have been one of the few pro bodybuilders I've known who understood what I would tell many pros: "Being a pro bodybuilder is not all about winning, getting first place, and being Mr. Olympia. It's about having a long, successful career."

Having never been a competitive athlete and understanding the drive to win and be first, that was easy for me to say. But I saw any number of athletes having better careers and lives than many of the people they had "lost" to.

With close to eight billion people on the planet, coming in sixth place — or sixteenth place — isn't bad.

NASSER EL SONBATY

Sometimes it didn't take months to get a Weider contract.

One day, when Egyptian-German pro bodybuilder Nasser El Sonbaty happened to be in my office, Joe Weider called. I took the call and let Nasser listen in on the speakerphone. Joe started to complain in his very distinctive voice about how Sonny Schmidt, a very good pro bodybuilder from Australia, couldn't seem to find his way around an airport and so was hopeless on the road as a Weider athlete as he was always getting lost.

I said, "Why not hire Nasser El Sonbaty? He speaks five languages!"

After faxing Nasser's resume from my office, Joe hired him. That was easy.

I had three house rules: No underage women; no recreational drugs; and no overnight visitors without my permission. Sometimes these were written down, and I even asked houseguests to sign off on them.

Then there was a fourth, unwritten rule that I just assumed was obvious and understood: If you were going to do a photoshoot at a gym, then it had better be Gold's Gym. It wasn't broken often, but it did happen. I blamed the photographers as much as the athletes, as they should have known better. That was the quid pro quo: You were expected to support the gym if you were a guest.

I also didn't like negativity and would send houseguests home early if their attitude was terrible. Some would call me Pollyannaish, but I had grown up in an era of optimism. The '50s, even with all the nuclear attack drills, were a relatively optimistic period given the meteoric growth of the US economy after the world war, perhaps with the belief that any new war could also be won. Even during the free speech tumult while I was at UC Berkeley, there was unimaginable optimism, especially in my area of study: architecture and city planning. It was believed that both industries could save the world — or at least the environment.

My grandparents were the most optimistic. Though I loved my parents and felt they loved all my siblings and me equally, my father's parents made the biggest impression. While my parents urged caution

— "Be careful, you might get hurt" — my grandparents were full of praise and told me I could do anything. I listened to them.

Strangely enough, just working in Beverly Hills when I first arrived in California was transformative. With its temperate climate, the air fragrant with the smell of orange blossoms, eucalyptus, and jasmine, and the views of the snow-capped San Gabriel mountains, it was like coming into the Garden of Eden. Even riding in an elevator or eating at a restaurant in that environment and overhearing others around me talking further reinforced that belief in myself. They didn't seem to be any different from me.

Maybe I can make it. Perhaps I can do something with my life.

NOT ALL WOULD BECOME FAMOUS

Not all of my houseguests became famous or even well-known in the fitness world, but that was all right with me. Not all of them got the dream they thought they wanted, but they thanked me for the experience just the same; I had saved them much time. And all seem to have fond memories of the trip to California, especially at that time of their life, usually in their twenties and usually their first time on a plane. In a matter of months, they realized what might have taken years in their hometown, namely that a bodybuilding career wasn't for them.

One of those people is Jeff Perrault, a bodybuilder I met working at a Gold's Gym in Yakima, Washington, when I was inspecting it for Gold's Gym Franchising.

Some time after Jeff left my home, he wrote this in a letter:

"The most important part of this letter is a formal 'thank you' that was meant to be sent your way a long time ago. Living at your beautiful home last summer and living the life that would create jealousy in every amateur bodybuilder worldwide was an experience that I'll never forget. The Lord definitely blessed me with that opportunity in meeting you at the Gold's Gym in the little town of Yakima. It perplexes me in thinking about the odds of that happening. It may be close to a statewide lottery. Sometimes when I thumb through various muscle magazines I smile to myself in disbelief; I was there, in the middle of it all. For that, I thank you, your kindness has inspired me to strive for excellence in whatever I end up doing in my lifetime. I'd like to stay in touch with you; you're a great role model."

Jeff had stayed at my home with Paco Bautista, a pro bodybuilder from Spain, and Scott Milne, a bodybuilder from Canada, who was picked for the TV show *Battle Dome* while staying with me. Besides Jeff's potential, another reason I invited him that summer was his ability to speak Spanish since Paco spoke very little English.

After a brief stint in law enforcement, Jeff is now helping with his family's agricultural business and married with three daughters. For some unknown reason, most of the bodybuilders I know have daughters, not sons, something that needs to be investigated.

Paco owns and operates a gym in Madrid today.

Several Gold's Gym franchise owners, or potential owners, stayed with me as well and had an experience similar to the one Jeff expressed but in a much shorter period, such as Patrick Neadow, the Gold's Gym Vancouver franchisee, and his wife, Kim.

In the space of a long weekend, Patrick was able to train with Gunter Schlierkamp, run by Weider's home in Hancock Park with me, and meet pro bodybuilder Jim Quinn and Mr. Olympia Dorian Yates while visiting Milos Sarcev's gym in Orange County. Perhaps Patrick paid me the ultimate compliment: He told me he could go back to Vancouver and tell his friends about his time in LA, but he thought no one would believe him.

SUPERHEROES

Crime fighting and firefighting are my former houseguests two most common occupations other than fitness. They chose not to pursue a competitive bodybuilding career or make a living in fitness in positions such as a personal trainer, gym manager, or owner.

Again, they were heavily influenced by the superheroes they saw in the media. Nine of the thirty top-grossing films in the world have used Marvel characters.

Jeff Perrault was going to be one of them when he returned to Washington state, like FBI agent Frank Castle in Marvel's *The Punisher,* all for a similar reason to the one he stated in his letter:

"240 pounds would be a great weight for a police officer. I will fulfill this goal sometime in the near future. I would feel like a crime-fighting superhero, much like the heroes that Marvel Comics artists have been creating for years. (Or maybe that's how I'd like to picture myself as I live vicariously through every 240-pound bodybuilder.)"

That was the sentiment of many of my houseguests, the driving force behind their desire to serve. Another large block of my houseguests were veterans who chose to enlist right after 9/11, such as Jason Pelletier and Steve Christman.

WRESTLING DEATHS

My houseguests had a lot in common. Some of them are kind of funny, like those who didn't like the taste or texture of tomatoes yet put ketchup on everything. While I didn't talk to many of their mothers, the ones I did would say things like, "You know he will need a fan blowing on him at night to sleep." I assured them that this wasn't my first rodeo, and every one of my bedrooms had a fan in it.

Then there were the more significant common traits. While some played football, most weren't into team sports. Most of them wrestled in grade school or high school. Many of them were encouraged to drop weight by their wrestling coaches to get an easier win. As a result, their growth was stunted. This typically resulted in a longer torso and shorter, thicker legs — perfect for a male bodybuilder. It's all about creating that "illusion" on stage, and having those proportions helped achieve that. Maybe it is because I am an architect that I naturally focused on that look.

The average American male is five feet, nine inches. The US is the only industrialized country whose male population has decreased in height, and no one knows why. Thirty years ago, that number was five feet, ten inches. By comparison, the average nineteen-year-old male in China is now more than three and a half inches taller during the same period.

One reason may be US grade school and high school wrestling programs. In the long term, this protocol hurts the athlete, whose growth will be stunted not getting the nutrients and the calcium needed for bones to grow.

One of the first things I would ask someone I met who I thought had potential was their shoe size. Most were surprised when I guessed their correct size, which was several sizes bigger than their friends who were the same height. I looked for big necks, big hands, and big feet, but feet were the easiest to measure. That's what I meant when I said it was all about genetics and what you did as a kid. It was Jim Quinn who said, "You know what they say about guys who have big hands and big feet? They wear big gloves and big shoes!"

When the ABC TV show *20/20* contacted the Gold's Gym

office in 1997 wanting to do an exposé on creatine, I took the call. Creatine had become widely available in 1993. The FDA was investigating whether any of the three wrestling deaths that year could be linked to using creatine.

I did what I could to change the narrative to be about the wrestlers who had died running around in rubber suits to make weight before matches. I told *20/20* that dehydration was the culprit, not creatine. If anything, creatine likely retained water in the muscle and probably saved lives.

Of all the supplement products I have seen during my twenty-five years with Gold's Gym, creatine certainly had been the most significant breakthrough, due primarily to Bill Phillips and his company, EAS. Bill was a pioneer and a marketing genius with his "Physique Transformation" promotion, something I would later modify for use in my gyms.

20/20 ended up blaming those deaths on the coaches in their drive for weight loss. For several years following that show, the NCAA changed the rules so that athletes could be as much as six pounds over the weight limit and still make weight. But the harm had been done.

I never met any male gym member who wished he were shorter. One of the biggest reasons for joining a gym was to get bigger because the person felt small and was self-conscious about his height. Osteoporosis will no doubt be an issue for many as they get older. Parents would rail against the use of steroids, but the simple fact of not getting enough calcium growing up was the bigger enemy to their child's health. And, of course, there is the short-man complex to overcome.

Adam Wheeler, one wrestler whose growth had not been stunted having to make weight, was a six-time USA Wrestling All-American. I helped sponsor him for the 2008 Olympics in Beijing. At the height of six feet, two inches, he became the first American ever to win a medal in wrestling at the Olympics by getting a bronze medal in Greco-Roman. Like quite a few bodybuilder/wrestlers I know, he is currently working in law enforcement.

JOHN CENA

Sometimes when I approached people or commented about what I saw in them, it was not appreciated.

When Howie Long joined the Los Angeles Raiders in 1981 at age twenty-two, Lyle Alzado, already a member, brought him in to join Gold's Gym. I was called to the front desk to sign off on the comp membership. I took one look at Howie — all six feet, five inches of him — and said, "If you work on that body, you might have a career in Hollywood."

Howie had been a big Boston brawler, not a gym rat. I think if I hadn't been behind the counter, and Lyle hadn't been standing there next to him, I would have been attacked and badly beaten up. But forty years later, I can report that Howie did make a few action movies and has been an analyst on TV, doing color commentary for the networks long after his thirteen-year career with the Raiders ended.

Like Howie Long, John Cena was from Massachusetts, just a few years younger. He was also a competitive bodybuilder and was visiting the Mecca while in LA during spring break.

I saw John working out in the gym but didn't want to bother him during his workout. When I approached him in the gym parking lot and gave him my business card, my first words to him were, "Have you ever thought about professional wrestling?" He surprised me by saying that it would be his "dream" and was all ears.

I didn't know it at the time, but like so many people on vacation, he was on a budget, and his hotel room was his rental car. But unlike most of the people I met and gave my card to, he didn't blow me off, and we agreed to stay in touch.

John reminded me of Matt Damon or Mark Wahlberg — only bigger. I think that after living in LA awhile, it's a natural tendency to identify people by their movie-star look-alikes, or doubles, and John reminded me of both of them. Matt Damon had been a recent visitor to the gym, so he was in my head. And I had met Mark Wahlberg at the Church of the Good Shepherd in Beverly Hills. When I turned around at the portion of the Mass after the Our Father prayer to greet those around me with the "sign of peace," there he was behind me, along with two other individuals whom I assumed were his assistants or bodyguards.

After Mass, I gave Mark my business card and invited him to Gold's Gym Venice. I can still remember him in the gym in his shorts, shooting something for Calvin Klein. Then he was Marky Mark, the singer, not Mark Wahlberg, the actor. He is also now Mark Wahlberg, the gym owner of the F45 fitness chain, which went public in 2021.

Like so many movie stars, Mark was a lot shorter than I had imagined — or maybe it just seemed that way because most of the people in my life were so big. Ironically, Cena would end up appearing in two movies where the comparison to Mark was made clear. In the comedy *Trainwreck,* someone compares him to Mark Wahlberg, and John objects, saying that he's the equivalent of "two Mark Wahlbergs." In the other movie, *Daddy's Home,* he has a cameo role at the end where he rides up on a Harley, with Mark looking devastated by his size.

At six feet tall, John would be shorter than most of his fellow wrestlers, but he had a great look — a telegenic look, in my opinion — and at 250 pounds, he would undoubtedly become more prominent and better built than most of them.

There was only one problem: his hair. He was completely bald when he took off his baseball cap that day we met. He had shaved his head while playing college football. He looked like the original bald Gold's Gym man, the one holding the bent barbell. I asked him to grow hair to be more marketable for wrestling.

In one of John's first letters after returning to Massachusetts to finish college, he wrote:

"I really look forward to working with you, no matter what the subject. It appears that you are very knowledgeable about the sport of bodybuilding and professional wrestling. I, therefore, have taken your recommendation to grow out my hair. Having shaved my head for the past six years, it will be a change, but I just want you to know that I trust you and your judgment."

People would give me a hard time about my focus on hair, but I was looking at the "total package."

After graduating, John returned to stay with me until he got on his feet. During this time, he experimented with different hairstyles, eventually ending up with a four-inch-wide blond mohawk, which was a huge hit when he worked the supplement booth in the lobby of

Gold's Gym Venice. John even showed his acting chops when he appeared in one of the first Gold's Gym commercials for television called "The Poser," in which he slips and falls coming out of the posing room. It was produced by Jack Fund, another brilliant former member of the Chiat/Day team.

Before that, John was a warehouse manager for Mass Movement, specializing in moving gym equipment. They had two mantras: "A dolly and a dream!" and "Making the world a better place to lift." It was started by another houseguest, Brad Baker from Canada.

Like his moving job, getting into wrestling back then was hard work; a wrestling prospect had to go to a local wrestling school and hope to get discovered by a scout from one of the big leagues. Fortunately, Rick Bassman had a great wrestling school in the area, and John could become part of that. Rick didn't charge John for the training because of my track record with other wrestling prospects like Sting and The Ultimate Warrior.

Within eighteen months of his arrival in LA, John had a contract with the Ohio Valley Wrestling league and moved to Louisville, Kentucky, where he was paid to train for a slot with the WWE.

Benjamin Franklin famously said, "Guests, like fish, begin to smell after three days." But five months seemed to be the right amount of time for many of my guests.

John remembers eight or nine other people staying at my home during that period. What's particularly amazing is after he made it to TV a couple of years later to wrestle, two of those people called me to ask if that was him on TV. My first reaction was to ask, "Who do you think it is?" He had transformed himself so successfully into such a larger-than-life character that they didn't recognize him or at least weren't sure it was him. That's how much of a mission he had been on, which is what he told Elizabeth, his high school sweetheart, when she came to Venice to stay with him in my "overflow house," the duplex I co-owned with Flex Wheeler. She didn't like Venice and returned home to Massachusetts. I told John that they would likely get married ten years later if it were meant to be. They married twelve years later, but the marriage lasted less than two years.

At the wedding of John's brother, Matt, I finally had a chance to meet John's parents. They were rather sheepish about meeting me, saying that when John left for California, they were getting a divorce, so his pursuit of a dream was not on their minds — neither was questioning who this older gentleman was with whom their son would be staying.

It was much more difficult getting into wrestling when John did it twenty years ago. I've encouraged the wrestling careers of nearly two dozen athletes, and it's much easier now as the WWE has a training center in Orlando where a candidate can audition for three days and learn immediately whether or not they have the possibility of a career with them. But even then, some of the talent I've sent them — individuals who passed the test — have turned down their offers, such as Calum von Moger and Sergi Constance.

Unfortunately, the WWE as a career path is not as highly regarded overseas as in the US. It's a little like winning the lottery. Both Sergi and Calum had a great look, and they blossomed while in the US but not in pro wrestling. I can't help but wonder what their careers would have been like had they gone the wrestling route, but of course, once chosen, you need to do "the work," as it's called in the wrestling world.

The most amusing response I've received to date was from the mother of a German bodybuilder I met at FIBO. After approaching her son and giving him my contact information, this is a portion of the message she sent me on Facebook in response — in somewhat broken English:

"Many people would be glad if they get such an offer, like your offer to Werner. But he is a person, who needs the security, that the financial things and all the other things around are ok.

He has been based here in Germany a professional future at work. Last year he got his master of chimney sweep as one of the youngest ever.

In Germany it is a good payed, difficulty and approved job.

Perhaps he can find a good sponsor and perhaps he can get his own gym in future, we will see what happens.

I haven't spoken English for a long time and I hope that you could understand me, nevertheless."

Her son was a professional chimney sweep. I didn't have the

heart to answer but would have loved to know how a big bodybuilder like her son could get down a chimney.

The American dream may not be what it was, but there is still a difference in how Americans dare to dream, whether in pro bodybuilding or pro wrestling. I've learned there's a vast cultural difference between America and the rest of the world.

John and his brothers wrestled at home when he was younger while watching people like The Ultimate Warrior on TV. Seeing pictures in magazines of two other former houseguests, Jay Cutler and Lee Priest, further increased his interest in bodybuilding. The media's role in inspiring and motivating generations of young bodybuilders in the US cannot be overstated.

CANADIAN BODYBUILDERS

I opened my home to seven amateur Canadian bodybuilders who became pros: Dave Fisher, Bruce Patterson, Scott Milne, Frank McGrath, Antoine Vaillant, Ben Pakulski, and Paulo Almeida. This seems even more remarkable than my luck with American bodybuilders because the odds were greater. The Canadian Bodybuilding Federation only gave out one pro card a year, although a Canadian could get one at the North Americans, which was open to citizens of the US, Mexico, and Canada.

Each one's path — each one's "arc," as the Hollywood screenwriters would say — provides a good lesson as to why I believe there is only so much one can do. I could open a door, but the individual must walk through it and make the journey independently. It's also the reason I don't blame myself if someone's career doesn't work out the way I hoped or would have liked it to have gone.

Dave Fisher

My first Canadian houseguest who turned pro was Dave Fisher, who I met in the Gold's Gym Venice parking lot in 1988. Like so many people I approached, there was the telltale sign that he was living in his vehicle: a pile of empty tuna fish cans outside his car door.

It wasn't Dave's first time at the Mecca. He had initially traveled from Calgary to Venice in 1983 at age eighteen, basically using "going to the Mecca of bodybuilding" as his excuse to leave home. This, too, I had heard before. After Dave returned to Canada that second time, I brought him down to LA a third time to work in one of the Gold's Gyms I was involved with in San Bernardino, where he worked with Dave Dearth and Dave's brother, Doug.

He is now a gym owner himself, having owned a gym in the Torrance area of LA for the past ten years.

Bruce Patterson

Bruce Patterson, who came after Dave, was probably the most homophobic of all my houseguests. When there were hard-wired telephones, my Venice house phone would get anonymous calls to pay the person who answered money to perform some gay fetish for the person on the other end of the line — Gay4Pay, it's called. Bruce would take the caller on, meet them, and beat them up if given a chance. Yet he did a couple of gay videos when he left my home and ruined any pro bodybuilding career he might have had.

When someone called me to tell me what Bruce had done, I didn't believe it. When I was sent the tape and viewed it, I was shocked because Bruce looked comfortable performing on camera.

When I asked Bruce why he did it, he said it was good money and thought no one would see it, to which I said, "Bruce, it's a video!"

And indeed, stills from those videos can be easily found on the internet. He did all this for $3,500.

Gay4Pay doesn't pay in the long term. During the HIV/AIDS period, it could have also been deadly.

Like everything else, the internet has changed how we interact. Things have come a long way from the "Santa Monica Muscle Service" days when it was next door to Gold's Gym Santa Monica and the Pussycat Theater. Now it has evolved to where it's virtual. Subscribers pay a fee, typically $5 to $20 a month, to view a feed of images on the OnlyFans site, ones that are too racy for Instagram. While an income of $5,000-$10,000 a month is more typical, some models and social media influencers earn $100,000 a month without meeting their clients in person. It seems anyone with a smartphone can become a pornographer.

Scott Milne

While Scott Milne was staying at my home to learn whatever he could to turn pro, he was discovered for the TV game show *Battle Dome*. He played the superhero character called Moose. Not the most exciting name for a superhero, but at six feet, three inches and close to three hundred pounds, Scott was cartoonish.

When Scott went back to Canada and won his pro card, he was later involved in a near-fatal car accident when his vehicle got stuck at a railroad crossing. He ended up with two crushed vertebrae, punctured kidneys, and a damaged spleen.

After being bed-ridden for two months, he was still 305 pounds. His doctors told him that he would have died if he hadn't been so big and in shape. This, too, was something I heard too many times. My former houseguests' most significant cause of death, or a life-changing accident, remains traffic accidents.

Scott died in 2020 at age forty-five. I can't help but think the toll the accident took on his body eventually caused such an untimely death. Ironically, it was because Scott couldn't stand the traffic in LA that he returned to Canada in the first place. This, too, I heard often.

Frank McGrath

Next came Frank McGrath from St. John's, Newfoundland, the farthest east you can go in North America, which I was surprised to learn is a four-and-a-half-hour time difference from LA.

To his credit, having blown his career, Bruce reached out to ask me to help Frank, who was on the verge of quitting competing, having not done well in the 2000 Canadians. Initially, the trip west was a tough sell for Frank and his family.

I invited Kristian, Frank's training partner, to Venice first to break the ice. It didn't go well.

It was a busy Thanksgiving weekend when he arrived, and I left him at the house with two other individuals already there, one of them fellow Canadian Scott Milne. The other visitor was Eric Poehler, a former training partner of Mike Francois. I thought they would entertain one another while I spent time with my family for the holiday. However, when I returned to LA, Kristian had left — fled, really — even involving the Canadian consulate in LA to get a plane ticket home.

One of the proven ills of smoking marijuana is increased paranoia. I later learned that Kristian had severe withdrawal problems from not having access to pot. He thought that drugs would be free-flowing on Venice Beach. When that wasn't the case, he went into severe panic mode, even complaining to the consulate that the place he was staying at had "locks on the doors." He had come from a small town where no one ever locked their homes. Venice was a strange place to him. It was also his first time going anywhere, his first time on a plane.

Kristian also had a disappointing first day in the gym as he later recalled in an email to me apologizing for his behavior:

"The one thing I had hoped to do was meet up with Lou Ferrigno, again and reacquaint myself with him, and simply tell him that I had made it, and to thank him for his encouragement, but when I approached him, he gave me a 'dirty' look and brushed me off. It seems my heroes aren't heroes at all, and I was very disappointed at that moment."

Unfortunately, that was the reaction most of my houseguests had upon meeting Lou "The Hulk" Ferrigno. The Hulk had been their motivation and superhero growing up.

Finally, I had to fly to St. John's to meet Frank's parents and convince them to let their son come to LA. It was 2002, and while I was on the board of Gold's Gym International, I was no longer an employee, so I had the time to travel.

Frank's mother, Gladys, said, "You know there are a lot of strange people in LA."

I told her, "Do you think there's anyone there who could make Frank do anything he didn't want to do?"

I was referring to Frank's forearms, which, at eighteen and a half inches, would have stopped anyone. Eventually, she and Frank's father acquiesced, and Frank followed me back to LA. In less than two years, he was Mr. Canada and a pro.

I was there in 2003. I think he would have won in 2002 if it hadn't been for a blood infection that nearly killed him, all because he wore old sneakers without socks while having a cut on his toe — Frank's own "Achilles' heel" moment.

Frank is another Canadian, like Sam Smith or Scott Milne, whose career was severely impacted by a vehicle-related accident. Besides totaling my Jaguar in a non-life-threatening accident on the streets of Venice — no small feat given the thirty-five mile-per-hour top speed limit — he also had a major, life-threatening wreck when he returned to Canada. Again, the doctors said the same thing: He would have died if he hadn't been in such great shape — and big.

Frank has had a magical career in terms of sponsorship, first by Universal Supplement's "Animal" line, where he became the character "Wrath."

Besides Frank, I sent many athletes to Universal: Antoine Vaillant, Evan Centopani, Brad Rowe, Roman Fritz, David Hoffman, and Derek Lunsford. In general, the supplement companies were great at concocting formulas but didn't handle who was hot and who was not in the bodybuilding world. I was happy to help.

Antoine Vaillant, Ben Pakulski, and Paulo Almeida

Antoine Vaillant, a French-Canadian bodybuilder, followed Frank and became a pro in 2012. Unlike Frank, he had no real father and was abused as a kid. A three-year bout with recreational drugs interrupted Antoine's career, but he managed to come out of that dark hole and place sixth in the 2020 Mr. Olympia in Orlando. When I asked him how he did it, he said he looked around at the people he was with at that low point in his life and realized he was different; he didn't belong there. He had a God-given talent and owed it to his Creator to do something with it.

I told many of the people I met, "You have a gift from God; use it!"

Ben Pakulski and Paulo Almeida followed. Ben didn't have much of a pro career but has used his pro status to transition into a terrific gym in Tampa, Florida, and create his own supplement line.

I introduced Paulo to Rich Piana. Thanks to Rich, Paulo at least had some exposure for a few years while Rich was alive.

Paulo had one of the best physiques — indeed, the best pair of biceps — I had ever seen. He is an excellent example of one of the guys I would sometimes see at bodybuilding events who didn't place high — or even was someone in the audience — who caught my eye instead of the winner onstage.

Such was the case in 2012 when I went to western Canada to see Antoine compete in the Mr. Canada contest. It was an incredible super heavyweight lineup, and Antoine was fortunate to win.

Who caught my eye was the competitor in eighth place: Paulo Almeida. I tried to find him after the show but to no avail. Like so many guys who are disappointed after a contest, he got out quickly to go home.

After that, I would go to one of the social media sites and type Paulo's name every so often. I did this for almost two years before Paulo's page came up. He had been on Facebook for about two weeks at that point. Social media was finally paying off.

Jeramy Freeman

My houseguests were utterly taken in by the superhero images they saw on TV and in movies and comic books. From the early *Hercules* movies with Steve Reeves to Superman to the Hulk to Mattel's Masters of the Universe to the superheroes from Marvel and people like The Punisher Jack Castle, they all played a part. And over the years, these superheroes kept getting more and more jacked. They went from big to freakish to cartoonish.

Pro bodybuilder Jeramy Freeman, one of my last houseguests in Venice, was even used as the model for Pixar's Mr. Incredible of *The Incredibles*. There were plenty of images to choose from, as photos of Jeramy were on magazine covers and in numerous articles in fitness magazines.

Jeramy and his wife, Kim, now have their own incredible family of three daughters, one even named Vera. Another bodybuilder with girls.

After operating a fitness facility in New York concentrating on a forty-two-day body transformation, he is now focusing on his supplement line. He is one of twenty-two former houseguests to start a supplement company, Freeman Formula. In their best years, they collectively did over $1 billion in sales, something I am very much impressed with, as Gold's Gym corporate's attempts at supplements never really reached any significant level. (Although, to our credit, we were often ahead of the curve. Pete was undoubtedly way ahead of his time with his protein powders in the late '70s.)

People who thought they knew the kind of people I typically would hire would ask, "Are you going to hire another one of those dumb bodybuilders again?" I wanted to find similar people; people who wanted to help others reach their goals. There were good and bad bodybuilders, just like there were good and bad of anything. The trick was to find the good ones.

Some of my houseguests would not be well-known at all but would become successful in their own way, mainly by becoming equity partners in Gold's Gyms in which I was involved, such as Jerry McCall with six Gold's Gyms in the Bay Area, Joel Potter with six Gold's Gyms in the Midwest, Jack and Leslie Wadsworth in Seattle with three, Tony Calhoun in Santa Barbara with three, Scott Kubitz with two clubs in El Paso, Rick Stephenson in San Diego, Gene LaMott and Steve Rance in Portland, and Jeff and Michele Fee in Long Beach.

My house, or houses — during my thirty-seven years living in California, mainly in Venice or Rancho Mirage — created a safe haven for my guests. In their hometowns, they might have been freaks, outcasts, but in Venice, they were with like-minded people who shared similar dreams.

Given that LA is the second-largest city in America, it probably comes as a surprise to many that it was a very welcoming place back then. People would, and still do, go there from all over the world with a dream. Some make it, some don't. But there was a lot of encouragement and support. If someone "makes it," then there is hope for all.

I saw this even when I went there as an architect in 1975. I was thirty years old when I designed the Beverly Hills Neiman Marcus, very young for a senior designer. That wouldn't happen in any other city in America, even in my hometown of Omaha. That job brought me to LA. By the time I was designing my third Neiman Marcus store, this one in Las Vegas, I was an owner of Gold's Gym and in the clothing business myself. Luck and persistence in equal measure. Fortunate to get the opportunity but then diligent enough to perform.

Perhaps one of my houseguests explained this phenomenon best when he saw my Mercedes convertible, the one I had taken over the lease for from Jim Hellwig, The Ultimate Warrior. I never bothered to put the hardtop on and garage the vehicle when it rained, so it was always open to the sky, even when I parked it on the street. My houseguest said, "If a person in my hometown saw that car parked on the street, they might throw trash in it or maybe even pee in it. Here, people look at a car like that and say, 'That's nice. I'm going to have a car like that one day and respect it.'"

Many people in La La Land dared to dream. They did not want to live their parents' lives.

And, indeed, the range of cars in the Gold's Gym Venice parking lots was breathtaking, everything from beaters to Lamborghinis and McLarens. When gym owners would ask me what the typical member was like, I would go with them to the parking lot, wave my hand at the cars, and say, "You tell me."

Sylvester Stallone made the grandest entrance of them all, usually in a stretch limousine along with a couple of bodyguards. I got served with a restraining order preventing Stallone from working out at Gold's Gym Venice after he was divorced from his wife, Brigitte Nielsen, who got "the gym" in the settlement. That's how vital Gold's Gym was in their lives.

Stallone ended up hiring one of the Venice trainers to set up a gym in his home, but it wasn't the same. Celebrities like Michael Landon from the *Little House on the Prairie* TV show, who had a gym in his home consisting of ten thousand square feet, told me home gyms didn't work; there was no energy.

GOLD'S GYM VENICE: A REVELATION

The biggest surprise for the houseguests pursuing competitive bodybuilding was that the big-name bodybuilders they saw working out in Gold's Gym Venice often weren't much bigger than they were. The two most common things I heard referring to the pros in the gym were, "They're not as big as I thought they would be," and, "They don't train any harder than I do." Almost all were seeing them for the first time in person.

The magazines had a way of presenting the "champions," as Joe Weider would call them, as larger-than-life characters. A bodybuilder who graces the cover of *Muscle & Fitness* is virtually assured of stardom. "You go in one end a muscle guy," said one bodybuilder, and "you come out the other end a mythological figure."

But by the end of their workout, everyone in the gym had shrunk in their eyes to the size of a mere mortal. Seeing them in person made them human. The people they saw were also often shorter than they had imagined, which also helped destroy the illusion.

The internet and social media have made most of the "stars" all too human by overexposing them with selfies and podcasts. No matter how many "likes" someone gets, nothing quite beats the power of a magazine cover.

Most of my houseguests were Catholic — at least baptized Catholic, not necessarily "practicing" Catholic. As an incentive to go to church, I would tell them that they could meet Arnold if they came with me to 9:30 a.m. Mass on Sunday at St. Monica's. Most took me up on my offer. After Mass, Arnold would stand on the steps outside the front of the church patiently greeting people, signing autographs, and taking photos with his fans. This was no easy task when he was governor as the security team was omnipresent, but Arnold did it anyway.

His wife, Maria, and the kids would stand off to one side, and I could see that they — or at least Maria — didn't understand his world as I did. What was beautiful about Arnold during those brief encounters was that he was always so complimentary, so supportive to my houseguests, saying things like, "You look FAN-TAS-TIC!" or, "You look unbelievable!" I was always encouraging, but it went a lot further when it came from Arnold.

After we would leave the church, I would take the guys to brunch somewhere in Santa Monica. That was the program every Sunday when I wasn't traveling: Mass followed by brunch. It was a good routine. So good that Sunday became a "cheat day," what is now termed "refeed" on social media. I encouraged the guys to go off their diet at least one day a week to stay sane and eat whatever they wanted, and that day was usually Sunday. An American brunch was a special treat, especially for foreigners. Then I would also suggest fasting on Monday. Intermittent fasting during the week now seems to be a popular way of dieting.

Most of my houseguests were in their twenties; a few were as young as nineteen. While thirty isn't old, it can be for bodybuilding, pro wrestling, or a modeling/acting career. The notion today seems to be that you have to be in your thirties to have a professional bodybuilding career, that it takes time, and you have to "pay your dues." From what I have seen, your thirties are a difficult time to go after a pro career, given the likelihood of injuries.

Paulo Almeida from Vancouver, Canada, is one of the few bodybuilders over thirty I encouraged, but he was over thirty when he started to pursue a pro card seriously.

When I had lunch with Kevin Levrone, one of the all-time great bodybuilders, and he announced that he was quitting bodybuilding and pursuing acting full time and wanted my help, I said, "Kevin, you're thirty-five. You're too old for Hollywood."

But Kevin didn't listen. In my opinion, Kevin should never have left his bodybuilding career as early as he did. It was unfortunate to see him try to do that much later at fifty-one. The results were not good. But it's wonderful seeing him being successful with his own supplement line given the wisdom that comes with age.

Back in 2017, when I spent thirteen months working in the former Gold's Gym in Battle Creek, Michigan, and going to events and contests with some employees and members, I saw millennials in full display, with everyone getting a trophy — or two or three.

I appreciate that contestants have goals and that what they are doing is certainly positive, but I also saw that for some it became obsessive to the point of being sad and destructive to their family life. The sport is wonderful but can be taken too far when the contestants expect to be the center of the universe at the expense of those who support them.

With the growing number of categories and pro cards given out (sold), contests nowadays have become money machines — $300 entry fees and $250 pro cards — with no heart.

I look at a lot of the competitors as victims of greed. As you can tell, I am an advocate of bodybuilding for everybody; I just hope the sport doesn't continue to exploit the contestant and gets back to the purity of the contest.

EVAN MARRIOTT: JOE MILLIONAIRE

Frank McGrath, one of the amateur Canadian bodybuilders who got a pro card, and Evan Marriott, who became Joe Millionaire, the first reality TV star, were the two houseguests who stayed the longest — almost two years total. However, Frank was at four different homes during those two years.

I typically approached every tall bodybuilder I saw in the gym about trying out for the WWE. There weren't many — maybe one or two a year.

When I first went up to Evan, he blew me off. Perhaps after seeing John Cena's early success, and while on the verge of being homeless, he contacted me to see if the offer of a place to stay was still open. It was.

While living at my home and going to wrestling school, I encouraged Evan to go on any "cattle calls" for acting or commercial work while he was there. One of those auditions was for *Joe Millionaire,* a new reality TV show and a novel concept at the time. The premise is that the women dating Joe thought they were going out with a man who was a millionaire but he was actually a broke construction worker.

Evan was a good-looking six feet, five inches and had a natural ability to act. He beat out nearly two thousand finalists. I thought a lot of that was the pitch I gave the producers. I told them most American viewers can't relate to some Harvard MBA candidate, and that Evan was more blue-collar, even wanting to be a pro wrestler, so he was the man to pick.

Forty-three million viewers saw the final episode. I watched the last episode on TV with him in the bedroom where he had spent most of those two years. He was even wearing the same outfit he had on in the show. It was a surreal moment.

Had Evan been willing to go to acting school, there's a good chance he would have starred in the next *Superman* movie and had a film career. As it was, his fifteen minutes of fame lasted about a year — but he did make $1 million.

There were several bodybuilders like Evan for whom I would say, "Your face and physique are your fortune — and future!" I don't know where that came from, but I looked at what they had as a God-given talent and something they should take advantage of and use.

It was easier for me to find potential pro bodybuilders, even pro wrestlers, than people in this "male fitness model" category. There are many beautiful women but not as many men whom the public could agree on who had "a look." But the men, like Evan, and unlike the women, would fight that beauty. Most were uncomfortable with it.

When I bought a second home in the desert area east of LA in 2001 to be near my parents, I decided to use my architectural skills and flip houses. I often had three places at a time — nine bedrooms, according to my way of thinking. During this period, Evan lived full-time in my home in Venice.

I wasn't sure where the world of bodybuilding was going but came across several people who I thought could have a career as a fitness model, which might lead to an acting career, where I thought Evan was going. Enough people were coming through my homes during that time that when one of them showed up at the local Gold's Gym in Palm Desert, the woman behind the desk said, "Oh, you must be from the model house." She wasn't referring to the typical "model house" in some new housing development. She was referring to the similar look they all had. It became a running joke. It did look like I was cloning people.

One of the first was Joey Gloor, a teenager when I first met him while inspecting a Gold's Gym in Illinois. Joey got some photoshoots that ended up inside or on the covers of a few fitness magazines. He went on to several TV shows, usually starring as a personal trainer, such as on MTV's *I Used to Be Fat*.

Klaus Riis from Denmark, David Rylah from Australia, and Mario Klintworth from Germany were my foreign houseguests during that time. All got photographed by the fitness magazines.

I had seen Mario working a booth when he was at the FIBO trade show in Germany. No one seemed to notice Mario in his home country — even the supplement company he worked for. But in America, he landed some magazine covers, being featured twice on the cover of *Muscle & Fitness* in the space of a few months, just like Gunter Schlierkamp had done — a rare feat.

THE ROLE OF FATE

The role of Fate — with a capital "F" — in my life is something I think about a lot. It also enters my mind regarding my relationships with others, especially with my houseguests or potential houseguests. Or maybe it can be called luck.

During the twenty-five years that I had such incredible luck picking the "winners," there was an equal number of individuals who I thought had just as much potential for getting a pro card but for whatever reason, perhaps due to luck, didn't achieve that goal. Erik Fromm's pursuit of his dream is one of the most heartbreaking.

In a letter from September 20, 1998, he wrote:

"Dear Ed,

I'm writing to let you know how much I appreciate everything you've done for me. After winning the Iron Man, I felt kind of lost. Then you wrote me the most motivating letter I've ever received. It made me decide to pursue my dreams. Now I find myself in grasping distance of one of my biggest goals. Thanks to you so many great opportunities have arrived. Even though I didn't make it all happen this year, I now know it is achievable. I truly feel in my heart I will be a pro. I will never train for second place. Ed, you're the man!

Your friend, Erik G. Fromm."

Then in an email nine years later, on April 10, 2007, Erik wrote:

"Ed, I sincerely apologize for letting you down and not being honest. You have inspired me to fulfill my potential from the moment we met. I just found myself lost after my divorce, and let my self-esteem slip completely away. I allowed myself to be surrounded by the wrong kind of people and took a path of isolation and self-destruction."

Erik died ten months later on February 28, 2008, at age thirty-six, from a fentanyl overdose. Apparently, it was being sold on the street as heroin in the area where he lived. He lived with Benjamin Loehrer, another former houseguest, in Minneapolis, coincidentally the same city where the singer Prince died under similar circumstances.

Benjamin had been a young bodybuilder with a dream like Erik's. Seeing Erik's struggle and the tragic end, he decided to change direction. He is now happily married with five kids and four gyms in Minneapolis.

PART III

THE EVOLUTION OF GOLD'S GYM

Board room meeting in Boca Raton, Florida, discussing the sale of Gold's Gym, 1999

THE ORGANIZATION AND DEVELOPMENT OF GOLD'S GYM

After World War II, the military profoundly influenced the operation of American business. It was the only organization most of the servicemen had ever known, and it shaped how they ran the companies they created after the war. Few had gone or would ever go to business school and earn a degree.

I had the Army in my past, which undoubtedly shaped how I thought a company might be run.

Pete, Tim, and I would set up departments for everything, even making them separate corporations. It made for a lot more accounting work but established legal separation that was deemed necessary in the litigious environment of American business. It worked. For example, the Venice gym was incorporated as the Bodybuilding Hall of Fame, Inc. (BBHF); merchandising was under Gold's Gym Merchandising, Inc. (GGM); and franchising was Gold's Gym Franchising, Inc. (GGF). GCK was for our book royalties. The parent company was Gold's Gym Enterprises, Inc. (GGE).

The company sounded big, but in reality, it was the mouse that roared. Our corporate staff never exceeded thirty people during our twenty years of being caretakers and developers of the brand.

When a female employee threatened to sue over sex and age discrimination, I pointed out that more than half of our employees were women, and a half-dozen were over fifty-five but didn't look it. Over half of the gym staff was composed of minorities, for which we received tax credits from the state.

I also had the experience of my architectural practice and saw how the profession was practiced by a half-dozen different architectural firms during the fourteen years I worked as an architect. One of them, Gensler Architects, was relatively new and small but would become the largest architectural firm in the world with revenue over $1.5 billion in 2019, more than double the next largest firm.

Art Gensler, who died in 2021 at age eighty-five, was widely credited with creating the blueprint for how many professional services firms organize and manage themselves today. He had a client-first approach and was not a starchitect.

As with my partners in the gyms or the people hired for corporate, I was not afraid to go after people who were more intelligent, more talented, or worked harder than I did. Pete, Tim, and I tried to hire good people, leave them alone, and let them contribute their talents. As General George Patton once said, "Never tell people how to do things. Tell them what to do and they will surprise you with their ingenuity."

Ironically, I left Gensler because I was not happy working with one of their clients: Carter Hawley Hale, the owner of Neiman Marcus at the time. I had initially designed the Beverly Hills store when Stanley and Richard Marcus were still involved. I succeeded with that box, a little less with the Neiman Marcus in Las Vegas that followed, and less still with the one in Orange County. The WASP accountants had taken over from the Jewish merchants.

Carter Hawley Hale was focused on the numbers and not the brand. They kept cutting budgets, saying they didn't have the money, even though I knew what margins were in the clothing business because I was in it myself with Gold's Gym. It was like printing money. The Venice gym pro shop consisting of eleven hundred square feet had revenue of $145 per square foot some months, especially during the summer, when busloads of Japanese tourists visited the gym.

After several leveraged buyouts, Neiman Marcus went into bankruptcy in 2020, with $5 billion in debt.

GROWING UP CATHOLIC

No doubt, the US Army influenced my thinking regarding the organization of the business. And being an architect taught me to put myself in the position of my client and address their needs and interests — the salesman's most important asset. But it was my experience growing up Catholic that had a profound effect on the look and feel of the gyms and my interest in helping others.

Both Pete and Tim went to Catholic grade school in Rochester, New York. I also went to a Catholic grade school, but then I went on to Creighton Preparatory School, a Jesuit high school in Omaha.

Perhaps the Catholic Church became a significant force in my life because it made such a positive impression on me when I was young.

One evening, when my parents and I were sharing a bottle of red wine at dinner, my eighty-six-year-old mother raised her glass and asked, "Did those priests ever abuse you?"

I do not know how long that question had taken for her to voice, but I was so shocked that I dropped my glass. I assured her that nothing terrible had happened and that if it had, I would have been strong enough to say and do something.

I had several classmates who had become priests, and as with the priests and nuns I knew growing up and would later meet in the gyms after inviting them in, I was impressed with their self-sacrifice and dedication.

Coincidentally, most business scholars believe that the roots of franchising can be traced to the Catholic Church in the Middle Ages, when tax collectors were allowed to keep a portion of revenues received from citizens. But my inspiration from being Catholic had to do with what I saw at individual parishes.

As many people did, no matter their religious affiliation, I would "shop" churches on the weekend. I would ask myself, "Why does a person choose one church over another, especially if they're all Catholic?" The answer was the quality of the experience, the quality of service, the built environment. That's what I would try to design and create in the gyms. As a result, I have visited many churches where I've lived and traveled.

Once I left working as an architect, the most extensive trip of the week might be a nine-mile drive from Venice into Beverly Hills to the Church of the Good Shepherd, the first church I attended when I moved to LA. I liked going to Mass there. It was a beautiful Spanish-style church from the 1930s right on Santa Monica Boulevard in the center of Beverly Hills. It was located next to a city park — a cactus garden — where I often went to eat lunch while working at an architecture firm located a few blocks away.

The message of the church made an impression, but perhaps because I am an architect, the physical components influenced me even more. How many times had I been at Mass when I couldn't hear the sermon because of the poor quality of the sound system?

Priests would tell me that the first thing they would do when coming into a new parish was to make sure they could be heard. Before the advent of Walkmans, iPods, Pandora, and Spotify, music in the gyms was crucial. The Church of the Good Shepherd had a great sound system providing beautiful music and even better sermons, most of the time given by Father O'Ryan or Father O'Brien, Irish-American priests right out of central casting. It might as well have been *The Bells of St. Mary's*, it was so magical.

It was even more magical because of all the Hollywood actors I would see there. One of the few TV shows I was allowed to watch growing up was *The Jackie Gleason Show* with my father. Another was *The Loretta Young Show* with my mother.

Mom wouldn't watch Jackie Gleason because of the Crazy Guggenheim character, who she found offensive. She said he made fun of disabled people. She was way ahead of her time.

Imagine my first Sunday in LA when I looked up from my pew and saw a woman who looked like an older Loretta Young. It was in fact Loretta Young, the person whose shows every week from 1953 to 1961 had made such an impression on me. They were mini morality plays highlighting the "golden rule" of Leviticus 19:18 that Jesus Christ quoted during his Sermon on the Mount: Love your neighbor as yourself.

Like Gold's Gym Venice, even the churches in LA had stars that added to their aura. I would invite many of the actors I met at church to train at Gold's Gym — after Mass, of course.

No one bothered the movie stars while inside that church in Beverly Hills. They were there to pray. I think that's what the celebrities liked about Gold's Gym Venice. They were there to work out, and everyone respected that. They were just one of the gang.

I remember helping actress Geena Davis. She was having trouble with the weight she was using, so I gave her a hand. I didn't say anything.

The next time I saw her, I was next to her on a treadmill, so I felt like I could talk. I said, "How are you doing, Ms. Davis? I'm one of the owners. Anything I could do to help, just let me know." She remembered me from the previous day and asked if I had recognized her. I said, sure. She seemed mortified and said she looked terrible that day. I reassured her she looked fantastic and told her how much I enjoyed *Thelma & Louise*.

While movie stars don't like to be bothered, I think they do want to be recognized. At the time, Jeff Goldblum, her husband, was also a member, along with Gregory Hines. They were two of my favorite celebrity members to run into at The Firehouse Restaurant when they weren't in the gym.

How I miss seeing Mr. Hines and having him be part of the gym community. He was the only celebrity member I can remember who insisted on paying for his membership after his first-year comp membership was up.

"I grew up poor. Now that I have money, I want to pay for the privilege of training here," he said.

MUSIC IN THE GYM

The importance of music in the gym came up one day at the restaurant Arnold owned next to his office in Santa Monica called Schatzi's, German for "honey."

Arnold owned the entire block. During the 1991-1992 period, he had taken over World Gym because of Joe Gold's health. Tim and I often had business lunches with staff and consultants there. Typical Arnold, he was a master at what is referred to in the restaurant trade as "touching the table," a personal visit to make sure the customers were happy. He made sure to let us know that he appreciated our business.

Arnold was loyal to Joe Gold because of their shared history when he first arrived in America, but there was little rivalry between us and either Arnold or Joe, or Mike Uretz, who ran the World Gym franchising program.

Arnold asked me why Gold's Gym was so busy and World Gym was not. I said it was the sound system. Arnold thought I was making a joke and laughed – but it was true. Joe Gold was still managing the club, so there was no music in the gym. It was as quiet as a church, which wasn't what most people wanted in a gym. You could hear a weight drop.

Pete Grymkowski even believed that loud music allowed the energy between individuals working out to be more easily transferred and shared. He may have been right. Gold's Gym Venice was always packed, and the energy seemed to be contagious.

When I would take over a gym, the first thing I would do was spend thousands – usually around $25,000 – on a great sound system to help give the gym energy. At certain times of the day, it could be more like going into a nightclub than a gym.

Because I had lived and worked in New York City, Studio 54, which was closed by then, was still an unforgettable memory. Just try to imagine Studio 54 in the mid-'70s without the music. I had also listened to organs in the great European cathedrals such as Chartres and Cologne. The music seemed to add yet another dimension to the physical grandeur.

The issue then became what to play on that great sound

system. In the early days, the most common topic of phone conversations with my managing partners of the gyms I was involved with was regarding complaints about the music. The best solution seemed to be having different types of music during the day. Typical operating hours were 5 a.m. to 11 p.m. during the week. The day could begin with mellow, easy listening music in the morning and end with heavy metal at night.

While the technology of listening to music has evolved to the point where almost everyone is tuned in to their devices, I think it has had a significant adverse effect on the gym experience as members are now engulfed in their own world and not part of a shared experience.

My inspiration for the Gold's Gym model seemed to be on the mind of at least one of the priests to whom I had given a comp membership.

I was at St. Monica's Catholic Church on Sunday morning along with a thousand other parishioners when the priest, Father Glassman, was giving the sermon. Father Glassman, who had no idea I was there, talked about how just as Gold's Gym has photos of the Olympians on its walls for inspiration (the current and former Mr. Olympia's), so, too, the Church had its stained-glass windows with pictures of the saints to inspire and motivate. (The gym walls were covered with photos and memorabilia, many of them autographed, of individuals who had come to Mecca and wanted to be remembered and leave something behind, perhaps to inspire others, something people seemed to love.)

St. Monica's was one of my favorite churches for Sunday Mass. As befits a model for the gyms, it had a great sound system and quality of service I could find almost nowhere else. Their congregation was composed of ten thousand families; ours had twelve thousand members.

THE WOW FACTOR

Other gyms began to come to the area to compete with Gold's Gym. Powerhouse Gym and World Gym were two well-known gym chains at the time that followed us into franchising. Their problem in competing with Gold's Gym Venice was that their facilities weren't bigger, and they couldn't expand in place. Gold's Gym Venice could evolve and change.

It was like comparing a chapel with a cathedral. It had a specific something so that when you walked into the gym, you felt the energy, you felt like working out. Among architects, it was called the "wow factor."

Don Ross, a former pro Mr. America and the author of *Muscleblasting,* described walking into the Venice gym this way in an article for *EXCEL* magazine in November 1990:

"The first thing you notice is a large number of each piece of equipment. A long line of calf machines, for instance. Some standing, some seated, and some bent at the waist. Each with a different leverage factor and a unique feel on the muscle. To the right is a long line of leg curl machines: seated, lying, standing, pulley, cam-driven.

"'My gosh!' You exclaim. 'Our gym just has a standing and lying machine for leg curls. With this tremendous variety, you have to make new gains working out here!'

"You look around and see many people working out. No matter how big and strong you are, there's somebody bigger and stronger to inspire you. No matter how inexperienced, there's someone in worse shape but rapidly improving, so you never feel out of place. You see famous actors and athletes training alongside business people and housewives. You see current world champion bodybuilders and champions from years before. Teenagers train alongside fitness enthusiasts in their sixties and seventies. Everybody fits in!

"As you walk halfway across the floor, you look to your left and see … Another huge room full of weights and equipment, and beyond that, a third room! Each of these rooms is a complete gym in itself! It takes about a week to get used to training here. Every day is an adventure in trying new equipment.

"After two weeks you are hooked. You don't want to go back to your very adequate gym that now seems substandard by comparison.

"Along with the workout experience is a pro shop and supplement counter for your workout needs. The very best nutritional counseling. Nutritionalysis is also available with counselors who practice what they preach. Famous bodybuilders and fitness personalities are on hand for one-on-one personal training.

"A posing room is located in the second room complete with lighting, surrounding mirrors, and a tape player to work on your presentation, or to view your progress.

"Aerobic machines, life cycles, stair machines, treadmills, and computerized rowers line the back of the second room and two mezzanines above the first room. At the time of this writing, a fourth room is being prepared exclusively for Cardiovascular fitness.

"A fourth room will soon open at Gold's Gym Venice (article published in November 1990). It will be primarily for cardiovascular activity, with many more aerobics machines and exercise classes. Gold's will continue to present new products.

"'We will never stand still!' declares Kimber.

"This is the Gold's Gym Experience. As exhilarating to the fitness faithful as the Kaaba is to the Islamic Pilgrims in Arabia's Mecca."

FROM BLACK & CHROME TO COLOR

Color was part of what made Gold's Gym different.

When the fitness industry started, the equipment in the gym spas had a chrome finish. In the hardcore gyms, it was black. I had seen white equipment in my father's medical office — and in hospitals — and thought white looked friendlier, less intimidating.

I asked Dan Block at Flex Equipment and Howard Briles at Icarian Strength Equipment to paint their machines white for the new gyms I opened in the Bay Area. They did, and white became a standard color. Blue, green, red, and yellow followed. The equipment companies also liked painting the machines. It became a way of differentiating their lines as we typically had a half dozen different brands in the gym simultaneously.

Eventually, a natural look with a standard metallic gray finish became the norm, solving the problem of the brighter colors getting nicked and showing their age. But it was an improvement over black.

By 1990, the Venice gym had expanded into all four building bays, which added to the experience. What was amazing was that every time we opened a new space, it was immediately filled with people, as if it had always been there. Many people coming into the first room with the main entrance thought that the first bay of the four-bay structure was it. Then, as they moved through that first room, they saw the door to a second room, and then another and another, all filled with different equipment and all kinds of people. It could be like a three-ring circus with photographers shooting in three of the four main rooms simultaneously.

All that visual chaos and stimulation resulted in sensory overload and made the gym a fascinating place to be. It was entertaining. It made working out more enjoyable, and the gym drew an eclectic crowd.

In the end, that mix of people ended up entertaining one another. It was another era, pre-digital, pre-social media. There were no smartphones. You went to the gym to discover what was happening and be part of the action.

THE MECCA

Theoretically, just as you could pray anywhere, so, too, you could work out anywhere. You didn't necessarily need a church or a gym to do either. This theory was certainly tested during the COVID-19 pandemic.

But just as the Jews had their temple in Jerusalem with the "holy of holies," the Catholic churches had their tabernacles behind the altars, where the body of Christ was kept so people could pray in a sacred place in the presence of their Creator.

Gold's Gym Venice was that kind of place for the fitness world: a holy ground for many who would come there to train from all over the world. It was the Mecca. They saw the gym as a temple where they could progress both in body and soul.

Many of the visitors to Gold's Gym, and quite a few of my houseguests, could legitimize their leaving — really, running away from — home to family and friends by saying they were going off to the Mecca of bodybuilding, just like a budding actor or actress might say they were off to Hollywood to get discovered.

When Chris Mitchell's mother died, and his father proved unsuitable and abusive, he left home right after high school and headed for Venice. His brother Drew followed. Both were houseguests for a short time while they figured things out.

There are many stories like theirs. Bodybuilding had saved their lives by giving them direction and purpose — and a place to go after leaving home.

Both are now happily married, each with one child, each vowing to be the father they never had. Chris is a professional gambler in Las Vegas. Drew is selling insurance in Cleveland and doing online fitness coaching. And he did finally get that pro card in 2021.

The word "Mecca" came to be used for gyms everywhere as the ultimate accolade to give a fitness facility, like Bev Francis's "East Coast Mecca" Powerhouse Gym on Long Island, previously a Gold's Gym. In Toronto, Canada, there was Dorian and Noah Hamilton's Pure Muscle & Fitness, "the Mecca of the North." There were similarly named facilities in Europe, like The Mecca Gym in Jaen and Granada, both in Spain. And in South America, in the unlikeliest places, like Curitiba, Brazil, with Overall Gym, "the Brazilian Mecca of Bodybuilding." Fitness fanatics understood what that word meant.

Variations of the name and logo became synonymous the world over with serious fitness. There was even a *God's* Gym, with Christ replacing the Gold's Gym man, to which our trademark attorney responded, "Thou shall not steal!" It was blatant trademark infringement.

In Italy, there were more creative versions of the Gold's Gym name and logo in at least thirty-one locations. Two especially appealed to my architect sensibilities. In one, the Gold's Gym man was replaced with Michelangelo's statue of *David*. In another, he was Leonardo da Vinci's iconic *Vitruvian Man*.

Our trademark attorney said we could send cease and desist letters to those located north of Rome regarding their infringement, but he wouldn't recommend doing anything with those south of Rome. But like the sellers of fake Rolex watches on Venice Beach, I figured people knew the difference, and I was flattered by the imitation.

When Gold's Gym started franchising in the Middle East, particularly Saudi Arabia, I was concerned about sending printed material with the word "Mecca" and photos of scantily clad men and women. But it all passed through customs without comment. Even the Arabs seemed to know the difference between their Mecca and our Mecca. And Gold's Gym Franchising has many success stories in the Arab countries where bodybuilding is listed as one of the top three sports activities.

GOLD'S GYM MOTION PICTURE & ENTERTAINMENT DIVISION

Gold's Gym Venice was more than just a place to take pictures. It provided the talent that the magazines, television shows, movies, and commercial casting agencies were looking for.

I remember casting directors for the TV shows *American Gladiator* and *Battle Dome* telling me that in one day of open auditions at Gold's Gym, they found almost all the talent needed for their new shows, after hiring three different agencies who had provided no candidates. Some of them had been houseguests, such as Billy Smith, Steve Henneberry, and Scott Milne.

Tim said what was different about Gold's Gym Venice was that "we were family." Just as a well-run parish tries to form a community, Gold's Gym tried to help its members.

In 1985, we set up a separate division of the company, designated as the Gold's Gym Motion Picture & Entertainment Division, to facilitate this family spirit, with Derek Barton at its head. Its mission was to get work in the entertainment and advertising industries for Gold's Gym members. It was indeed a great name, and it did do much good.

Derek had experiences in the entertainment industry performing stunts and with professional voice acting, acting, and stand-up comedy. Tim met Derek through a softball league they were in due to Tim's early venture into acting. Tim had always wanted to be an actor, but while I thought his acting was terrific, his looks were considered average by the industry — at least according to his agent.

Derek became a vital part of the team, especially at the annual Gold's Gym conventions, where his skills as an MC made all the difference in the world. Derek later spearheaded groundbreaking advertising for the gyms with ad campaigns that had never been seen before in the fitness industry.

Agencies and photographers would contact Derek to satisfy their requirements, but some even called my home back when there were telephone landlines. I remember one of my startled houseguests,

Tom Varga, who answered the phone at my beach house when I wasn't there.

Tom had a conversation with Mike Niveaux of *Ironman* magazine that went something like this:

Mike: "Is Ed there?"

Tom: "No."

Mike: "Would you like to do a photoshoot for an equipment company? It would pay $1,000."

Tom: "Sure, but you don't even know me. You don't know who I am. You haven't seen me."

Mike: "You must be good. You're staying at Ed's house."

So, Tom ended up doing the shoot, looking great, and making some money. Mike was happy as well.

And Tom did go on to get a pro card, becoming one of the 102 pros who stayed at one of my homes.

David and Peter Paul, The Barbarian Brothers, are some of the early characters who would help create the "magic" of Gold's Gym and who, in turn, Gold's Gym helped with this entertainment agency and service. There would be many who followed in their path.

From the first day they walked into the gym, they were unforgettable: identical twins, six feet tall, each weighing at least 265 pounds, dressed in work boots, bib overalls, and lumberjack shirts. They had come from somewhere back east and had an air of mystery around them — and occasionally a bad odor as well.

As an *LA Times* columnist said in an interview with them (which they were late for), "Would you expect a barbarian to wear a watch and be on time? To wash?"

In the article, The Barbarian Brothers said, "We're built better than Schwarzenegger, we're as funny as Eddie Murphy, and we're twins on top of everything else!" And they had dyslexia, to boot.

When they walked into the gym the first time while it was still in Santa Monica, they said they wanted to train but had no money. No questions were asked. They looked like they belonged. They were given free memberships.

When Brockway Moran & Partners bought Gold's Gym in 1999, David complained to me that they now had to pay. I said, "Maybe after 20 years, it's time."

David Paul, who died in 2020, was also one of the most creative photographers the bodybuilding world had ever seen.

PERSONAL TRAINERS

The sense of family that Pete, Tim, and I tried to create extended to the people in the gym making a living as personal trainers.

We waited until 1993, almost ten years after it all began, to start charging rent. This was fourteen years before the smartphone era, and even pagers were in limited use, so the front desk was overwhelmed with calls from clients trying to contact their trainers — this being LA, most likely to tell them they were stuck in traffic and running late.

We needed more front desk personnel to handle the calls. And we needed to organize it so that everyone was certified, carried insurance, and was CPR trained.

Darin Lannahan and Mike Ryan, our dual managers at the time, proposed an initial rent of $250 a month. This worked out very well since we were about the only gym on the Westside of LA that allowed outside personal trainers, something I failed to understand — and I still don't. How someone could think they could afford to have someone like Charles Glass or Mike O'Hearn on their payroll when they were getting $250 a session alludes me.

During the twenty-five years that Pete, Tim, and I were involved, I don't remember one lawsuit involving a trainer. They made the gym safer and helped members get results, which is the surest way to keep them.

When we exited the company in 2004, 125 personal trainers were paying $475 a month rent, totaling almost $60,000.

THE START OF GYM LICENSING

With the help of my father, I purchased an existing gym in San Francisco from Denny Malloy and Bob Fischer and opened up the first licensed Gold's Gym on June 16, 1980. Coincidentally, it was almost the same size of the gym on Second Street in Santa Monica. Most of the equipment was also made by the same individual, George Pipasik, who had helped Joe Gold make most of his equipment.

Like Gold's Gym in Santa Monica, it was way ahead of its time with its size and equipment. There was even irony in the name. The previous owners felt that if they couldn't be Gold's Gym, they would be the next best thing to gold, so they called it Diamond Gym. Ironically, later, when foreign passport control officers would ask me what my business was, and I would say, "the gym business," they would often misconstrue what I said as the "gem business" and would want to learn more, like if I was carrying diamonds into the country.

My early success in San Francisco encouraged me to get involved in other gyms in California. San Jose, Reseda, San Diego, and Walnut Creek followed. I faced local competition in all these areas but thought having the Gold's Gym name and a larger, better-equipped facility would make them successful. For the most part, it did.

I used to tell my houseguests to "give it three years." If they hadn't realized their goal in that time frame, then it was time to move on. The same rule applied to my gyms: If they weren't successful in three years, they would probably never be, the demographics usually being the most significant factor.

After the success of the first three licensed gyms in California and Florida, I told Pete and Tim that what the country needs is a chain of heavy-duty gyms instead of those hoity-toity gyms, like the spas.

As Pete traveled the country and world as Mr. World, he was often asked what Gold's Gym is like. Since most people can't come to the Mecca, Pete thought, why not bring the Mecca to them?

Tim interjected, "We also want to be a significant force in promoting bodybuilding. While the Howdy Doody gyms act ashamed of the bodybuilders and discourage serious workouts, we want the world to be aware of the benefits of bodybuilding for everybody."

Thus "Serious Fitness for Every Body" was born.

Why even franchise at all? Why not own all the facilities? Pete and Tim had no interest in owning any gym other than the one in Venice. I was willing to explore other options, but that took capital, which usually meant working partners. But even this had its limitations. Some markets just aren't big enough to warrant a corporate-owned or an absentee owner investment.

I remember going to a small town in Wisconsin and stopping at a gas station to ask for directions or more likely buy a map. This was in the days before smartphones and GPS. This was the way I usually started when visiting owners and inspecting clubs. Fortunately, perhaps because of my architectural background, I had a great sense of direction, which had served me well in the Army in Vietnam.

When I asked the gas station attendant if he knew where the Gold's Gym was, the young man said proudly, "We only have one. It's down the road along with the one McDonald's," and pointed to the way. No doubt, just as this wasn't a town where corporate McDonald's wanted to plant a flag, they were happy to have a locally owned store instead. So was Gold's Gym. Pete and Tim didn't like to travel but would thrill to the stories I had when I returned from my trips. We were proud of our gyms, like they were our children who had made it.

Initially, the program started as a licensing operation. Three things constitute a franchise: a registered trademark, a fee paid for the use of that mark — essentially a royalty — and a business plan.

There was no manual or guide to operating a gym in the beginning. It was all new. My early business partners were only half-joking when they asked, "Where's the manual?" When they would tell me later that they would never have gone into the business if they'd known all its complexities, my response would be, "That's why I didn't tell you!"

I wanted them to interpret Gold's Gym for their market. They weren't bound by any tradition. I guess I was trusting people and not process.

In the beginning, there was even some discussion about combining food service with the gym operation as part of "the package." When Gold's Gym moved back to Venice in 1981, it changed the neighborhood, transforming the dining choices from none to a half-dozen, although it took some time.

Places like The Firehouse Restaurant, The Rose, and Omelette Parlor were particularly successful in catering to our members and visitors to the Mecca because they offered a novel experience. Ordering egg whites for breakfast or a burger made from ostrich or buffalo meat was impossible in some areas of the US in the '80s where everything was fried. Tom Wilson, our longest-serving gym manager, even got a number of the restaurants to name some of the healthy choices on the menu after Gold's Gym and give discounts to our members.

Getting a nutritious meal along with a workout would have been ideal, but that would have added an extra degree of complexity. And like so many things, the world has changed so that healthy food on the menu is the new normal, along with the calorie count.

Google is now the next-door neighbor to The Rose. The menu at The Rose would hardly be recognizable to a Gold's Gym member back then — or appealing or affordable. Under "Pasta & Grains," you can now order "sweet corn agnolotti: Mexican style street corn, cotija, cilantro" for $28, something you could also find up the street at a food truck for $4. Their version of the "The Gold's standard" for breakfast costs $20 and consists of "braised bacon, two eggs sunny-side-up, fried potatoes, country bread, butter, and seasonal jam."

Tackling the foodservice industry is one thing. Dealing with a new service industry like fitness is quite another.

The entry system — how one is admitted to the gym — is an excellent example of the changes over four decades. Initially, I used a sign-in sheet and Rolodex to check in members. How a person prints and signs their name is unique versus a membership card, even one with a barcode, that multiple people can trade and use. (This is how most states verify the authenticity of mail-in ballots in today's elections, the process that was so hotly contested in the 2020 US presidential election.) So, when a member joined, that information was completed on a Rolodex card along with their membership number. When the individual came into the gym for their workout, they signed in, writing in their number and printing or signing their name. When that person was in the gym, the front counter personnel's job was to confirm that person's status.

More elaborate systems followed: eye readers, fingerprint readers, barcodes that display the member's face on a computer screen, and now cameras that can not only recognize the individual's face but, thanks to COVID-19, check their temperature as well. All this over the span of forty-two years.

A Rolodex is now on display as a relic from another era at the Cooper Hewitt Smithsonian Museum in New York City.

But while technology has revolutionized the check-in process, the most critical person in a gym is still the person the potential or existing member sees when walking into or leaving the facility. People who might be visiting the city for a short time would say to me that the most attractive and friendliest people they met had been the ones behind the front counter of the gym. That's the way it should be.

We even had an entirely new category of employee: "weight picker-upper," later termed "floor supervisor." For this thankless task, Tim and I hired physically challenged individuals to whom members would be more likely not to react too negatively when asked to please pick up their weights.

Some of these employees might have been seen as the polar opposite of the individuals working up front, but they had unique talents and could be disarmingly charming. I later learned that one of them was a "stunt dick" — another category of employee I had never heard of before — who was working in the porn industry in the Valley when he wasn't working for Gold's Gym. While he seemingly wasn't as attractive as the front counter staff, it turned out that he had his own exceptional talent from the waist down.

THE GROWTH OF GOLD'S GYM LICENSING

The interest in the licensed gyms was steady. It helped that we started like McDonald's with a small, yearly licensing fee of $1,400. (McDonald's started with $950 in 1955.) Steady enough that Paul Grymkowski, Pete's brother, was hired, and he came out from Rochester to head up the licensing program. In 1989, Rich Minzer became his assistant.

After I became the first licensee in the middle of 1980, three more followed by the end of the year: Rick Hall's Gold's Gym in Pompano Beach, Florida, another one of mine in San Jose, then San Diego. That number doubled in 1981, enough for a Gold's Gym convention held in conjunction with the American Bodybuilding Championships at Caesars Palace.

By the end of 1982, there were fifty-six Gold's Gym licensees located in the following states: Colorado, Ohio, Kentucky, Utah, New Mexico, Minnesota, Mississippi, Alabama, Illinois, Hawaii, Oregon, Maryland, Washington, Texas, Vermont, Michigan, Pennsylvania, Nevada, Tennessee, Iowa, and Connecticut. The Gold's Gym name was well-known enough that we even had interest from Canada, Italy, and Denmark.

The convention was again held that year at Caesars Palace along with the National Physique Committee's USA contest.

In the early days of Gold's Gym licensing, we were closely tied in with the bodybuilding community. Perhaps following Arnold's example, we never forgot our roots. We were the authority on fitness.

Eric & Howard Levine

Eric Levine and his brother, Howard, led the way in Canada.

After traveling the world while working for Club Med, Eric was advised that Venice would be the perfect place to unwind. So, in 1980, at age twenty-four and without even a high school diploma, he got a place at the Windward Village apartment complex near Muscle

Beach, with neighbors in his building such as Tom Platz, Ron Teufel, and Robby Robinson, some of bodybuilding's greats. All it took was a visit to the apartment complex's swimming pool to realize that it was another world. It might as well have been Jurassic Park with all the monsters.

A visit to Gold's Gym would further change Eric's perspective. Whether you were a housewife, a professional, an actor, or a bodybuilder, you were just one of the boys or girls in an environment that was motivational but fun.

Today you don't need to leave home to be entertained, but back then, even if you weren't training, you would want to go to the gym to be entertained and inspired, to see bodybuilders and celebrities not acting like celebrities. But once inside, it was almost impossible not to want to join in. The energy was infectious. Like so many visitors to Gold's Gym Venice, Eric was hooked. He wanted to take the magic back to his country, where Joe Weider was a distant memory but still a memory to Eric's father in his hometown of Montreal.

But Ontario was a bigger market. So, in 1984, Eric created a small ad promoting the prospect of a Gold's Gym coming to Canada. He set up an office with just a wooden packing crate and a phone and waited for the phone to ring. It never stopped ringing.

His marketing got many men, and especially women, to believe in the bald muscleman and share his passion that, like Club Med, offered an escape from reality — at least in its ads.

One of his TV commercials, "The Art of the Human Body," was so good that the Cannes Film Festival borrowed it and used it in a worldwide competition, where it came in second.

Eric and Howard formed a company, Super Gym Advertising, and started selling ad material to other Gold's Gym operators. They went on to open three more Gold's Gyms, varying in size from twelve thousand to twenty thousand square feet, before finally selling ten years later in 1994.

But then, like several other former Gold's Gym owners, Eric became a modern "Johnny Appleseed" for fitness. Ray Wilson, his mentor and one of the early pioneers in the fitness industry, said to go west. So, off Eric went to Asia, populating it with California Fitness gyms for the next twenty-three years, starting in Hong Kong, then Singapore, Taiwan, Korea, Thailand, Vietnam, and China.

THE REAGAN YEARS AND CHANGES IN THE REAL ESTATE MARKET

In 1979, *Time* magazine made Ayatollah Khomeini Man of the Year. He had helped make President Jimmy Carter a one-term president after his handling of the Iran hostage crisis — and the economy. But in 1980, *Time* made Ronald Reagan its Man of the Year, and with his election and a revitalized economy declared "the dawning of a new morning in America."

It had helped that President Carter put Paul Volker in charge of the Federal Reserve. But most importantly, like Margaret Thatcher in Great Britain, Reagan helped create a sea change in attitude, a can-do spirit that encouraged many of our future gym owners to be young entrepreneurs.

By the end of 1982, the United States was beginning what would be called the Great Moderation: a quarter-century of steady growth, low inflation, booming financial markets, and recessions that were rare and mild. Gold's Gym would grow to 704 locations during this period.

There were profound shifts in the real estate world; the banks were downsizing while the supermarkets were upsizing. Branch banks were going from ten thousand square feet to five thousand. To better compete with superstores like Walmart, supermarkets began giving up their forty-thousand-square-foot locations to move into buildings with sixty thousand square feet or more. A demising wall could split that forty thousand square feet into two spaces of twenty thousand square feet each, which would be perfect for the new prototype Gold's Gym Venice had created by 1989.

Three of the Gold's Gym locations I was personally involved with were in former Bank of America branches that were ten thousand square feet. And most of the other gyms I had a stake in — ones that were twenty thousand square feet — were in former grocery stores.

This new, freed-up space was significant because mall owners did not welcome gyms in the beginning. They were as oblivious then as they seem now about the changing demographics. They thought our members spent all their time in the gym, tying up parking spaces for hours, and didn't eat in restaurants. I tried to assure them that our majority male demographic with disposable income was desirable — and that they did enjoy pizza.

It also helped that the Gold's Gym "one-gym-fits-all" model lasted for almost three decades, roughly from 1981 to 2010. Gold's Gym Franchising did not allow a franchisee to be involved in another fitness facility brand, just as McDonald's would not permit an operator to own a Taco Bell or some other fast-food operation. There was the obvious concern about "trade secrets," but during those thirty years, there wasn't the need for the range of fitness options that make sense today. If I were involved with gym franchising now, I would allow an owner to have at least three different gyms in the same market: low-priced, medium-priced, and high-end.

It only makes sense to essentially own your competition when it doesn't compete with what you are offering in another kind of facility. The soap, auto, and hotel industries are great examples of how this brand extension can work: one company owning several competing brands with nearly identical products. How many people know that the same company that owns Equinox Fitness Centers also controls SoulCycle and the SNAP chain of low-cost gyms?

THE GROWTH OF THE CONVENTIONS

By the end of 1983, there were eighty-four Gold's Gym locations, and the convention was held at the Inn of Santa Monica. Many businesses were popping up all over America with the last four digits of their phone number, 4653, listed as GOLD.

With 130 clubs by the end of 1984, it was back to Caesars Palace. In an attempt to satisfy East Coast owners due to a survey we did, the convention moved to Miami in 1985, with 176 Gold's Gym locations at year-end. The convention stayed in the east for the following two years and then moved to the Marriott at LAX for the next six years, between 1988 and 1993.

In 1994, we started having guest speakers at the convention, beginning with my friends Bart Conner and Nadia Comaneci, to whom I had sold my first home in Venice. Legendary college basketball coach Jim Garrick followed the next year; then came NFL great quarterback Fran Tarkenton and, after him, Don Shula.

Except for 1997 and 2001, when the convention was at the Fontainebleau Hotel in Miami, we produced lavish conventions in the major strip hotels in Las Vegas between 1994 and 2003, even giving our owners two or three free room nights. The sit-down dinners or buffets we sponsored had seating for around eight hundred people, and attendees at our trade show reached a high of fourteen hundred when we were in Las Vegas. As long as we changed hotels, our franchisees were happy to return to Sin City year after year.

Since we were a health and fitness business, it seemed incongruous at first, but no place else in the world does service quite like Las Vegas. There were many lessons to be learned there, especially by our foreign owners. While none of the hotels would share with us how our owners did at the gaming tables, they did say that their room service business went through the roof when we were in residence.

We typically shared the hotel with one or two other large groups having their conventions. There were some fun juxtapositions, like the Bull Riders of America or the organization of Black colleges of America. We even shared The Mirage Hotel one year with McDonald's franchisees. We showed them something new, and they broadened our perspective as well.

The hotels also used that time of the year — usually July — to take their promo pics since they could be assured of an unusually high number of attractive people and hard bodies around the pool or in the casino.

That time at the pool or around the gaming tables also provided more valuable interaction between our owners than was likely achieved in the seminars we put on. We also had a very good franchise in Las Vegas with Brad Neste, a Canadian contractor, and his wife, Wanda, who had moved to Palm Springs initially, like many "snowbirds" from Canada, in the winter. Brad and Wanda became king and queen of the desert locations, with eighteen clubs in Palm Springs, Las Vegas, Temecula, and Phoenix. Brad designed and built the gyms. Wanda initially taught aerobics.

They seemingly gave up having children to have gyms. They told me that every morning for them was like a boardroom meeting around the kitchen table.

JOE WEIDER OPENS WEIDER FITNESS GYMS

In the spring quarter of 1991, *California Centers* magazine announced that Weider Enterprises would open one hundred Joe Weider Fitness Gyms in California: "The gyms would range from 10,000 to 20,000 square feet and will be located in shopping centers or stand-alone buildings," they reported.

I had warned Joe and Betty that it wouldn't be easy, and indeed it collapsed after a couple of years, resulting in numerous lawsuits, which I tried to help Joe resolve. The individual Joe had hired was even going after existing Gold's Gym franchises trying to "convert" them, which is illegal under franchise law. I asked Joe to stop this.

In a letter to me on June 25, 1991, he said:

"Please be advised that I have instructed Weider Franchising Inc. management staff that they are not to solicit your gym owners trying to convert them to Joe Weider Fitness Gyms."

I had given WWE's Vince McMahon similar advice when Vince considered buying Gold's Gym.

That wouldn't be the last time I would have that kind of conversation with wrestlers. When the pro wrestler Sting and his partner, Lex Luger, came to me and said they were going to drop the Gold's Gym name for their club in Atlanta and start a new gym chain to be called Main Event Fitness, I told them it wasn't a good idea.

After managing my gym in the Valley, Sting had become quite a successful wrestler, like his former partner, The Ultimate Warrior. Their logic was that since they were in a gym almost every day of their lives, they knew the business. I told them that while I eat out at a restaurant nearly every day, that does not mean I could own or operate a restaurant.

Their "chain" closed after two clubs.

FROM LICENSING TO FRANCHISING

There was no convention in 1996 because we were making the transition from licensing to franchising.

When Gold's Gym became a franchise business in California, it became one nationwide. Gold's Gym had a commanding lead of 150 clubs over the number two gym, Bally. World Gym had half that number, and Powerhouse half of that. The line between license and franchise had become blurred. In some states, like New York, Gold's Gym was considered a franchise from the start, one reason GGF avoided that state in the early days. Iowa was another state we avoided.

As GGF and its franchises learned more, information was passed on to new owners culminating in the start of a three-day Gold's Gym University on October 22, 1996, with the start of franchising. We felt the ethical, indeed, moral obligation to share as much as our owners, and we had learned to help ensure as much success as possible for the new franchisees. New franchisees were finally getting that "manual," which ended up being three inches thick. Ironically, a lot of it became obsolete the moment it was printed. That's how much the gym business was changing.

The most apparent aspect of this change concerned the size of the facility, which had an impact on the sales per square foot and gross revenue. The gyms had developed naturally into three classifications: A, B, and C categories.

The "A+" facilities grossed $1.5 million a year, which was similar to a typical McDonald's at the time. An "A" gym had yearly revenue of $1.08 million; a "B+" was at $960,000; "B" at $720,000; "C+" at $480,000; and a "C" at $ 360,000, for an average of $774,000 per gym.

The net margin ranged from ten percent with the lower gross revenue to twenty-four percent with the higher-grossing gyms. Payroll ranged from a high of thirty-three percent of gross income to a low of twenty-five percent — typical for a fast-food franchise, but a gym's profits were much higher.

When GGF was sold to Brockway Moran & Partners, the minimum size requirement had grown to fifteen thousand square feet

– not large in comparison to some big-box clubs today but often easily the largest fitness facility in most markets. And even in the major markets, a fifteen-thousand-square-foot Gold's Gym might have a bigger workout floor and more equipment than a more substantial competitor, like a YMCA or public recreational center.

Back then, bigger was better when it came to gyms. This metric may be changing in this post-pandemic world, but back then, it was the reason the nearby Powerhouse Gym and World Gym in Venice did not compete successfully with Gold's Gym. They were much smaller.

We welcomed diversity, and we were not afraid of new ideas. While wisely increasing the square footage requirement over the years, we allowed individual Gold's Gym owners the freedom to interpret Gold's Gym for their market. We believed you could have unity without uniformity.

My first gym in San Francisco is a good example. While many gyms provided a babysitting service for the children of their members, that didn't make much sense in San Francisco. But currently, the successor gym to that first location located at 1001 Brannon Street has a "Doggie Day Care" room for its members' pets, something that makes sense and that I have seen nowhere else.

TERRITORIES & EQUIPMENT

There were some painful lessons to be learned early on, like territory. While anchor stores can compete at the opposite ends of a typical American mall, and auto dealerships can go head to head on an "auto row," it's not a good idea for gyms to be across the street from each other, something our first licensee in Las Vegas learned.

Another mistake: Giving too large a territory or too large a territorial option. Our licensee in Columbus, Ohio, is an example of this. We gave the first Gold's Gym owner there a radius of sixty miles. He never did more than the one club and quickly got outflanked by the competition: the World Gym locations owned by Jim Lorimer. Lorimer partnered with Arnold for the annual Arnold Classic, during which they completely took over the city.

Fortunately, most owners were interested in opening only one club with a smaller radius, usually five miles. And most of our multiple operators did a very responsible job of developing territories, like John and Kirk Galiani in the greater Washington, DC area. They would be a critical component to the next phase of Gold's Gym's existence.

By the time of one of my last meetings as president of GGF in 2001, I had learned enough to be leery of any individual seeking the franchise rights for an entire country — in this case, Saudi Arabia.

Ali Mahmoud, chairman of the Gold's Gym group operating in Egypt, had just opened their second location on a boat barge overlooking the Nile River in the center of Cairo. It had an over-the-top Egyptian pharaonic theme, was over twenty thousand square feet, and cost $2 million. I thought if anyone should be branching out in the Middle East, it should be them.

When an attorney from Chicago — the center of the legal world for franchising because of McDonald's — called and asked if I would mind meeting him and his client on a Saturday, I said, sure. You can never learn less. And working on Saturday was no different from working on a weekday.

We agreed to meet for a late lunch at the Polo Lounge at The Beverly Hills Hotel on Sunset Boulevard in the center of Beverly Hills. The lunch lasted several hours, during which the Saudi prince, the client, explained to me how he saw an American-style gym working in a Muslim country.

Having designed two homes for Saudi princes while working as an architect, I was familiar with the cultural differences but didn't let on. Instead, I let him go on discussing his interpretation of Gold's Gym, like entirely separate facilities for the men and women or closing the gym down three or five times a day while members went into the aerobics room to pray.

I didn't like where the meeting was going. I began to sense that he intended to hold the franchise for a large territory and then sublicense his rights to others. The sublicensees, in turn, might sell off parts of their territories to a third level of operators. He could also collect a sizable franchising fee upfront for each one. This happened to several American fast-food operations in foreign countries with disastrous results.

So, when the prince asked if there was a Gold's Gym location nearby to see, I jumped at the chance to end the meeting with a tour. I told him that the closest Gold's Gym was about five miles away in West Hollywood. So, he called up his — or the hotel's — convertible gold Rolls-Royce for us to jump into and go to Gold's Gym Hollywood on Cole Avenue near Santa Monica Boulevard.

It was a Saturday evening, so the energy walking into the gym was electric, much like walking into Gold's Gym Venice — or Studio 54. It had the wow factor and the bodies; there were many gay men getting pumped up to go out that evening to the clubs nearby.

This was twenty years after the start of HIV/AIDS. A considerable percentage of the members were on steroids and growth hormone to combat the disease, so there were many impressive physiques to see as we walked into the gym.

The prince's first reaction was, "Where are all the women?"

Trying to keep a straight face, I said, "This is our Saudi model."

And sure enough, when we went upstairs to see the group exercise studios, they were entirely packed with women taking ZUMBA and other kinds of aerobic classes in the three studios — a lot for a Gold's Gym. It had just as much energy as the gym floor below. I said, "See, it works!"

I didn't end up selling a franchise, but it had been an enjoyable day.

One landmine GGF avoided, which many fast-food franchises didn't, was getting involved with exclusive suppliers, which would eventually be deemed illegal. GGF worked with many vendors who offered a discount to franchises, but our gyms were not required to buy exclusively from that list. Pete, Tim, and I firmly believed that no one equipment company "made it all" or did everything perfectly.

In August 1993, *Club Industry* magazine, the fitness industry's trade journal, ran a cover story titled "Muscling IN," which talked about "Muscle-Head" gyms sprucing up for broader appeal. Supposedly, studies showed that hardcore bodybuilders make up just three to five percent of the overall exercise population. It was thought to be a tricky balance to achieve, to appeal to both the bodybuilding clientele and the general public. And that the "Big Three" gym chains — Gold's Gym, World Gym, and Powerhouse Gym — will have to do that if they are serious about broadening their market reach.

We seemed to have no problem doing that. Maybe our three percent was like McDonald's "heavy users": people who ate there more than once a week. Our core group probably used the gym six days a week, creating energy — and traffic. And it was by not being afraid to adapt and change, like adding cardio equipment or group exercise, that helped.

The growth of Gold's Gym Franchising looked like the thirty-degree triangle on my drafting table. It was straight-line growth from one to 535 gyms when we sold for the first time in 1999. My large desk, made out of a four-by-six-foot sheet of plywood, was something I had retained since high school and was located in the corporate offices along with my drafting tools.

The architecture industry was just going from pencil and paper to computer when I left the profession in 1985. It was a painful transition for the last firm I worked for. They lost millions of dollars trying to make the switch. However, I still "played" architect for many new owners, marking up their plans, so the table and equipment came in handy. I never took the place of the local architect the franchisee may have hired, but I was happy to review their work.

I wanted local input. I didn't want a cookie-cutter approach to the design of the gyms. GGF was not producing fast food. Though I was part of gym franchising, I didn't like what franchising had done or was doing to America and the world. When I was on the road, I would seek out one-of-a-kind restaurants to eat at and avoid the fast-food franchises.

Even the big shopping malls were part of the mauling of the American landscape; they were "Westfield Malls" with no sense of place. I didn't like the buildings that LifeTime Fitness, 24 Hour Fitness, and LA Fitness were erecting — the ones with the so-called broader appeal.

Perhaps it was because of the lesson I had learned from the Catholic Churches I had visited over the years; they were all Catholic, yet they each had their character and place. Any building can be a temple — a church — if you make it one.

GOLD'S GYM: A CLOTHING COMPANY

Gold's Gym Enterprises was a clothing company masquerading as a gym chain back in the '80s. When *Sporting Goods Business* listed fifty of the top athletic apparel companies, Gold's Gym was number twenty. This was certainly true up until 1989, when Gold's Gym Merchandising started licensing products when demand outstripped our ability to supply. We hit on several unusual items such as fanny packs, cotton-Lycra shorts, and baggy pants.

The color combinations that people wore were often so crazy that I called them the "Easter egg" people, but they were big hits. If a person wore a matching top and bottom, it looked more like pajamas than workout gear.

Because of those baggy pants, Joe Bozich came on board to run GGM in 1985.

While majoring in mathematics at Vanderbilt University, Joe won the NCAA National Bodybuilding Championships, essentially Mr. Collegiate America.

I contacted Joe and brought him to LA to work at my gym in Reseda in the Valley. When Joe showed me how to save thirty-five cents on the manufacturing of a pair of baggy pants, we hired him to head up the clothing division along with the help of Ray Bolton, who showed him some of the ropes of the "schemata business." He also got Gold's Gym into shoes: the Classic and the Gladiator.

Indeed, more people have worn the Gold's Gym brand than worked out in the gyms. It was a name people wanted to be associated with.

A good quality T-shirt could be bought and silk-screened for $2.25. That, in turn, could be sold to a Gold's Gym franchise for $4.50. They, in turn, could keystone it and sell it for $9.95.

Everyone made money. It created a win-win situation because the person wearing it also advertised the brand.

It was hard keeping up with the demand in the late '80s. The clothing industry wasn't like it is today. The suppliers were primarily concentrated in the southeast US then, and there weren't the foreign options that exist today.

For the first ten years of the business, we had to change banks every year to increase our lines of credit as a new bank would offer a higher line of credit to get us to switch. Factoring the receivables wasn't working because entities like Macy's took ninety days to pay.

So, in 1989, we began licensing out the brand. In the spring of 1990, we licensed American Marketing Works (AMW), which Marvin Winkler owned, for the clothing. They had licenses for Body Glove, Disney, and Speedo, along with a three-hundred-thousand-square-foot warehouse. They seemed reliable, but they went belly up between the summer of '90 and the start of '91, never really getting started with our line.

Joe had gone to work for them but then left for Stedor, the parent company of Carolina Fashions, in Greer, South Carolina, which took over the licensing. When Joe left them in the early '90s, he became a spokesperson for Weider Enterprises and Mattel Corporation and then founded Knights Apparel in 2001. By 2009, Knights passed Nike to become the largest apparel supplier in the $4.5 billion licensed college products industry.

Joe was named Ernst & Young's Entrepreneur of the year and, in 2010, along with Warren Buffet and Bill Gates, was nominated as one of the top one hundred "Game Changers" in the country by *The Huffington Post* for his ethical business model, Alta Garcia.

Pete, Tim, and I were never afraid to hire someone who was smarter or would work harder than we did.

GOLD'S GYM NUTRITION & SUPPLEMENTS

In 1987, David Zelon, who had been a tireless worker and an essential factor in the success of our bodybuilding contests, started Muscle Camps in New Jersey. It was a bodybuilding version of the popular summer camps I was familiar with when I lived on the East Coast.

A year later, Weider hired him to produce Pro Muscle Camps at Loyola Marymount University in LA, where it ran for six years during the summer months. It also gave Weider a chance to make use of his sponsored athletes. And it was a boon to Gold's Gym Venice with all the added traffic and tourists, and the several thousand students enrolled each summer.

David had hired Chris Aceto, a young, twenty-year-old student majoring in applied exercise science at Springfield College to be one of the instructors. As I saw with Neal Spruce in my San Francisco gym, nutrition was becoming more and more critical.

So, when Chris came to see me looking for a job, I gave him an office and phone with one of our secretaries to further his stay in California. He would go off to various Gold's Gym locations to help install the "Nutritionalysis" program we were developing. Then Joe Weider called Chris and asked him to write a column, and he was off and running.

Chris was instrumental in the success of many athletes, including some of my houseguests such as Jay Cutler, Paul DeMayo, and Mike Francois. He is still a much sought-after "guru" in today's fitness world.

Marc Missoreck was another one we hired from the Muscle Camps. Marc, a graduate of the University of Pennsylvania's Wharton School of Business, became director of product licensing from 1993 to 1997, helping it grow into numerous new areas and enhance the value of the license both for gym owners and vendors. Marc currently produces the most significant fitness expos in the US with The Fit Expo.

NEAL SPRUCE & NUTRITIONALYSIS

Like Joe Bozich, Neal Spruce was another great department head I was fortunate to find. And, like Joe, he seized the opportunity I gave him.

I saw Neal win the Mr. Western States in 1981 and offered him a job at Gold's Gym San Francisco, working with the other bodybuilders I had hired: Jon Loyd, Barry Clothier, Bob Reis, Steve Rance, and Bill Cambra.

Neal had left home early and was passed around six foster homes before turning sixteen. He joined a Bay Area biker gang to survive. However, sports and fitness saved him when he became a member of his high school's football team. Then Gold's Gym became the family he never had.

Neal had an exceptional knowledge of nutrition, especially for the time. Every membership Neal sold came with a handwritten diet.

From 1982 to 1987, Neal held nutrition seminars and did grand opening appearances in the Bay Area. I shared with Pete and Tim my thoughts regarding offering Neal a position to head up the sagging Gold's Gym nutrition department.

Neal moved to Venice in 1987 and created a computerized nutrition program that included supplements, first for Venice and then the licensees. It was a first of its kind.

Neal and Billy Smith, whom I brought to Venice around the same time, assembled a solid staff and installed over three hundred franchises with "Nutritionalysis" between 1988 and 1994. We trademarked the name and worked with some medical doctors and top bodybuilders to develop a questionnaire and body fat analysis to help people understand their bodies and requirements.

Neal left in 1994 after we licensed this program to John Logsdon, a brilliant chemist, pharmacologist, and pioneer in the nutritional supplement industry and founder of Old Fashioned Natural Products (OFNP).

After leaving OFNP, Neal started APEX Nutrition, which was later combined with 24 Hour Fitness and eventually sold. Neal then bought the National Academy of Sports Medicine (NASM) and two other sports performance companies in 1997 to build NASM into the world's largest provider of sports, exercise, and fitness education and certification. Neal also created the "bodybugg," an early forerunner of the performance watch.

DotFIT, Neal's latest venture into the supplement industry, which he started in 2008, is currently in fifteen hundred locations and represented by forty thousand sport and fitness professionals.

Billy Smith came to my attention when he won a local Gold's Gym Classic bodybuilding contest in his home state of Maryland in 1987. It happened to be at the same time that the new TV show *American Gladiators* was looking for talent, and so I invited Billy to LA for the tryouts. At six feet, three inches and 265 pounds, he became "Thunder" on the show, which ran for seven seasons.

Like so many of my visitors with alcoholic parents, Billy was ready to leave home and start a new life in California. But while growing up, he had become an expert on nutrition while trying to help his diabetic brother, so he became not only a gladiator but a vital part of the Gold's Gym nutrition and supplement program. Along with Neal, he installed the Gold's Gym Nutritionalysis program in hundreds of our franchises even while touring for the show. He competed as Thunder in numerous American cities as the TV show went on the road.

His partner and future wife in all of this was Cathy Sassin. Cathy had a degree in exercise physiology from UCLA and was working as a pharmaceutical rep when she met Billy at Gold's Gym Venice. Billy asked her to join the Gold's Gym nutrition team, and later, she herself became a gladiator, starring as either "Panther" or "Jett" on the show.

Years before producing *Survivor, Shark Tank,* and *The Apprentice* — and helping launch Donald Trump — Mark Burnett was a struggling, wannabe movie producer when he approached Gold's Gym in 1994. He had arrived in California from England and was looking for sponsors for "Team American Pride." That team would be competing in a race and test of human endurance called "Raid Gauloises." He had seen its success on television in Europe with as many as forty international teams competing and thought that might be duplicated in the US with an American team. But for that, he needed money — and a team.

Gold's Gym gave Mark sponsorship money and, after Derek

Barton's encouragement, a key player: Cathy Sassin. Besides her physical ability, Cathy's leadership qualities earned her a place on the team as the only woman. In one of the first races, Cathy and two of her Navy Seal teammates beat all eighteen international teams in front of them in six grueling days in the jungles of Borneo.

Cathy would go on to compete and carry the Gold's Gym banner all over the world in another twenty "eco-challenges," placing in the top three eighty percent of the time. That's the kind of person we would hire.

After Neal left, Cathy Sassin became director of Nutritionalysis and, along with Billy, developed a nutrition program called Intra-Fit to service Gold's Gym members. Derek managed to supply a steady stream of celebrity entertainers and athletes for Cathy and Billy to advise, thereby helping cement Gold's Gym's place as the "authority on fitness."

In 1993, we licensed Golden Era for fitness drinks: performance iced tea, isotonic quencher, All-Day Energy, and Gold Water. While the company didn't go anywhere with the products, I had the feeling that we were ahead of the market, ahead of the curve, as sports drinks are more significant than ever today.

CELEBRITY GYM OWNERS

The '90s, the second decade of Gold's Gym Franchising, saw the beginning of "celebrity franchisees," like fighter Ken Norton, baseball players Pete Rose and Reggie Jackson, singer Jermaine Jackson, entertainers Barbara Mandrell and Ben Vereen, football players Archie Manning, Joe Klecko, Kevin Greene, and Ron Jaworski, and pro wrestler Ric Flair.

It was flattering. Some wanted to be tied so closely with the brand that they wanted to name the facility in such a way as to highlight that, as in "Archie Manning's Gold's Gym," something the trademark attorneys didn't like because it weakened the brand. Derek Barton did a brilliant job of diffusing this situation by telling the celebrity that while they undoubtedly had their fans, not everyone may love them, whereas everyone loved Gold's Gym.

Sometimes being tied to a celebrity had unintended consequences. When Pete Rose, manager of the Cincinnati Reds and baseball's all-time hits leader, was being investigated for illegally betting on major league games, it turns out that the payphones inside the Cincinnati Gold's Gym that he was part owner of were being bugged. The action by the FBI unintentionally uncovered that Mike Fry, the primary Gold's Gym owner, and two of his associates — Don Stenger and Paul Janszen — had been involved in selling recreational drugs, primarily cocaine.

Stenger and Janszen, who were both excellent bodybuilders, had been former houseguests of mine but, as it turned out, had also been houseguests of Pete Rose. Janszen claimed that Rose asked him to set up a cocaine ring and include him. As a result of the taping, the IRS and the DEA got involved in the FBI sting.

Mike Fry and Don Stenger pled guilty to tax evasion and cocaine trafficking charges. Fry served an eight-year sentence, and Stenger ten years.

Gyms were a convenient way to hide or launder money before the widespread use of ACH, or automated clearing house transactions also called Electronic Funds Transfer (EFT), for collecting monthly dues directly from a member's bank account.

After a while, I was so negative on celebrities that when my partners in the Portland area Gold's Gyms wanted to hire Kobe Bryant as a spokesperson, I said it would be better — and safer — to engage his mother. Several months later, in July 1993, Kobe was charged with assaulting a woman in his hotel room in the middle of the night, and he became damaged goods. Fortunately, in his case, he could revive his image before tragically dying in a helicopter crash. O.J. Simpson, a member of Gold's Gym Venice, could not do the same.

Luckily, most of our franchisees weren't outside investors, like the celebrities who hired managers to run their businesses. I felt the genuine Gold's Gym celebrities were the franchisees with multiple locations who had been in business a long time and who so graciously shared what they had learned with prospective owners.

Two of the best were brothers Angel and Willy Banos, Cuban Americans who had previously owned three women's shoe stores. They had a passion for fitness. After nearly thirty-five years, they are still running Gold's Gym, with twenty locations in the greater LA area.

All the celebrity owners have long since disappeared.

Gold's Gym was blessed with many wonderful franchise owners whose backgrounds added to the mix and created much dynamism for the brand. While World Gym and Powerhouse Gym undoubtedly had some talented operators, Gold's Gym seemed to have more — at least that's what it looked like when they went head to head in shared markets.

In the beginning, one of the biggest surprises was that very few of the early franchisees were existing gym owners. I assumed they would want to be part of something bigger and benefit from a national brand. But those owners probably felt they were doing well enough on their own, so why change? As a result, the new Gold's Gym franchisees came from all walks of life, perhaps the only common denominator being a belief and passion in fitness.

Most of the working partners in the gyms I was involved in were bodybuilders or powerlifters. Naysayers would give me a hard time and say things like, "Are you going to hire one of those dumb lifters again?" every time I would start to open a new gym. I would respond by saying, "There are good and bad lifters, just like there are good and bad of anything."

I tried to find the good ones. It also helped to find a working team or a group of shareholders with varied interests or skills so that the company benefited from a sort of brain trust. I don't believe one person can wear all the hats well. Silicon Valley has proven that collaboration is better, that it's not possible to go it alone. It's not likely that one person could be a marketing genius while being good at human resources, facility design, equipment selection, building leases or purchases, etc.

All of my businesses were Chapter S corporations or LLCs, which meant the profits or losses flowed to the shareholders who were responsible for the taxes.

It was for everyone's benefit to make intelligent decisions. The working shareholders also had to realize they wore two hats: employee and director. Essentially, they had to be ready to fire themselves if they weren't doing a good job. This also applied to salaries. Just because the gym manager might also be a shareholder didn't mean that they should be paid more than the industry rate for that position.

It helped that the businesses could be capitalized for a relatively reasonable amount of money in the early days of the gym business. Coincidentally, that cost of entry to get in my first four gyms — Venice, San Francisco, San Jose, and San Diego — was $100,000. So, for $1,000, one of my employees in Gold's Gym SF could become a one-percent shareholder. Naysayers would scoff at that, but one percent of something is worth more than one hundred percent of nothing.

Jerry McCall, who started with two percent of the former Gold's Gym in San Jose, at one point owned one hundred percent of six gyms in the greater San Jose-Bay Area.

Jerry was a bodybuilding competitor who came to me after placing fifth in the Mr. America and said, "I don't think I'm ever going to be Mr. Olympia; maybe I should learn the gym business." He now lives across the street from Larry Ellison in Woodside, California, one of the wealthiest towns in Silicon Valley.

I had a college degree from UC Berkeley, but it was in architecture. It didn't matter. I wasn't even sure how many of the thousands of people I hired had high school or college degrees over the years. Resumes and diplomas were not things I focused on, which is ironic because, when I was in college, I was always told how significant a degree was. But I never bothered with that requirement when I hired someone even to be a managing partner of one of the gyms I was personally involved in. I just asked them to tell me a little about themselves, their life story.

The biggest group was composed of nine with four partners in Portland, Oregon. To this day, I couldn't tell you the educational background of any of my managers or partners, except perhaps Joel Potter's, the manager of the six former Gold's Gyms in Nebraska and Michigan. Joel skipped his high school graduation yet speaks and writes better than anyone I have ever met.

GOLD'S GYM MOSCOW

While the concept of an American brand franchising in a foreign country was unknown — even strange — in the '70s, it began to be accepted in the '80s at the start of Gold's Gym's expansion overseas.

The foreign gyms that worked were the ones that had both an American and a native as partners, or a native who had traveled and understood the US to a significant degree.

"You've got to know the territory," as they say in *The Music Man*. Gold's Gym Moscow was a great example of this.

I thought you should know when you were in a Gold's Gym in a foreign city. It was something I thought would enhance the brand's value: the novel experience you could have with Gold's Gym while traveling. Our franchises would build Warren Buffett's famous "moat" by offering business travelers a consistent experience in terms of equipment, cleanliness, and service.

Still, the interpretation of what that looked like would be at the owner's discretion. For example, Gold's Gym Moscow had a coat check room with a full-time employee to take, among other things, the full-length fur coats of some of its members. That was one-of-a-kind. Ironically, the large facility of forty thousand square feet was located in the former "Palace of Young Pioneers" a couple of miles from the Kremlin. Vladimir Lenin's wife had conceived it as the world's largest recreational complex. Now it was a Gold's Gym.

I grew up during the height of the Cold War, with the Cuban missile crisis. The good nuns at Our Lady of Lourdes Grade School, which I attended in Omaha, had regular shelter-in-place drills in the event of a nuclear attack. They also had us praying the rosary every day "for the conversion of Russia."

My initial visit to the former evil empire was something I could hardly wrap my head around. While more capitalist than Catholic, my first thought was that the prayers worked. My second thought after landing at the Moscow airport in 1996, five years after the collapse of the Soviet government, was wondering whether their missiles would have worked. It didn't help that the Marriott Hotel I was staying at had brown-colored cold, and sometimes hot, running water.

I had talked with bodybuilders who had traveled to Russia to compete and found very little to eat. Did the typical American bodybuilder know more about what was going on in Russia than Henry Kissinger and the US State Department? It seemed that way when I was in Vietnam, and now it sure looked that way when I was in Russia.

At the grand opening, I asked the partners what had been the hardest thing to teach the Russian employees. The Russian partner said, "to smile." At which point, one of the staff who overheard us talking said, "You Americans smile too much!" Like Americans, Russians are not shy about expressing their feelings, one thing I loved about them.

I answered, "We have a lot to smile about!"

The main partners were Paul Kuebler, Vladimir Grumlik, Jake Weinstock, Alexi Spirin, and Drew Steichen, a combination of Americans and Russians. Paul and Vladimir were thirty-one. Jake was only twenty-five.

Like many of our franchisees, Paul and Jake had backgrounds with major American accounting firms. Jake was a full-time consultant to Ernst & Young; Paul with Anderson Consulting.

There was a long timeline to open the gym:

- May 1995: Kuebler and Weinstock decide to launch a fitness center in Moscow, where they had met six months earlier.
- November 1995: First commitment by private investors.
- December 1995: Investors back off when Communists win in parliamentary elections.
- June 1996: Yeltsin's prospects improve. Boston's Commonwealth Property Investors commits $1 million. Other investors follow.
- July 1996: Four days before Yeltsin wins the presidency, the partners sign a twenty-five-year agreement for the gym site.
- July 20, 1996: Construction begins.
- September 1996: Nike agrees to sponsor and build the basketball court.
- October 1996: Club starts accepting members; within a month, four hundred are enrolled.

They had concluded they would need one thousand members paying $1,500 to $2,500 annually to break even, and three thousand members to earn returns that could attract Western capital.

Just as the first McDonald's in Moscow had the highest revenue of any McDonald's at the time when it opened, so, too, Gold's Gym Moscow became the highest-grossing Gold's Gym of which I am aware, doing $12,000,000 its first year with six thousand members at $2,000 each — cash.

GOLD'S GYM JAPAN

My visit to inspect the first couple of Gold's Gym facilities in Japan elicited an entirely different cultural reaction than I had experienced when I visited Russia.

When I visited Japan in 1969 on R&R from Vietnam, I was shocked to see open trenches on the floor inside the toilet stalls in the public restrooms. Users were expected to squat down and defecate into the void. If they needed toilet paper, they were expected to bring their own — not much different from Vietnam except for the walls of the stall.

When I visited Tokyo twenty-five years later, I found myself in a hotel room with a $5,000 Toto toilet that was so complicated to use that it was intimidating. It reminded me of the iconic toilet scene in the movie *2001: A Space Odyssey*.

A lot had changed. The Gold's Gym locations I visited in the greater Tokyo area were equally as impressive physically. The gyms had perfectly duplicated the look and feel of Gold's Gym Venice, even copying the branding we had in Venice over the mirrors.

When Eiji Tezuka, the master franchisor for Japan, asked me what they could do better, I said, "You could teach us. The level of service and cleanliness in your gyms far exceeded anything I have seen in the States. There is much of the Japanese culture and 'sensibilities' that could benefit a new and reinvigorated Gold's Gym."

In twenty-five years, Eiji has grown Gold's Gym to one hundred locations all over Japan.

The success in Japan demonstrated that an American gym chain was exportable to a foreign culture.

I think Gold's Gym succeeded because we relied on the wisdom and courage of hundreds of entrepreneurs, some of whom I was fortunate to have as business partners, such as Steve and Carol Rance, Jack and Leslie Wadsworth, Jeff and Michele Fee, Joel Potter, Tony Calhoun, and Jerry McCall. They all had an economic incentive and a common standard regarding the equipment, pricing, and cleanliness, but nothing else about them was the same. While they had a passion for fitness and helping people, none of the early franchisees were "gym people." Being part of something new, they were not bound by tradition. They came from different worlds.

When a couple who ran a mortuary wondered if they would be good franchisees, I said, "Well, you certainly know the service business." Then there was the couple from Lubbock, Texas, who owned an amusement park. They, too, would provide a unique outlook to their interpretation of Gold's Gym, no doubt making it fun.

TSI AND 24 HOUR FITNESS BUY GOLD'S GYM FRANCHISES: 1994-1999

Appropriately enough, the most challenging years Gold's Gym Enterprises would face began on January 17, 1994, with a natural disaster: the Northridge Earthquake, which was centered about twenty miles north of Venice. It was the deadliest and most destructive earthquake during my time in California. Significantly, it was also the only year income from the Venice gym ever dropped. Not even a half dozen recessions had impacted the gym revenue.

I had this theory that gyms were "cheap entertainment" during tough times that also offered the additional benefit of a person getting in shape for when employment rebounded.

I can still remember Mike Francois running into my bedroom that morning, yelling, "Ed, Ed, I think we're having an earthquake!" I told him to stop running around and get under a doorway. Up until that point, Mike had been considering moving to California from Ohio to further his pro bodybuilding career.

People in California are warned to have certain supplies on hand in the event of an earthquake, including food and water. That was not one of my problems. I had plenty of both in the house with Mike at my home and two other bodybuilders. This was when distilled water was considered necessary for "pre-contest." It was only available in gallon jugs, so plenty of water was on hand. That trend continues to this day — at least as far as the size of the container is concerned. It's still a gallon jug, but now it's filled with regular water, probably containing an intra-workout mix of branched-chain amino acids (BCAAs).

Most of the gyms I was involved with opened at 5 a.m. Only one of the clubs, Gold's Gym Northridge, opened at 4:30 a.m., specifically at the request of Jake Steinfeld, then well-known for his *Body by Jake* show on CNN. The shaking started at 4:31 a.m. and, along with the immediate aftershocks, caused part of the roof structure to collapse at that club. A beam fell onto the gym floor, pinning and crushing the leg of one of the members who was on a flat bench.

Incredibly, he already had one broken leg, and the steel beam landed on his good leg and broke that as well. He sued, but the accident was declared a force majeure, an act of God — Fate — and he lost. But like the Venice gym, it would take over a year to recover because so many members' lives had been upended.

During this time, Gold's Gym Merchandising was involved in a lawsuit with its former licensees for clothing and accessories who had been terminated for insolvency. The earthquake caused the 10 Freeway to pancake in several places between the Westside and Downtown, so I had to take surface streets to the courthouse for five months.

When the jury decided in our favor in August 1994, I asked its members in the post-trial question and answer session what was important in making their decision. They said it was seeing Pete, Tim, or me every day in court fighting for our business. That drive had been difficult but worth it.

The other side made few appearances in person. They had basically rolled the dice, hoping for an easy win. But we were in the fight of our lives. That trial, along with decreased royalty revenue from the sportswear, cost the company nearly ten years of retained earnings.

Another immediate casualty of the earthquake was the interest in a second location. That search had started a few months earlier. The building we were looking at in the Playa del Rey section of LA — midway between Venice and LAX — was one of the hundreds of brick structures that suffered partial collapse during the earthquake. Pete said he thought it might be a sign that we shouldn't proceed with a second location. Tim and I agreed.

This highlights the problem of a business being too regional: having all its eggs in one basket. That was not our problem, as GGE's revenue was coming in from all over the US and, indeed, the world by this time. But then something happened: Two other large gym chains started buying up our US franchises.

They were two big regional players, and they owned all their clubs, which meant they had access to plenty of money. One was Town Sports International (TSI) on the East Coast. The other was 24 Hour Fitness on the West Coast.

Three forces were at work: First, the franchise system was

fourteen years old, and some of our owners wanted to sell or retire; second, it's less risky to buy an existing operation because you know what you were getting; and third, since this was something new in the fitness industry, the purchase price could often be less than building from scratch — a greenfield.

Realistically, a breakeven point for a new fitness facility could be reached in eighteen months, but that's an average. Sometimes it takes less time, but it could also take longer. Some gyms never make money. The beauty of buying an existing operation is that you know what you are getting, and you can cherry-pick the best.

Losing a gym is not like losing a fast-food operation. Once those markets would be lost, Gold's Gym would be out of the area for a long time. The only way to stem the loss was for GGF to find a way to buy the clubs themselves. But for that, it needed a lot of money.

INITIAL PUBLIC OFFERING

As we had learned during our first ten years of business trying to finance the clothing operation, banks are not in the business of loaning money unless you don't need it. One alternative to banks is an Initial Public Offering (IPO). It is one of the most effective ways for a struggling young company to gain access to money. However, the negative is that the founders may give up control.

One of the requirements for an IPO was having financial statements audited by one of the "Big Six" accounting firms. (There are now four.) This was enough of a prospect at one point that we hired one of those entities to audit our books. The outcome was that the individual doing the audit, George Jackson, became so enamored with our company that he left the firm and came onboard as our controller and eventually a Gold's Gym franchisee.

But when 24 Hour Fitness announced it would be doing an IPO, it raised that option again. We knew that their IPO would mean they would have even more money to damage our franchise operation. They later withdrew from the IPO because they were being investigated for RICO violations, but the initial threat was real.

Concurrently, the Gold's Gyms in Portland, Oregon, of which I was a board member and shareholder, decided to explore the possibility of raising money with its IPO. Like so many successful businesses, its problem was that it needed money to grow. Leaving too much money in a Chapter S corporation, or LLC, created a significant tax liability for the shareholders. Yet, there is the need to grow the business. It isn't all about greed. It's about survival. As they say, "If you're not growing, you're dying."

Other gym operations saw the initial success of Gold's Gym Portland and tried to duplicate it. Gyms are in the service business, and location and convenience are essential. A member may end up using only one location, but multiple locations are a big selling point.

Gold's Gym Portland had started innocently enough with one club in downtown Portland in 1989 in a spectacular building: a former screw factory with thirty-five-foot ceilings. Steve Rance, who with his wife, Carol, had been a wonderful partner in several of the gyms in California, had moved to Portland because of the special needs of their daughter. He called me and said the gyms he saw in Portland were so primitive they even had rope pulleys. He thought a Gold's Gym would work well there.

The initial capitalization was $100,000 from me and four sets of partners. (All the others were married couples.) We borrowed or leased the remaining start-up capital, mainly based on personal financial statements. But by 1994, Northwest Fitness, Inc. was operating five Gold's Gyms in the greater Portland area with gross revenue of $7 million and a profit of nearly $2 million. Even so, lending institutions were leery of loaning the company money, so Northwest Fitness, Inc. began looking into an IPO. However, they discovered that while the concept was fine, what was needed was a critical mass of at least $25 million in gross revenue.

Portland would have to combine with one or more other Gold's Gym operators. The largest group of eleven in Dallas and Houston, owned by Bruce Nickel and Mike Schankenberg, had over $25 million. But then 24 Hour Fitness bought the operation.

As a result, we asked Piper Jaffray Securities to make a presentation at our 1995 convention showing how the owners might become part of something bigger via an IPO. It would help raise capital to grow while allowing owners some short-term liquidity and increased long-term valuation of their businesses. Many of the Gold's Gym owners who were being bought were leaving a lot on the table by selling for too small a multiple of EBITDA ("Earnings Before Interest, Taxes, Depreciation, and Amortization," a standard way of measuring financial performance).

With the help of several firms like Piper Jaffray, we explored the IPO option in different parts of the country with a dozen or more Gold's Gym operators. There were a half dozen meetings in places like Kansas City, Omaha, and even at Piper Jaffray's headquarters in Minneapolis. A short time after that meeting, Charlie Lannin, who had left Piper Jaffray by then, came to me to say that he represented a group of Gold's Gyms still interested in doing an IPO. But one of the main restrictions of the financier, Citicorp, would be a right of first refusal to purchase corporate should it ever come up for sale. I knew Pete would never agree to this as it would limit our options, so I said no.

Lannin then came back with this question: "What would it take to buy corporate?"

I felt obligated to bring this question to Pete since he was the majority shareholder. Pete surprised me and said that given market conditions (as he saw them), he would sell Gold's Gym Enterprises, Inc. and related companies for $40 million.

To make that number palatable for the various suitors, I broke it down: $15 million for the business and $25 million for the brand. It represented a very high multiple (for a gym business) of thirteen times EBITDA, but the buyer was getting a brand: Gold's Gym.

What is Coke without the Coca-Cola brand? Sugar water.

Gold's Gym was just another gym with weights, but it was the authority on fitness for thirty-four years. There was a great deal of equity in the name. In 1999, Omnibus Research did a telephone research study of two thousand US consumers and found that Gold's Gym is the "clear and present top-of-mind brand awareness leader in the health club/gym category. Among 18 to 34-year-olds, 80% were aware of Gold's Gym."

Along with our franchises, we had branded a unique service in the health club industry. We developed a relationship and emotional bond with our clientele through this branding, enhancing their trust and confidence in the gym. This high customer loyalty leads to better retention rates for our existing members and means a lower cost of acquiring new ones.

But trying to get that many entrepreneurs to work together was not easy. And it was also the dot-com era, when valuations were ridiculous for high-tech companies. Companies that had never made a profit were selling for astronomical multiples. They were high-tech. Gold's Gym was the ultimate low-tech. It doesn't get much more basic than a twenty-five-pound weight plate. But Martha Stewart and the WWE (World Wrestling Federation at the time) were going public, so why not Gold's Gym?

A public company would ensure that the entrepreneurs of Gold's Gym would own Gold's Gym. But the problem with doing an IPO then for a health club was there were no existing stocks on Wall Street whose performance could be used as a guide in appraising Gold's Gym. Unfortunately, unlike today when Life Time Fitness, Beachbody, Xponential Fitness, F45, and iFIT Health and Fitness have all gone public, Bally Total Fitness and Sports Club LA were the only publicly traded health club companies, and their business models were different. But by 1998, their stocks were at record highs.

Nevertheless, Paul Grymkowski reached out to Sports Club to see if we could become part of an existing publicly traded company.

The Sports Club Company had just gone public in 1994, generating $42 million in capital. Mike Talla, its president, said the stock offering made The Sports Club Co. the first high-end club to go public.

Thirteen clubs were included in the stock offering: two Sports Clubs, six Spectrum Clubs, and five Sports Connection Clubs. The three chains had a combined total of about 38,000 members.

Paul Grymkowski thought he had struck a deal with them. It was even announced on September 17, 1997, in the *LA Times* but was abruptly canceled.

In a surprise move, two years later, Sports Club sold the Spectrum Clubs to Brentwood Associates for $49 million in September 1999, seemingly concentrating on the high-end market with "urban country clubs."

After that option failed, I reached out to Bally.

BALLY TOTAL FITNESS

Bally had been spun off of Bally Manufacturing in January 1996. It had not been doing well, showing a profit of $800,000 on revenue of $694 million while the casinos had an operating profit of $104 million on revenue of $619 million.

Bally had a bad reputation with its $9 memberships – so bad that Equifax stopped reporting delinquencies.

The industry had changed a lot during the previous fourteen years, but Bally had not changed with it.

In August 1995, Bally tried franchising by offering up to ten percent of its 340 clubs for purchase by outsiders. But its franchise fees were outrageous: an upfront fee of $40,000, three percent of that entity's annual revenues for a royalty fee, four percent toward an advertising fund, and eight percent for various Bally-run "backroom services" such as bookkeeping and collections, something at which they were notorious. A total of fifteen percent. By comparison, today's major fitness chain franchises are charging around seven percent. Still too high, in my opinion, but half of what Bally hoped to get.

Following a bad first couple of years after being spun off, Lee Hillman, age forty, a former CFO and treasurer at Bally, was put in charge in 1997. In October of that year, he announced plans to follow a "dry club" model, eliminating pools, running tracks, and racquetball courts, redefining its position in the marketplace as "fitness only."

By March 1998, Bally had 320 clubs in twenty-seven states and Canada and was labeled "the largest (and only nationwide) commercial operator of fitness centers in the US." But Gold's Gym, with its franchisees, actually had more locations in more states: forty-six.

I wrote to Lee in November 1997 to suggest a merger of the two entities, something I thought would benefit both. But Lee felt we wanted too much for our business and didn't want to meet and talk. Yet, four years later, in April 2001, Bally purchased Crunch Fitness's nineteen facilities for $90 million in cash and a stock-for-stock merger.

Doug Levine, the founder of Crunch Fitness, said, "We are

confident that Bally will foster our creativity and excellence with greater resources and more Crunch-branded facilities to capitalize on the strong growth potential of our unique, consumer-driven concepts."

A year after that, Lee Hillman quit, and Bally Fitness went into bankruptcy twice and then finally out of existence. Bally's share price had gone from about $30 to twenty-two cents a share in 2004. The company was delisted in 2007. When it went into bankruptcy the second and final time in 2008, it had $45 million in cash and $800 million in debt, on which it defaulted.

During this four-and-a-half-year period, I sent out 175 packages to different entities, hoping that one of them would be the white knight Gold's Gym needed to stop the bleeding, the loss of our gyms. Our FedEx bill hit a high of $15,000 one month.

Tim was involved in some of those meetings and gave me full support. We often spent time working with a group only to be low-balled at the end after an all-out effort. The potential buyer might have said something like, "It looks to me like you have no choice but to sell to us," after first leading us on and then giving us a low number. When that would happen, Tim and I would say we did have a choice and get up and leave.

Most of the people we met lacked integrity. In the back of my mind, I often thought of a favorite quote from Warren Buffett, "The Oracle of Omaha": "Somebody once said that in looking for people to hire, you look for three qualities: integrity, intelligence, and energy. And if you don't have the first, the other two will kill you. You think about it; it's true."

This was also a difficult time at corporate. I felt like the shepherd crying wolf so often that no one believed the sale of the business was real. This uncertainty was enough to create much turmoil within the company. Pete even proposed restructuring the company in 1997, giving department heads more say in how the company was being run, and a PR company was hired to make the announcement.

Between January 1997 and January 1998, GGF had a net gain of three gyms. The pressure was on to do something. At the end of 1998, we tried to put together a "poof IPO" by combining a dozen franchises to create a single company that would go public — poof! — the moment it is created.

On August 14, 1998, Pete, Tim, and I signed a letter of intent with Platinum Fitness to pursue this plan. A letter was sent to all franchise owners explaining the benefits and offering them a chance to participate with the following objectives: an opportunity to grow, a way to gain liquidity, and a more viable option to exit their business in the future.

There were 185 Gold's Gyms in the hands of fifty-five companies. We had some wonderful operators in different parts of the country, which was essential as it would not be considered a regional offering. Seventy of the more mature gyms in this group represented candidates for going public. The average square footage was around 22,500 square feet, with gross revenue averaging $1,350,000 ($112,500 per month) and net income before taxes at $337,500, or twenty-five percent of gross revenue.

But IPO activity in September 1998 was the lowest in twenty years. Piper Jaffray couldn't commit to going public, and some owners did not want to be part of the deal if going public wasn't an assured reality. Piper Jaffray had been recently purchased by US Bank — Bally's bank — and wasn't high on health clubs. 24 Hour Fitness had also missed its window.

With the delay, other suitors were coming out of the woodwork. By March 1998, I was dealing with eight. The last deal of $40 million in cash and stock fell through at the end of 1998, so that number turned out not to be real.

On March 1, 1999, we received an offer of $24 million. The next day, Houlihan Lokey Howard & Zinkin made an offer of $28 million. But then a group I had been dealing with in 1997 — just before the submission from The Sports Club — came back with an offer of $32 million.

KIRK AND JOHN GALIANI

From 1994 to 1999, one franchise headed up by the Galiani brothers — John and Kirk — experienced explosive growth.

Kirk was born in 1965, the same year Gold's Gym was founded. John was two years younger. They had a background in real estate, which no doubt helped their rapid rise. Their chain of Gold's Gym locations in the greater Washington, DC, area reached a total of eleven in a short time.

Most importantly, they wanted to do something with their business, and they had met someone who could show them how to do that: Tim Spillane, a thirty-two-year-old director at PricewaterhouseCoopers Securities (PWC), the investment banking subsidiary of the giant accounting firm.

Combining the more mature gyms in this group with what GGE could contribute resulted in a size that met the critical mass requirement of at least $50 million in gross revenue to attract a private equity partner. Most importantly, ninety-five percent of their income was from monthly dues collected electronically. Had this not been the case, I don't think the deal would have happened.

Before the wide use of this technology around 1995, gyms always been suspect because they were a cash business. The profitability of both entities was also good as measured by EBITDA. GGE's combination of companies was thirty-seven and a half percent; the Galiani's group was forty-one percent.

We had our first meeting with PWC on March 29, 1999. By late May, a young and talented team from PWC was already beginning to contact investors and lenders.

Pete, Tim, and I signed a letter of intent to sell GGE on April 21, 1999. A little over three months later, on June 30, Lior Samuelson of PWC informed Pete that they had selected Brockway Moran & Partners, located in Boca Raton, Florida, as the financial partner.

Brockway operated a $200 million private equity fund; principal investors included Goldman Sachs & Co., Brinson Partners, PPM Worldwide, General Electric Capital, and Donaldson, Lufkin, & Jenrette. Financing for the transaction was to be provided by Heller Financial, Inc., a Chicago-based commercial finance company.

Kathy Mankin, the Brockway Moran partner I initially dealt with, was the only woman I presented to in my four-and-a-half-year search. Along with Kathy, the other Brockway associate I first met was Mark A. Eidemeuller, who coincidentally had fond memories of being a member of a Gold's Gym in Pittsburgh when he was in school.

Haters made negative comments about the nature of the deal because the Galiani brothers had a last name ending in a vowel, and Brockway Moran was based in Florida. It's almost funny if it weren't so sad.

Derek Barton used to joke at our conventions that all the East Coast gym owners had last names ending in vowels — and though that was mostly true, the Galiani brothers were far from that world. And even though Brockway was located in Florida, not in New York City or some other financial hub, they were a legitimate private equity firm handling billions of dollars in various funds — and they had integrity.

Just as there were haters in the bodybuilding world, so, too, there were haters in the wings, even for the Gold's Gym deal.

BROCKWAY MORAN & PARTNERS

Peter Brockway and his team came to Venice to "kick the tires" in July 1999. He was coming from Florida and hadn't done many West Coast deals, so LA was relatively new to him, as he showed by his first comment to me when he walked into our Venice office: "We sure lucked out on the weather."

I replied, "Actually, it's like this every day."

It was the perfect summer weather: seventy-five during the day, fifty-five at night, and plenty of sunlight, what so many people think about when they hear "sunny Southern California."

His remark brought back memories of my getting off the plane in 1975 and noticing that the baggage claim at LAX was stainless steel cylinders out in the open, off the tarmac. What a concept, I thought: The weather outside is the same as the weather inside, so there's no need for an enclosure. And indeed, none of my homes in LA, nor the Venice gym, had air conditioning.

Brockway Moran & Partners invested mainly in entities catering to the consumer, but Gold's Gym was still unusual. When I walked through the gym with Peter, he said, "I feel so insecure."

I said, "Trust me, you're the most secure person in here."

It was one of those *Wizard of Oz,* man-behind-the-curtain moments. I was reminded of Bob Paris's first book, *Gorilla Suit,* which is how he described all the muscle he put on.

Peter had on his suit and tie. I had on my blue blazer — one of six I owned — and a tie. That was my "body armor," my suit that I wore almost every day for twenty years, so much so that in the early '80s, when no one knew my name, I garnered the nickname "Blue Blazer," which ironically went on to be the moniker used by professional wrestler Owen Hart.

When an impending sale was announced on July 27, 1999, at the annual convention in Las Vegas at the Rio Hotel, many still didn't believe it would happen, including our outside accounting and legal advisors. Pete gave me roughly thirty days to get the deal done.

I returned to Venice after the convention and gave the merger and acquisition (M&A) attorney at Hambrecht & Quist in Orange County I had been working with a call. When I told him the required timeline, the attorney said he couldn't do it, that he was too busy. It was the height of the dot-com boom. I told him he was fired.

I got out my Rolodex and spun it around, looking for attorneys. My fingers ended up on the card of a lawyer I knew at Buchalter, Nemer, Fields & Younger. As the third-largest law firm in LA at the time, I thought they would have someone to help me. I called that person up and asked if they did M&A work. The attorney said he didn't but that the firm had someone who did, and he connected me with Bill Jarblum.

When we started talking, I asked Bill to tell me a little bit about himself, just like I did when I would hire someone. When Bill got to the part about how his parents had fled Nazi Germany, I told him he could stop. We quickly had a meeting of the minds.

At times, I can have a sort of "reverse prejudice." Bill asked if I was one of those good Catholic boys who likes to surround himself with Jewish accountants and attorneys. I confessed and said yes and asked how many were on his team. Bill said eleven of the twelve attorneys who would be working on this were Jewish.

I asked Bill how much of a retainer he would need to get started. Bill said $10,000. I sent $15,000, and we were off and running. Less than four weeks later, I met Bill at LAX to fly to O'Hare in Chicago to get the deal done.

When I showed up at the sidewalk outside American Airlines's terminal four at LAX, Bill was there with his wife and their tiny white poodle. I was surprised but amused. Bill explained to me that he always traveled with his wife and dog. He had also arranged all the travel. I'm not sure whether Bill used frequent flyer miles to upgrade, but the three of us were in business class and on our way to O'Hare.

When we arrived in downtown Chicago, we were greeted with the sight of hundreds of life-sized, painted fiberglass cows that were part of the "Cow Parade" art installation all over the city. The Ritz-Carlton would be home for a week, another upgrade I had not expected. Although having worked on the design of several hotels in my past, I could only marvel at how complacent the management was as it looked like the hotel had not been refurbished or updated in decades.

Despite that disappointment, I only wish I could have spent

more time in the hotel room, as the days at the then Sears Tower were long. Because of that, everyone was told to dress casually. When Bill and I walked out of the elevator on the fifty-ninth floor dressed in casual black, I heard one of the receptionists proclaim, "You can sure tell this is an LA deal." I guess we had dressed appropriately.

Some fifty attorneys and accountants were on that floor in three of the largest conference rooms I have ever seen. They would work nearly a week of days and some all-nighters to complete the merger and sale. Brockway Moran's Chicago law firm, Latham & Watkins, played host for the Galiani's attorneys, who had come from Atlanta. And then there was Bill and me. The rest of Bill's team was back in LA.

It should have been an enjoyable time for me, but Pete was making life difficult — with Paul's encouragement. Pete didn't like the non-compete clause — or at least the number of pages in the agreement, which, with all the exhibits, was nearly three and a half inches thick.

It had never occurred to me that after twenty years, Pete would now want to work or be involved with something that would compete with the new company, which was to be called Gold's Gym International (GGI). Pete told me that if I could get that portion of the agreement, the non-compete, down to three pages, he would sign it. I did.

The project was given the code name "Hercules." Tim Spillane, Stuart Layzell, and Masha Korunsky represented PricewaterhouseCoopers Securities. Peter Brockway, Kathy Mankin, and Mark Eidemueller were there for Brockway Moran & Partners, and Chris Rossi for Pepper Hamilton LLP's law firm. William Avery, Ben Muraskin, and John Shannon were with Alston Bird. This Atlanta law firm represented the Galiani group of Kirk and John Galiani, Jeff Skeen, and Ross Byington. Tim Eichenlaub represented Heller Financial, which was providing financing.

It was the beginning of the internet, and communication was being done through email. I remember Kathy Mankin, like a patient teacher or den mother in one of our first organizational meetings, instructing "us boys" on the danger of hitting "reply all" when one meant to hit "reply." It was all new to me, and I appreciated the instruction.

Pete's brother, Paul, was making matters difficult. Even though he was only a one percent shareholder, he was in Pete's ear. During one of those critical last hours, Paul was with Pete and Tim in the Venice office on speakerphone with me and Bill in Chicago. Paul brought in a former partner in the David Delehant law firm, which Pete, Tim, and I had used for most of the previous twenty years.

Two years earlier, he had left the firm, claiming that David was guilty of malfeasance, but I could not determine what that was. It seemed he was just trying to get our business, which was typically over half a million dollars in some years.

Paul Grymkowski had a similar personal reason – again, in my opinion, his job. He was making things very difficult.

Paul was nearly apocalyptic about the looming "Y2K" problem many talked about, the transition to the next century. Many thought it would be a disaster, that businesses would cease to run smoothly. Spoiler alert: The world transitioned with very little problem.

Bill had wisely sent over one member of his team to be there in person. Pete drove to the meeting from his home in Victorville, which can take two hours, even with light traffic. At first, Pete was reluctant to go into Venice. But when I divided how much money he was about to make by the mileage and came up with a dollar amount per mile that he would risk losing if he didn't make the trip, Pete changed his mind.

THE BEST LITTLE WHOREHOUSE IN TIJUANA

Pete came into the meeting wearing a T-shirt from his favorite house of ill repute in Tijuana. Incredibly enough, the young attorney from LA's large Iranian Jewish community whom Bill had sent was familiar with the very same place. They immediately bonded over that, especially when the attorney told Pete all the numbers he knew regarding that particular business.

Meanwhile, Paul's counsel, who was the epitome of a WASP attorney, picked away at minutiae in the contract, which Pete's newfound friend quickly shot down, much to Pete's delight. I think, had it not been for that Tijuana connection, the deal would never have happened. That was a heart-stopping moment.

The document was officially signed on Saturday, August 21, 1999. The baton, or dumbbell, had been passed. The sale document with exhibits was six hundred pages. It was quite a difference from the ten-page document – including exhibits – that Pete, Denny Doyle, and I had signed twenty and a half years earlier to buy Gold's Gym, Inc. from Ken Sprague. The business had grown and gotten more complicated.

Joe Gold said he could never have dreamt that the business could have been sold for such a high number and said that Pete, Tim, and I had built Gold's Gym into what it was at the time of the sale: a great company. "You know, in a strange way, they made me famous," he said. He also said that "in any business, you get to a certain level and can't go higher. You need other people to help you reach the next level."

It was nice of him to say that. There was even a time when we entertained combining the two chains, but it was too late as many of our franchisees were competing with a World Gym in their home market.

After an exhausting week in Chicago, I returned to Venice that weekend. The following Monday morning, I was in our accounting office with Jennifer Buehler, our controller, and Joel Morse, our outside accountant, to receive notice that the money from the sale had been wired into GGE's account at City National Bank in Beverly Hills. This is the magic moment in selling a business that some compare to having sex.

Once the money transfers hit, Joel supervised the disbursement of funds into the bank accounts of Pete, Tim, Paul, and me. I indeed would describe it as one of the most amazing feelings I have ever had.

It wasn't until the following Friday — five days later — that I heard from Pete by phone. Pete's first words were basically, "Where's my money?" but in much more colorful language. I told Pete it had been in his bank account since Monday. Where had he been? "Tijuana" was Pete's response.

Paul Grymkowksi and Rich Minzer, Paul's assistant, were the only two employees who decided not to come on board with the new owners. In the final sale document, they claimed to have an agreement with GGF to be paid commissions on the renewal of franchises, whether or not GGF employed them. We denied there was any such agreement.

More than that, they sued for pay they felt they were owed, namely future commissions — commissions they wouldn't have been there to service. Tim and I thought the lawsuit was baseless and that Pete should take care of his brother. But in the end, we agreed to pay a settlement to see it go away.

With the two of them gone, I became president of franchising, which would mean the longest hours and most travel I had ever done in my life. With my associate, Kent Lenhoff, we would sell three times the number of franchises Paul and Rich would typically sell in a year. Brockway Moran & Partners would add nearly 170 more franchises during the next five years, 105 of those added during the eighteen months Kent and I worked together.

I would take heat for some of the people we would give a franchise to who did not seem financially qualified. But I had learned that money wasn't everything, especially with the celebrity owners. I was looking for passionate people who would work hard to achieve their dream.

After the failure of Jermaine Jackson's Gold's Gym in London, I licensed a British subject whose family had come from

India. Not exactly your stereotypical British citizen, but it was the Indian British who seemed to be the ones in London who were willing to work long hours and understood the service business.

After a year as president of Gold's Gym Franchising, Gene LaMott, who had been one of my partners in the Gold's Gym locations in the greater Portland area and was now president of GGI, asked me to step down. He said I didn't know gym franchising. I told him, "I believe I only invented it."

Gene told me they had hired Ben Amante, who had previously worked in franchising at Midas Muffler. I asked him when the last time he bought a muffler was. Gene and others after him would make the same mistake: hiring people from outdated or defunct industries and business models.

I'll never forget what my grandfather told me when I told him how in awe I was of him for having been vice president in charge of operations when he ended his career at Union Pacific Railroad. This position made him responsible for the lives of over sixty thousand workers.

"Son, the smart ones left for the airlines," he said.

They couldn't replace me overnight, so it wasn't until May 2001 when I finally left work at GGF. But Gene and Ben made it as difficult as possible for me to work, like deciding to remodel the offices or take a year to reimburse me for travel expenses.

Gene was one of my last houseguests during this time, staying in my last home in Venice for almost a year. I later learned that he violated his employment agreement with Brockway Moran, as he was supposed to relocate with his family to LA from Portland. Instead, he chose to fly back to Portland on Thursday and return to LA the following Sunday, a routine he would have during most of his time with GGI.

TRT HOLDINGS BUYS GOLD'S GYM INTERNATIONAL

Brockway Moran's plan had always been to grow GGI and then sell it in five years, which is precisely what they did.

Though I was one of seven members of the board Brockway Moran had established to head up the Gold's Gym investment, I did not have a vote in the sale of GGI. It was left to a separate committee headed by Gene.

My preference was for a group working with Tony Robbins. The mind-body connection while exercising had always fascinated me, and Tony Robbins could undoubtedly have been the person to explore that. It can be as simple as the person working the front desk telling the member the benefit they gained from the visit to the gym that day. But the Robbins' bid — one of seventeen — was rejected by Gene in favor of a group out of Texas.

The *LA Times* does a terrific job covering the entertainment industry but tends to overlook a lot of local, home-grown businesses. In the twenty-five years I was part of Gold's Gym, I only remember three other articles mentioning the Venice gym or its franchise business.

The fourth time was in the business section on Tuesday, June 15, 2004, with the headline: "OWNER OF OMNI HOTELS TO BUY GOLD'S GYM." The article began with, "The owner of Omni Hotels is hoping to add some new muscle to Gold's Gym International Inc., the fitness chain made famous by a bodybuilder named Arnold Schwarzenegger."

The article went on to report incorrectly that, "When Joe Gold sold the gym in 1979, it was to two other bodybuilders and an architect. 'It is a highly fragmented industry, and no company runs more gyms than Gold's,' Terry Philen, TRT's CFO, said. TRT Holdings, based in Irving, Texas, was formed in 1989 by Texas oil explorers Reese Rowling and his son, Robert."

Supposedly, billionaire Robert Rowling was playing cards with three of his friends when they agreed to put in around $40 million each to buy Gold's Gym for $158 million. Rowling eventually bought out his partners and involved some of his family in running the gyms. GGI then went through a succession of CEOs, seven over sixteen years: LaMott (2004-2006), Schnabel (2006-2008), Weaver (2008-2009), Snow (2009-2011), Watkins (2011-2013, Bean (2013-2016), and Zeitsiff (2017-2020).

They had the resumes but not the passion. Two of the executives were even charged with sexual harassment, one of whom went to jail for domestic violence.

They also weren't part of a team. They were just CEOs. Peter Drucker's *The Practice of Management* described the ideal CEO as an outside person, an inside person, and a person of action. Not one person but a leadership team. Maybe Pete, Tim, and I were that team. And though many of them went to prestigious business schools where I'm sure there were courses in creating a brand, Gold's Gym seemed to be less in the news than when Pete, Tim, and I were behind it.

There wasn't one person on TRT's board of directors with any history in the gym business. It was like WeWork not having someone with experience in real estate on its board, which was the case — and a recipe for disaster.

People would joke that our quarterly newsletters only came out two or three times a year. Still, in hindsight, they were a better means of communication than what TRT did during the blossoming of the internet and email.

In a 1996 newsletter, Derek Barton, who was then our director of public relations, advertising, and promotions, announced that Gold's Gym was coming to the internet, where "over 80 million people have access to the World Wide Web, and this number continues to grow at an astounding rate."

When Pete, Tim, and I sold in 1999, only seventeen percent of our owners even had email addresses. By 2004, when I was still an owner in some Gold's Gym locations, I would have welcomed weekly, even daily, email blasts from corporate. Instead, I was lucky to receive one email every few months.

During the seventeen years TRT owned GGI, I only received one phone call from someone in the corporate offices, and that was to ask if Gold's Gym had ever given Hulk Hogan an award. We had. I think that because I was so closely associated with the bodybuilding community, I had been ostracized, and now they wanted to give an award to Hulk Hogan, whose life by then had become one of those "celebrity nightmares."

In addition, I was banned from Gold's Gym Venice because I had raised such a stink in the pro shop regarding the quality of the merchandise. Many of the products still had old-fashioned labels in them, the kind that drive people crazy by scratching them in the back of the neck. In today's marketplace, everyone who is anyone silkscreens that information on the clothing. What does it matter if it adds another ten cents to the cost if you're charging between $20 and $30 for a T-shirt that can still cost under $3 to make?

Some people thought of us as the Three Stooges. We thought we were the Three Muscleteers. I was always very proud of what the three of us had accomplished but often wondered what a Harvard or Stanford MBA could do with the business. As it would turn out, with the hindsight of eighteen years after selling: not much. Some would say it takes a lifetime to overcome a Harvard education. Maybe they are right — perhaps that's one reason people like Bill Gates, Matt Damon, and Mark Zuckerberg left early.

It's a fact that many "C" students go on to hire "A" students to fulfill their dreams. Put your energies where your passion is, and let that passion become contagious to others around you. We shared one common goal of making Gold's Gym the very best it could be. Pete and Tim barely finished high school. My college degree was in architecture.

Tim and I were an effective team in managing the company's money; we knew the numbers. Given the weather in LA, membership income didn't vary as much as it did in other areas of the country with extreme weather, so we were fortunate as far as wild swings in revenue were concerned.

Before electronic payments, cash flow was a primary concern for owners. Monthly dues changed everything because even if there was a blizzard that closed the gym for a day or two, drafts from the members still went through, removing the cyclical nature of membership income.

Every Tuesday, our controller, Jennifer, would give us a printout of the payables. Tim and I would go over it with her and decide who or what was most important to pay. Jennifer would often remark that it was a waste of paper to give us the bank balances because Tim and I always seemed to have a good intuitive feel of where we were with the various accounts. Because each company was a separate legal entity, they had their own bank accounts, so her job was more complicated.

On Wednesday, Jennifer would bring us the checks to sign. Two signatures were needed, something we never gave up except with payroll, when a payroll service took over. On Thursday, the checks were mailed out. It worked.

It doesn't matter how great a business is if you don't manage the cash flow. Many times, even up until the end, Pete, Tim, and I would hold our paychecks to help with that.

Gold's Gym International declared bankruptcy in 2020. The pandemic was given as the reason, but GGI had made many bad decisions before taking this drastic action. Among other things, it had raised royalties to a percentage that effectively amounted to a sevenfold increase for most franchise owners. As a result of that action, they lost hundreds of great operators.

Once a gym franchise is lost, it will likely be a long time before another new one can open successfully. One possible reason to buy a business might be that the buyer thought the company could be run better and add value.

One would think that when buying an existing franchise operation, the obvious way to grow and add value would be to buy up existing, successful franchisees when the time to sell arrives. But rather than purchasing successful owners who wanted to sell and retire, TRT bought non-Gold's Gyms, even oversaturating several markets with too many locations.

The Gold's Gyms in Nebraska I was involved with dropped the name because of the high royalties. They became Blue Moon Fitness. GGI bought some clubs in that market to compete. They lost millions of dollars doing that.

Before the COVID-19 quarantine, GGI had begun selling off corporate locations that were losing money, including those they had purchased in Omaha and then another ten in St. Louis.

During the sixteen years that TRT Holdings was the caretaker of the Gold's Gym brand, they had a net loss of twenty-four clubs. Gold's Gym had gone from 704 locations in 2004 to 680 in 2020, with four hundred of those in foreign countries. They were investors who had no vision.

GGI had planned to sell its assets to TRT Holdings for $80 million through a chapter 11 bankruptcy plan and not an auction. But the gym's creditors came forward and asked the judge for a "market check" to seek better offers for the assets. TRT then became a stalking horse, or lead, bidder but was unsuccessful.

In October 2020, the bankruptcy court accepted the high bid of $100 million for GGI. It came from RSG, the company headed by Rainer Schaller, the founder of McFit Gyms in Europe, the one who said that Gold's Gym Venice inspired him to open his first McFit Gym in Germany in 1997.

Gold's Gym had indeed come full circle.

REFLECTIONS

Ray Kroc said, "If a corporation has two executives who think alike, one of them is unnecessary."

That certainly wasn't our problem. Pete, Tim, and I were entirely different from one another. I had book smarts; Tim and Pete had street smarts. I never missed an election; Tim and Pete never voted.

We never socialized outside the business. It wasn't until after we sold in 1999 that Tim and I visited Pete at his home in Victorville, and that was because Pete had just had triple bypass open-heart surgery.

I only saw Tim at one of his homes once, when his house and property constituted the third largest zoo in LA County, something that eventually made him have to move.

I had never married. Pete had been married three times with three children. Tim had been married four times and had six children. As Tim would say: "Ed, you have your gyms, I have my wives and kids — and animals."

Some people thought Pete, Tim, and I were greedy — always taking, never giving — but by charging only $3,500 to $5,000 a year for a franchise, we were being generous. We created a lot of wealth, a lot of newly minted millionaires. There were quite a few Gold's Gym owners who made more than either Pete, Tim, or me. I knew this for a fact. Our gyms had combined revenue of over $1 billion with their three million-plus members.

We, along with our franchises, could be proud of what we were doing, how we were making our money. We provided a service, creating a clean, well-equipped place to share with other human beings to make them healthier and happier about how they felt about themselves, perhaps adding years to their lives while improving the quality of life of their years.

This has been my mission statement from day one: "Nothing pleases me more than a group of adults who can work together, provide a good service, make some money, and have some fun doing it."

If you're not making money, it isn't fun. And since our twenty-five-pound plate isn't any different from their twenty-five-pound plate in this business, service is essential. It's a simple business but not an easy one. It's as simple as treating every member as we would be treated — again, the Golden Rule.

This was the mission statement Pete, Tim, and I had for Gold's Gym: "To enhance the quality of life in the communities we serve through our fitness philosophy, facility programs, and products and to instill in the lives of people everywhere the value of health and fitness."

While Pete, Tim, and I were a somewhat dysfunctional team, we somehow managed to hold it together for twenty years and grow the chain to 534 clubs before selling the first time to Brockway Moran. Perhaps it was always asking what is good for Gold's Gym that made us successful. We tried to create a win-win situation, and our business relationships were like family, like our relationships with the gym members. We each had our own lives but one common goal with Gold's Gym.

Pete, Tim, and I had a tradition of caring. We just wanted to build the best gym possible for our members. We started with a local, hardcore gym that happened to have been in Venice Beach during the golden age of bodybuilding. We ended up becoming the Mecca.

VISITORS

I did not start out with the goal of creating the first gym franchise of its kind. But once started, it was my goal that during the twenty-five years me and my two partners owned Gold's Gym, it would be the largest gym chain in the world. I did it with the help of my houseguests, who make Gold's Gym Venice the Mecca and the most famous gym in the world.

Aalsma, Alex
Abadie, Brian
Abitz, Alvin
Albrechrt, Achim
Alexander, Kristian
Allen, Erin
Almeida, Paulo
Anthony, Derek
Antorino, Mike
Apperson, Lee
Arntz, Jason
Ballenger, Alex
Barnhart, Logan
Bartlett, JB
Baker, Brad
Batista, Paco
Baye, David
Beard, Chris
Beaver, Doug
Becht, Marcus
Becht, Monica
Beckrich, Brandon
Benagli, Thomas
Bengtsson, Ulf
Bennet, Chris
Bereckzki, Krisztian
Bergsma, Mike
Berkankamp, Glenn
Billow, Dave
Black, Rick
Blanchard, Caleb
Blatz, Heather
Blatz, John
Blauhut, Eli
Blewitt, D'Marko
Blount, Greg
Boeving, Christian
Bohn, Lambert
Bohnstedt, Steve
Bognar, Greg
Bolen, John
Boonzaayer, Martin
Boos, John
Boozell, Derrick
Borden, Steve
Boucher, Kenny
Bourlett, David
Bozich, Joe
Braun, PJ
Breznik, Tony
Brown, Matt
Bucci, Joe
Bunce, Casey
Burzacott, Matt
Butler, Richard
Caldarelli, John
Callaghan, Sid
Campbell, Leisa
Cambra, Bill
Caputo, Dean
Cardillo, Steve
Carmichael, Leigh
Catapanto, Gianluca
Cellini, Chris
Cellini, Shea
Cena, John
Cena, Matthew
Centopani, Evan
Champagne, John
Chancey, Mel
Chase, Bill
Cheeney, Richard
Cherrier, Martial

Christie, Kevin
Christman, Steve
Church, Dan
Ciotti, Rick
Cline, Matt
Clothier, Barry
Cockel, Gene
Combs, Kyle
Comeaux, Greg
Commerford, Vinny
Connell, Brian
Cook, Chris
Corbell, Craig
Coulombe, Louis
Cowan, Dudley
Cowgill, Allison
Cowgill, John
Creador, Scott
Creighton, Steve
Crull, Brian
Cutler, Jay
Cutler, Kerry
Cupae, Sam
Cutri, John
Cziurlock, Roland
Dagen, Jeff
Datiz, Javier
Davey, Bill
Davis, Shawn
DeAngelis, Joe
Dearth, David
Dearth, Doug
DeFendis, John
Demairs, Michele
DeMayo, Paul
DeMelo, James
Demetriou, Chris
Demetriou, Con
DeMey, Berry
DeMora, Shane
Denison, Steve
Dennis, Ralf
Dente, Gerard
Dente, Linda
DePolo, John
Dillon, Pat
Dodson, Chris
Dorsey, David
Dreer, Billy
Duffy, Chris
Defresne, Matthew
DuVall, Mat
Dwelle, Jeff
Eakman, Sam
Ebel, Bruce
Ebel, Suzi
El Sonmbaty, Nasser
Elliot, Joel
Ellis, Aaron
Enders, Dave
Erickson, Brett
Erickson, Christer
Erpelding, Mark
Everson, Cory
Everson, Jeff
Federal, Alexander
Feroce, Seth
Ferrante, Michael
Ferris, Dick
Fisher, Dave
Fisher, Ken
Fol, Bob
Fortier, Julie
Fortier, Patrix
Francois, Mike
Frankly, Dan
Freeman, Jeramy
Freeman, Kim
Fritz, Roman
Fromm, Erik
Fury, Remy
Fux, JP
Gable, Denny
Galiani, Kirk
Galiani, John
Garceau, Tyler
Gaspari, Rich
Gay, Donny
Gay, Francois
Genkinger, Chris
Genkinger, Kay
Gentle, Marty
Gille, Lance
Glonek, Paul
Gloor, Andreas
Gloor, Joey
Godderz, Jessie
Golias, Craig
Golini, Jeff
Gosch, Bob
Gosch, Kay
Goss, Gary
Gothager, Stephan
Graham, Brian
Greene, Sean
Griner, Chad
Groux, Claude

Grundy, Guy
Grymkowksi, Pete
Hagan, Scott
Hagan, Steve
Haik, Ryan
Hall, Kevin
Hall, Melissa
Hallo, Debbie
Hamblet, Jim
Hampton, James
Hans, Joey
Hanscomb, Chris
Hansen, Camron
Hansen, Frank Harald
Hansen, Thomas
Hartl, Stephan
Harrison, Ian
Harrop, Robert
Hatcher, Dale
Hayes, Pat
Heim, Randy
Helgessen, Samuel
Hellwig, Jim
Henderson, Grant
Henneberry, Steve
Henriksen, Gordon
Hernon, Phil
Hildebrand, Frank
Hildreth, Mark
Hill, Daniel
Hillier, Robin
Hillman, Jordan
Hnatyschak, John
Hoffman, David
Hindalov, Danny
Hollibasugh, Brad
Holstine, Joe
Homka, Brian
Holston, Joe
Holston, Jon
Horvath, Istvan
Horvath, Kiss
Howell, Terry
Huber, Jurgen
Huber, Karin
Hubon, Mike
Hughes, David
Idziak, Ryan
Insko, Jim
Jackson, Michael
Jansiewicz, Austin
Janszen, Paul
Jarvis, Cari
Jaudes, Michael
Jewell, Todd
Joba, Elek
Johnson, Zak
Johnson, Diane
Jones, Greg
Justis, Chris
Kallbach, Heiko
Karlsen, Sven
Karlsen, Nanna
Kardell, Mats
Kardell, Cecilia
Karrengarn, Dirk
Kehr, Mark
Ketchens, Rod
Kerr, Bart
Kickinger, Roland
Kimberly, Dale
King, Jeff
Kiss, Jeno
Kleeves, Mike
Klein, Scott
Klintworth, Mario
Kocikowkski, Micheal
Konex, Louis
Koontz, Rod
Korte, Stephan
Korte, Regina
Kovacs, Greg
Kovacs, Kim
Kozma, Joe
Krader, Steve
Krautgartner, Alred
Kruck, Debbie
Krueger, Kurt
Kubitz, Scott
Kurtz, Kreed
Kwiatkowski, Tobias Johann
LaMott, Gene
Lannaghan, Darin
Lanzillo, Pat
Larson, Doug
Layton, Joe
Lee, Jimmy
LeMasters, Eric
Leonard, Gary
Lewis, James Flex

Lewis, Coty
List, Arne
Livingstone, Scott
Loehrer, Benjamin
London, Jack
Long, Jeff
Lohr, Peter
Lopez, Justin
Lowden, Matt
Loyd, Jon
Lundmark, Thomas
Lyman, Craig
Maddron, Aaron
Maddron, Brandy
Malm, Eddie
Marcello, Steve
Mariano, George
Marriott, Evan
Marshall, Mark
Marshall, Doria
Martin, Gerard
Martini, Mike
Masters, Don
Matarazzo, Mike
Matechat, Steve
Matz, Ron
Matz, Regina
McCarver, Dallas
McCombs, Leslie
McGrath, Frank
McKenzie, Steve
McLean, Chris
Means, Joe
Medeiros, Steve
Meeko, Joe
Mello, Rob
Mendenhall, Matt
Mentis, Jim
Mies, Erica
Mileski, Ray
Miller, Kurt
Milne, Scott
Mitchell, Chris
Mitchell, Drew
Moen, Gabe
Morale, Glen
Mordetsky, Chris
Moyzan, Eddie
Mueller, Marcus
Murray, Brian
Natalie, Mark
Nazario, Joe
Neadow, Patrick
Neadow, Kim
Nerseveen, Toril
Neugabauer, Alfred
Newman, Dennis
Newman, James
Nicoletto, Scott
Nobert, Kevin
Oluk, Steve
Opiela, Larry
Orton, Randy
Osborne, Chris
Ostler, Nick
Ourama, KP
Oxford, John
Page, Tony
Pakulski, Ben
Palmucci, Don
Palumbo, Dave
Paolini, Lucio
Paris, Bob
Patterson, Bruce
Patterson, Angie
Paul, Kent
Paulsen, Geir
Paulsen, Bjarne Borgan
Paulsen, Toril Nerseveen
Pavelka, Jessie
Pearson, Michael
Pelletier, Jason
Penn, William
Perrault, Jeff
Petters, Scott
Pfister, Dan
Phares, Dylan Wayne
Piana, Rich
Place, Brett
Pellechia, Jimmy
Poehler, Eric
Ponder, Roy
Poulin, Jeff
Pratt, Craig
Priest, Lee
Prince, Melissa
Prince, Selby
Prince, Tom
Pruitt, David
Pruitt, Mercedes
Puckett, Dan
Puder, Daniel.
Quinn, Jim
Quinn, Mike
Ralf, Dennis
Rance, Steve
Rance, Carol

Rance, Lindy
Rangel, Lionel
Ratliff, Sean
Rawlings, Mark
Raymer, Marvis
Register, Bill
Reis, Bob
Relyea, Bill
Riss, Klaus
Myren
Rivers, Spenser
Roberts, Matthew
Robinson, Eddie
Robinson, Skip
Rodriquez, Unai
Sarobe
Rosbo, Gunnar
Rottermund,
Kevin
Rowe, Brad
Roy, Rich
Ruhl, Markus
Rylah, Brad
Rylah, David
Rytter, Ove
Sager, Lori
Sager, Rob
Samoluk, Todd
Santiago, Ernie
Santiago, Julio
Santoriello,
Franco
Satz, Guy Russell
Savolainen,
Marko
Scalesse, Jerry
Scarcella, Mike
Schlierkamp,
Gunter
Schlierkamp,
Carmen
Schnitker, Kevin
Schwan, Devon
Schwartzer, Jeff
Schweyher,
Ronnie
Scholtz, Armin
Segers, Sigg
Sehr, Mike
Sepe, Frank
Sergovsky,
Dennis
Shiflett, Jeff
Simpson, Chris
Smallwood, Billy
Smith, Bobby
Smith, Billy
Smith, Brian
Smith, Jimmy
Smith, Sam
Smolinski, Tim
Smullen, Jeff
Sneed, Jeff
Snowhill, Viggo
Spinello, Joe
Spinello, Jose
Spruce, Neal
Stadele, Doug
Stasiak, Shawn
Stenger, Don
Steyskal, Dan
Stevens, Dave
Stevenson, Rick
Stevenson,
Agnatha
Stewart, Rober
Stipich, Shawn
Strydom, Gary
Stymiest,
Ephraim
Sullivan, Mark
Summers,
Maverick
Schwarzenegger,
Dennis
Swenson, Robert
Alexander
Tappon, Rob
Teachout, John
Tenuta, Tim
Terilli, John
Terra, Victor
Terry, Kyle
Terry, Rob
Teufel, Ron
Thomas, Joel
Thorn, Rocky
Thorvildsen,
Tommi
Tiahart, Leif
Titus, Craig
Tomasini, Kevin
Tomasini, Stacey
Touchstone, Tom
Trigili, Nick
Troccoli, Joe
Turnage, James
Turner, Jet
Underwood, Tim
Valente, Rick
Vaillant, Antoine
Van,
Amersterdam Ed
Van Beck, Nick

Varga, Tom
Vassil, Frank
Velcich, Andy
Verret, Brad
Viator, Casey
Vitale, Nick
Vitale, Nicole
Van Aachen, Hanni
Voss, Michael
Vrabel, Mike
Wadsworth, Jack
Wadsworth, Leslie
Walterscheid, Roger
Watson, Mike
Weidel, Adam
Wells, Scott
Wendt, Ryan
Wentz, Doug
Wheeler, Flex
Wheeler, Josh
Whitehead, Derek
Whitley, Keith
Wicks, Chad
Wiebelt, Marco
Williams, Joe
Wilson, Scott
Wintterle, Aaron
Wisniewski, Tony
Wojcik, Travis
Wolf, Dennis
Wolf, Katja
Wood, Ashley
Wooten, Danny
Wooten, Brandon
Yablon, Mike
Yersky, Brian
Young, Jason
Young, Scott
Zachry, Dave
Zajac, Eddie
Zak, Trevor
Zak, Rob
Zechmeister, Tom
Zona, Same
Zuccoloto, Troy
Zuri, Remi

TOTAL: 528
Pro Bodybuilders: 102
Pro Wrestlers: 21
Gym Owners: 67
Supplement Company Owners: 22
Deceased: 59

AUTOGRAPHS

Perhaps following the example of the stars in Hollywood, fitness celebrities sold or gave away autographed photos at the events they attended. Here are some that were given to me by my houseguests.

Craig Titus | Dennis Wolf

Ben Pakulski | David Hawk

Nassar El Sonbaty Neal Spruce

Gary Strydom

Gunter Schlierkamp

Flex Wheeler

Ian Harrison Debbie Kruck

Michael Francois Paul DeMayo

Thomas Bengali JP Fux

Diana Dennis

Gunnar Rosbo

Berry de Mey

The Ultimate Warrior

Cory Everson

Denis Sergovskiy

Joe DeAngelis Jim Quinn

Erik Fromm

Paco Bautista

John Defendis

Robert Harrop

Robby Robinson & Billy Smith

Jon Loyd

Daniel Hill

Eddie Robinson & Ed Connors

Scott Milne

Jack & Leslie Wadsworth

Jay Cutler

Stephan Hartl

ABOUT THE AUTHOR

Edward Krueger Connors Jr. was born on May 6, 1945, in Omaha, Nebraska. After receiving a Bachelor of Architecture degree from the University of California, Berkeley, Ed served in Vietnam with the U.S. Army.

On February 28, 1979, Ed, along with two partners, purchased the single Gold's Gym in Santa Monica, California. On June 16, 1980, Ed opened up the first gym franchise ever. Before exiting the company in 2004, the chain grew to become the largest gym chain in the world.

Ed is currently designing a new gym model for the post-pandemic era. He enjoys reading and traveling in his free time. Visit www.edconnors.com.

THE THREE MUSCLETEERS is also available as an e-book for Kindle, Amazon Fire, iPad, Nook and Android e-readers. Visit creatorspublishing.com to learn more.

○ ○ ○

○ ○ ○

Made in the USA
Las Vegas, NV
16 August 2022